The Child Psychotherapy Treatment Planner, Fourth Edition

Practice*Planners*® Series

Treatment Planners

The Complete Adult Psychotherapy Treatment Planner, Fourth Edition
The Child Psychotherapy Treatment Planner, Fourth Edition
The Adolescent Psychotherapy Treatment Planner, Fourth Edition
The Addiction Treatment Planner, Third Edition
The Continuum of Care Treatment Planner
The Couples Psychotherapy Treatment Planner
The Employee Assistance Treatment Planner
The Pastoral Counseling Treatment Planner
The Older Adult Psychotherapy Treatment Planner
The Behavioral Medicine Treatment Planner
The Group Therapy Treatment Planner, Second Edition
The Gay and Lesbian Psychotherapy Treatment Planner
The Family Therapy Treatment Planner
The Severe and Persistent Mental Illness Treatment Planner
The Mental Retardation and Developmental Disability Treatment Planner
The Social Work and Human Services Treatment Planner
The Crisis Counseling and Traumatic Events Treatment Planner
The Personality Disorders Treatment Planner
The Rehabilitation Psychology Treatment Planner
The Special Education Treatment Planner
The Juvenile Justice and Residential Care Treatment Planner
The School Counseling and School Social Work Treatment Planner
The Sexual Abuse Victim and Sexual Offender Treatment Planner
The Probation and Parole Treatment Planner
The Psychopharmacology Treatment Planner
The Speech-Language Pathology Treatment Planner
The Suicide and Homicide Risk Assessment & Prevention Treatment Planner
The College Student Counseling Treatment Planner
The Parenting Skills Treatment Planner
The Early Childhood Education Intervention Treatment Planner
The Co-Occurring Disorders Treatment Planner

Progress Notes Planners

The Child Psychotherapy Progress Notes Planner, Third Edition
The Adolescent Psychotherapy Progress Notes Planner, Third Edition
The Adult Psychotherapy Progress Notes Planner, Third Edition
The Addiction Progress Notes Planner, Second Edition
The Severe and Persistent Mental Illness Progress Notes Planner
The Couples Psychotherapy Progress Notes Planner
The Family Therapy Progress Notes Planner

Homework Planners

Brief Therapy Homework Planner
Brief Couples Therapy Homework Planner
Brief Employee Assistance Homework Planner
Brief Family Therapy Homework Planner
Grief Counseling Homework Planner
Group Therapy Homework Planner
Divorce Counseling Homework Planner
School Counseling and School Social Work Homework Planner
Child Therapy Activity and Homework Planner
Addiction Treatment Homework Planner, Third Edition
Adolescent Psychotherapy Homework Planner II
Adolescent Psychotherapy Homework Planner, Second Edition
Adult Psychotherapy Homework Planner, Second Edition
Child Psychotherapy Homework Planner, Second Edition
Parenting Skills Homework Planner

Client Education Handout Planners

Adult Client Education Handout Planner
Child and Adolescent Client Education Handout Planner
Couples and Family Client Education Handout Planner

Complete Planners

The Complete Depression Treatment and Homework Planner
The Complete Anxiety Treatment and Homework Planner

PracticePlanners®

Arthur E. Jongsma, Jr., Series Editor

The Child Psychotherapy Treatment Planner, Fourth Edition

Arthur E. Jongsma, Jr.

L. Mark Peterson

William P. McInnis

Timothy J. Bruce, Contributing Editor

WILEY

JOHN WILEY & SONS, INC.

To my daughters and sons-in-law, Kendra and Erwin vanElst and Michelle and David DeGraaf, who give themselves creatively and sacrificially to the task of parenting my grandchildren, Tyler, Kaleigh, Justin, and Carter.

—A.E.J.

To Zach and Jim, who have expanded and enriched my life.

—L.M.P.

To my three children, Breanne, Kelsey, and Andrew, for the love and joy the bring into my life.

—W.P.M.

To Lori, Logan, and Madeline, for everything.

—T.J.B.

CONTENTS

▼ indicates that the chapter contains Objectives and Interventions consistent with those found in evidence-based treatments.

PRACTICE*PLANNERS*® SERIES PREFACE

Accountability is an important dimension of the practice of psychotherapy. Treatment programs, public agencies, clinics, and practitioners must justify and document their treatment plans to outside review entities in order to be reimbursed for services. The books and software in the Practice*Planners*® series are designed to help practitioners fulfill these documentation requirements efficiently and professionally.

The Practice*Planners*® series includes a wide array of treatment planning books including not only the original *Complete Adult Psychotherapy Treatment Planner, Child Psychotherapy Treatment Planner,* and *Adolescent Psychotherapy Treatment Planner,* all now in their fourth editions, but also *Treatment Planners* targeted to a wide range of specialty areas of practice, including:

- Addictions
- Behavioral medicine
- College students
- Co-occurring disorders
- Couples therapy
- Crisis counseling
- Early childhood education
- Employee assistance
- Family therapy
- Gays and lesbians
- Group therapy
- Juvenile justice and residential care
- Mental retardation and developmental disability
- Neuropsychology
- Older adults
- Parenting skills
- Pastoral counseling
- Personality disorders
- Probation and parole
- Psychopharmacology

- School counseling
- Severe and persistent mental illness
- Sexual abuse victims and offenders
- Special education
- Suicide and homicide risk assessment

In addition, there are three branches of companion books that can be used in conjunction with the *Treatment Planners,* or on their own:

- *Progress Notes Planners* provide a menu of progress statements that elaborate on the client's symptom presentation and the provider's therapeutic intervention. Each *Progress Notes Planner* statement is directly integrated with the behavioral definitions and therapeutic interventions from its companion *Treatment Planner.*
- *Homework Planners* include homework assignments designed around each presenting problem (such as anxiety, depression, chemical dependence, anger management, eating disorders, or panic disorder) that is the focus of a chapter in its corresponding *Treatment Planner*.
- *Client Education Handout Planners* provide brochures and handouts to help educate and inform clients on presenting problems and mental health issues, as well as life skills techniques. The handouts are included on CD-ROMs for easy printing from your computer and are ideal for use in waiting rooms, at presentations, as newsletters, or as information for clients struggling with mental illness issues. The topics covered by these handouts correspond to the presenting problems in the *Treatment Planners.*

The series also includes:

- Thera*Scribe*®, the #1 selling treatment planning and clinical record-keeping software system for mental health professionals. Thera*Scribe*® allows the user to import the data from any of the *Treatment Planner, Progress Notes Planner,* or *Homework Planner* books into the software's expandable database to simply point and click to create a detailed, organized, individualized, and customized treatment plan along with optional integrated progress notes and homework assignments.

Adjunctive books, such as *The Psychotherapy Documentation Primer* and *The Clinical Documentation Sourcebook* contain forms and resources to aid the clinician in mental health practice management.

The goal of our series is to provide practitioners with the resources they need in order to provide high-quality care in the era of accountability. To put it simply: we seek to help you spend more time on patients, and less time on paperwork.

ARTHUR E. JONGSMA, JR.
Grand Rapids, Michigan

ACKNOWLEDGMENTS

I have learned that it is better to acknowledge your weaknesses and to seek out those who complement you with their strengths. I was fortunate enough to have found the right person who brings his expertise in Evidence-Based Treatment to this project. He has contributed wisely and thoughtfully to greatly improve our *Adolescent Psychotherapy Treatment Planner* through his well-informed edits and additions to our content, to bring it in line with the latest psychotherapy research. He has been thoroughly professional in his approach while being a joy to work with, due to his wonderful sense of humor. I have said to many people since beginning this revision, "This guy really knows the literature!" For a person like me, who has spent his career in the psychotherapy trenches, it is a pleasure to get back in touch with my science-based roots by working with a Boulder Model clinician-scientist. I take my hat off to you, Dr. Tim Bruce. You have taken our product to a new level of contribution to the clinicians who are looking for Evidence-Based Treatment guidance. Your students are fortunate to have you for a mentor and we are fortunate to have you for a Contributing Editor. Thank you!

I also want to acknowledge the steady and perceptive work of my manuscript manager, Sue Rhoda. She stays on top of a thousand details while bringing the disjointed pieces of this work to a well organized finished product. Thank you, Sue.

A.E.J.

I want to acknowledge how honored I am to have had this chance to work with Art Jongsma, his colleague Sue Rhoda, and the staff at John Wiley and Sons on these, their well-known and highly regarded, treatment planners. These planners are widely recognized as works of enormous value to practicing clinicians as well as great educational tools for students of our profession. I didn't know Art when he asked me if I would join him on these editions, and the task he had in mind, to help empirically inform objectives and interventions, was daunting. I knew it would be a challenge to retain the rich breadth of options that Art has offered in past editions while simultaneously trying to identify and describe the fundamental features of identified empirically supported treatments. Although I have trained in empirically supported treatment approaches, contributed to this literature, and used them throughout my professional career, I recognize that our product will be open to criticism. I can say that we have done our best to offer a resource to our colleagues and their clients that is practical, flexible, and appreciates the complexities of any of the treatment approaches it conveys. And in the process of working with Art and Sue toward these goals, I have found them not only to be consummate professionals, but also thoughtful, conscientious, and kind persons. It has been a great pleasure working with you, Art and Sue, and a privilege to call you my friends.

T.J.B.

INTRODUCTION

ABOUT PRACTICE*PLANNERS®* TREATMENT PLANNERS

Pressure from third-party payors, accrediting agencies, and other outside parties has increased the need for clinicians to quickly produce effective, high-quality treatment plans. *Treatment Planners* provide all the elements necessary to quickly and easily develop formal treatment plans that satisfy the needs of most third-party payers and state and federal review agencies.

Each *Treatment Planner:*

- Saves you hours of time-consuming paperwork.
- Offers the freedom to develop customized treatment plans.
- Includes over 1,000 clear statements describing the behavioral manifestations of each relational problem, and includes long-term goals, short-term objectives, and clinically tested treatment options.
- Has an easy-to-use reference format that helps locate treatment plan components by behavioral problem or DSM-IV™ diagnosis.

As with the rest of the books in the Practice*Planners®* series, our aim is to clarify, simplify, and accelerate the treatment planning process, so you spend less time on paperwork, and more time with your clients.

HOW TO USE THIS TREATMENT PLANNER

Use this *Treatment Planner* to write treatment plans according to the following progression of six steps:

1. **Problem Selection.** Although the client may discuss a variety of issues during the assessment, the clinician must determine the most significant problems on which to focus the treatment process. Usually a primary problem will surface, and secondary problems may also be evident. Some other problems may have to be set aside as not urgent enough to require treat-

ment at this time. An effective treatment plan can only deal with a few selected problems or treatment will lose its direction. Choose the problem within this *Planner* which most accurately represents your client's presenting issues.

2. **Problem Definition.** Each client presents with unique nuances as to how a problem behaviorally reveals itself in his or her life. Therefore, each problem that is selected for treatment focus requires a specific definition about how it is evidenced in the particular client. The symptom pattern should be associated with diagnostic criteria and codes such as those found in the *DSM-IV* or the International Classification of Diseases. This *Planner* offers such behaviorally specific definition statements to choose from or to serve as a model for your own personally crafted statements.

3. **Goal Development.** The next step in developing your treatment plan is to set broad goals for the resolution of the target problem. These statements need not be crafted in measurable terms but can be global, long-term goals that indicate a desired positive outcome to the treatment procedures. This *Planner* provides several possible goal statements for each problem, but one statement is all that is required in a treatment plan.

4. **Objective Construction.** In contrast to long-term goals, objectives must be stated in behaviorally measurable language so that it is clear to review agencies, health maintenance organizations, and managed care organizations when the client has achieved the established objectives. The objectives presented in this *Planner* are designed to meet this demand for accountability. Numerous alternatives are presented to allow construction of a variety of treatment plan possibilities for the same presenting problem.

5. **Intervention Creation.** Interventions are the actions of the clinician designed to help the client complete the objectives. There should be at least one intervention for every objective. If the client does not accomplish the objective after the initial intervention, new interventions should be added to the plan. Interventions should be selected on the basis of the client's needs and the treatment provider's full therapeutic repertoire. This *Planner* contains interventions from a broad range of therapeutic approaches, and we encourage the provider to write other interventions reflecting his or her own training and experience.

Some suggested interventions listed in the *Planner* refer to specific books that can be assigned to the client for adjunctive bibliotherapy. Appendix A contains a full bibliographic reference list of these materials, including these two popular choices: *Read Two Books and Let's Talk Next Week: Using Bibliotherapy in Clinical Practice* (2000) by Maidman Joshua and DiMenna and *Rent Two Films and Let's Talk in the Morning: Using Popular Movies in Psychotherapy, Second Edition* (2001) by Hesley and Hesley (both books are published by Wiley). For further information about self-help books, mental health professionals may wish to consult

The Authoritative Guide to Self-Help Resources in Mental Health, Revised Edition (2003) by Norcross et al. (available from The Guilford Press, New York).

6. **Diagnosis Determination.** The determination of an appropriate diagnosis is based on an evaluation of the client's complete clinical presentation. The clinician must compare the behavioral, cognitive, emotional, and interpersonal symptoms that the client presents with the criteria for diagnosis of a mental illness condition as described in *DSM-IV*. Despite arguments made against diagnosing clients in this manner, diagnosis is a reality that exists in the world of mental health care, and it is a necessity for third-party reimbursement. It is the clinician's thorough knowledge of *DSM-IV* criteria and a complete understanding of the client assessment data that contribute to the most reliable, valid diagnosis.

Congratulations! After completing these six steps, you should have a comprehensive and individualized treatment plan ready for immediate implementation and presentation to the client. A sample treatment plan for Attention-Deficit/Hyperactivity Disorder is provided at the end of this introduction.

INCORPORATING EVIDENCE-BASED TREATMENT INTO THE *TREATMENT PLANNER*

Evidence-based treatment (that is, treatment which is scientifically shown in research trials to be efficacious) is rapidly becoming of critical importance to the mental health community as insurance companies are beginning to offer preferential pay to organizations using it. In fact, the APA Division 12 (Society of Clinical Psychology) lists of empirically supported treatments have been referenced by a number of local, state and federal funding agencies, which are beginning to restrict reimbursement to these treatments, as are some managed-care and insurance companies.

In this fourth edition of *The Child Psychotherapy Treatment Planner* we have made an effort to empirically inform some chapters by highlighting Short-Term Objectives (STOs) and Therapeutic Interventions (TIs) that are consistent with therapies that have demonstrated efficacy through empirical study. Watch for this icon as an indication that an Objective/Intervention is consistent with those found in evidence-based treatments.

References to their empirical support have been included in the reference section as Appendix B. Reviews of efforts to identify evidence-based therapies (EBT), including the effort's benefits and limitations, can be found in Bruce and Sanderson (2005), Chambless and colleagues (1996, 1998), and Chambless and Ollendick (2001). References have also been included to therapist- and client-oriented treatment manuals and books that describe the step-by-step use of noted EBTs or treatments consistent with their objectives and interventions. Of course, recognizing that there are STOs and TIs that practicing clinicians have found useful but that have not yet received empirical scrutiny, we have included those that reflect common practice among experienced clinicians. The goal is to provide a range of treatment plan options, some studied empirically, others reflecting common clinical practice, so the user can construct what they believe to be the best plan for their particular client.

In many instances, EBTs are short-term, problem-oriented treatments that focus on improving current problems/symptoms related to a client's current distress and disability. Accordingly, STOs and TIs of that type have been placed earlier in the sequence of STO and TI options. In addition, some STOs and TIs reflect core components of the EBT approach that are always delivered (e.g., exposure to feared objects and situations for a phobic disorder; behavioral activation for depression). Others reflect adjuncts to treatment that are commonly used to address problems that may not always be a feature of the clinical picture (e.g., assertive communication skills training for the social anxious or depressed client whose difficulty with assertion appears contributory to the primary anxiety or depressive disorder). Most of the STOs and TIs associated with the EBTs are described at a level of detail that permits flexibility and adaptability in their specific application. As with previous editions of this *Treatment Planner,* each chapter also includes the option to add STOs and TIs that are not listed.

Criteria for Inclusion of Evidence-Based Therapies

Not every treatment that has undergone empirical study for a mental health problem is included in this edition. In general, we have included EBTs the empirical support for which has either been well established or demonstrated at more than a preliminary level as defined by those authors who have undertaken the task of identifying EBTs, such as Chambless and colleagues (1996, 1998) and Nathan and Gorman (1998, 2002). At minimum, this requires demonstration of efficacy through a clinical trial or large clinical replication series that have features reflective of good experimental design (e.g., random assignment, blind assignments, reliable and valid measurement, clear inclusion and exclusion criteria, state-of-the-art diagnostic methods, and adequate sample size). Well established EBTs typically have more than one of these types of studies demonstrating their efficacy as well as other desirable features, such as demonstration of efficacy by independent research groups and specification of client characteristics for which the treatment was effective. Because treatment literatures for various problems develop at different paces, treatment STOs and TIs that have been included may have the most empirical support for their problem area, but less than that found in more heavily studied areas. For example, Cognitive Behavioral Therapy (CBT) has the highest level of empirical support of tested psychotherapies for Childhood Obsessive-Compulsive Disorder (OCD), but that level of evidence is lower than that supporting, for example, exposure-based therapy for phobic fear and avoidance. The latter has simply been studied more extensively. Nonetheless, within the psychotherapy outcome literature for OCD, CBT clearly has the highest level of evidence supporting its efficacy and usefulness. Accordingly, STOs and TIs consistent with CBT have been included in this edition. Lastly, just as some of the STOs and TIs included in this edition reflect common clinical practices of experienced clinicians, those associated with EBTs reflect what is commonly practiced by clinicians that use EBTs.

Summary of Required and Preferred EBT Inclusion Criteria

Required
- Demonstration of efficacy through at least one randomized controlled trial with good experimental design, or
- Demonstration of efficacy through a large, well-designed clinical replication series.

Preferred
- Efficacy has been shown by more than one study.
- Efficacy has been demonstrated by independent research groups.
- Client characteristics for which the treatment was effective were specified.
- A clear description of the treatment was available.

There does remain considerable debate regarding evidence-based treatment amongst mental health professionals who are not always in agreement regarding the best treatments or how to weigh the factors that contribute to good outcomes. Some practitioners are skeptical about the wisdom of changing their practice on the basis of research evidence, and their reluctance is fuelled by the methodological problems of psychotherapy research. Our goal in this book is to provide a range of treatment plan options, some studied empirically, others reflecting common clinical practice, so the user can construct what they believe to be the best plan for their particular client. As indicated earlier, recognizing that there are interventions which practicing clinicians have found useful but that have not yet received empirical scrutiny, we have included those that reflect common practice among experienced clinicians.

A FINAL NOTE ON TAILORING THE TREATMENT PLAN TO THE CLIENT

One important aspect of effective treatment planning is that each plan should be tailored to the individual client's problems and needs. Treatment plans should not be mass-produced, even if clients have similar problems. The individual's strengths and weaknesses, unique stressors, social network, family circumstances, and symptom patterns must be considered in developing a treatment strategy. Drawing upon our own years of clinical experience, we have put together a variety of treatment choices. These statements can be combined in thousands of permutations to develop detailed treatment plans. Relying on their own good judgment, clinicians can easily select the statements that are appropriate for the individuals whom they are treating. In addition, we encourage readers to add their own definitions, goals, objectives, and interventions to the existing samples. As with all of the books in the *Treatment Planners* series, it is our hope that this book will help promote effective, creative treatment planning—a process that will ultimately benefit the client, clinician, and mental health community.

SAMPLE TREATMENT PLAN

ATTENTION-DEFICIT/HYPERACTIVITY DISORDER (ADHD)

Definitions: Short attention span; difficulty sustaining attention on a consistent basis.

Susceptibility to distraction by extraneous stimuli and internal thoughts.

Repeated failure to follow through on instructions or complete school assignments or chores in a timely manner.

Poor organizational skills as demonstrated by forgetfulness, inattention to details, and losing things necessary for tasks.

Goals: Sustain attention and concentration for consistently longer periods of time.

Regularly take medication as prescribed to decrease impulsivity, hyperactivity, and distractibility.

Parents and/or teachers successfully utilize a reward system, contingency contract, or token economy to reinforce positive behaviors and deter negative behaviors.

Parents set firm, consistent limits and maintain appropriate parent-child boundaries.

SHORT-TERM OBJECTIVES

THERAPEUTIC INTERVENTIONS

1. Complete psychological testing to confirm the diagnosis of ADHD and/or rule out emotional factors.

1. Arrange for psychological testing to confirm the presence of ADHD and/or rule out emotional problems that may be contributing to the client's inattentiveness, impulsivity, and hyperactivity; give feedback to the client and his/her parents regarding the testing results.

2. Take prescribed medication as directed by the physician.

1. Arrange for a medication evaluation for the client.

2. Monitor the client for psychotropic medication prescription compliance, side effects, and effectiveness; consult with the prescribing physician at regular intervals.

3. Parents and the client demonstrate knowledge about ADHD
symptoms.

1. Educate the client's parents and
siblings about the symptoms of
ADHD.

2. Assign the parents readings to
increase their knowledge about
symptoms of ADHD (e.g., *Taking
Charge of ADHD* by Barkley;
Your Hyperactive Child by Ingersoll; *Dr. Larry Silver's Advice
to Parents on Attention Deficit
Hyperactivity Disorder* by Silver).

3. Assign the client readings to
increase his/her knowledge
about ADHD and ways to manage symptoms (e.g., *Putting on
the Brakes* by Quinn and Stern;
*Sometimes I Drive My Mom
Crazy, but I Know She's Crazy
about Me* by Shapiro).

4. Parents maintain communication with the school to increase
the client's compliance with
completion of school assignments.

1. Encourage the parents and
teachers to maintain regular
communication about the client's
academic, behavioral, emotional,
and social progress (or assign
"Getting It Done" in the *Child
Psychotherapy Homework Planner,* 2nd ed. by Jongsma, Peterson,
and McInnis).

5. Utilize effective study skills
on a regular basis to improve
academic performance.

1. Teach the client more effective
study skills (e.g., clearing away
distractions, studying in quiet
places, scheduling breaks in studying).

2. Assign the client to read *13 Steps
to Better Grades* (Silverman) to
improve organizational and study
skills (or assign "Establish a
Homework Routine" in the *Child
Psychotherapy Homework Planner,* 2nd ed. by Jongsma, Peterson,
and McInnis).

6. Increase frequency of completion of school assignments, chores, and household responsibilities.

1. Assist the parents in developing a routine schedule to increase the client's compliance with school, chores, or household responsibilities.

2. Consult with the client's teachers to implement strategies to improve school performance, such as sitting in the front row during class, using a prearranged signal to redirect the client back to task, scheduling breaks from tasks, providing frequent feedback, calling on the client often, arranging for a listening buddy, implementing a daily behavioral report card.

3. Encourage the parents and teachers to use a behavioral classroom intervention (e.g., a school contract and reward system) to reinforce appropriate behavior and completion of his/her assignments (or employ the "Getting It Done" program in the *Child Psychotherapy Homework Planner*, 2nd ed. by Jongsma, Peterson, and McInnis).

7. Implement effective test-taking strategies on a consistent basis to improve academic performance.

1. Teach the client more effective test-taking strategies (e.g., reviewing material regularly, reading directions twice, rechecking work).

8. Delay instant gratification in favor of achieving meaningful long-term goals.

1. Teach the client mediational and self-control strategies (e.g., "stop, think, listen, and act") to delay the need for instant gratification and inhibit impulses to achieve more meaningful, longer-term goals.

2. Assist the parents in increasing structure to help the client learn

to delay gratification for longer-term goals (e.g., completing homework or chores before playing).

9. Parents implement the Parent Management Training approach in which parents utilize a reward/punishment system, contingency contract, and/or token economy.

1. Teach the parents a Parent Management Training approach (e.g., a reward/punishment system, contingency contract, token economy), explaining how parent and child behavioral interactions can reduce the frequency of impulsive, disruptive, and negative attention-seeking behaviors and increase desired behavior (e.g., prompting and reinforcing positive behaviors; see *Parenting the Strong-Willed Child* by Forehand and Long; *Living with Children* by Patterson).

2. Teach the parents how to specifically define and identify problem behaviors, identify their reactions to the behavior, determine whether the reaction encourages or discourages the behavior, and generate alternatives to the problem behavior.

3. Teach the parents how to implement key parenting practices consistently, including establishing realistic age-appropriate rules for acceptable and unacceptable behavior, prompting of positive behavior in the environment, use of positive reinforcement to encourage behavior (e.g., praise), use of clear direct instruction, time out, and other loss-of-privilege practices for problem behavior.

4. Assign the parents home exercises in which they implement and record results of implementation exercises (or assign "Clear

Rules, Positive Reinforcement, Appropriate Consequences" in the *Adolescent Psychotherapy Homework Planner,* 2nd ed. by Jongsma, Peterson, and McInnis); review in session, providing corrective feedback toward improved, appropriate, and consistent use of skills.

5. Ask the parents to read parent training manuals (e.g., *Living with Children* by Patterson) or watch videotapes demonstrating the techniques being learned in session (see Webster-Stratton, 1994).

DIAGNOSIS

Axis I: 314.00   Attention-Deficit/Hyperactivity Disorder, Predominantly Inattentive Type

ACADEMIC UNDERACHIEVEMENT

BEHAVIORAL DEFINITIONS

1. History of overall academic performance that is below the expected level according to the client's measured intelligence or performance on standardized achievement tests.
2. Repeated failure to complete school or homework assignments and/or current assignments on time.
3. Poor organizational or study skills that contribute to academic underachievement.
4. Frequent tendency to procrastinate or postpone doing school or homework assignments in favor of playing or engaging in recreational and leisure activities.
5. Family history of members having academic problems, failures, or disinterests.
6. Feelings of depression, insecurity, and low self-esteem that interfere with learning and academic progress.
7. Recurrent pattern of engaging in acting out, disruptive, and negative attention-seeking behaviors when encountering difficulty or frustration in learning.
8. Heightened anxiety that interferes with client's performance during tests or examinations.
9. Excessive or unrealistic pressure placed on the client by his/her parents to the degree that it negatively affects his/her academic performance.
10. Decline in academic performance that occurs in response to environmental factors or stress (e.g., parents' divorce, death of a loved one, relocation, move).

—. _____

_____

—. _____

_____

—. _____

_____

LONG-TERM GOALS

1. Demonstrate consistent interest, initiative, and motivation in academics, and bring performance up to the expected level of intellectual or academic functioning.
2. Complete school and homework assignments on a regular and consistent basis.
3. Achieve and maintain a healthy balance between accomplishing academic goals and meeting his/her social, emotional, and self-esteem needs.
4. Stabilize moods and build self-esteem so that the client is able to cope effectively with the frustrations and stressors associated with academic pursuits and learning.
5. Eliminate the pattern of engaging in acting out, disruptive, or negative attention-seeking behaviors when confronted with difficulty or frustration in learning.
6. Significantly reduce the level of anxiety related to taking tests.
7. Parents establish realistic expectations of the client's learning abilities and implement effective intervention strategies at home to help the client keep up with schoolwork and achieve academic goals.
8. Remove emotional impediments or resolve family conflicts and environmental stressors to allow for improved academic performance.

—. _____

_____

—. _____

_____

—. _____

_____

SHORT-TERM OBJECTIVES	THERAPEUTIC INTERVENTIONS
1. Complete a psychoeducational evaluation. (1)	1. Arrange for psychoeducational testing to evaluate the presence of a learning disability, and determine whether the client is eligible to receive special-education

services; provide feedback to the client, his/her family, and school officials regarding the psychoeducational evaluation.

2. Complete psychological testing. (2)

2. Arrange for psychological testing to assess whether possible Attention-Deficit/Hyperactivity Disorder (ADHD) or emotional factors are interfering with the client's academic performance; provide feedback to the client, his/her family, and school officials regarding the psychological evaluation.

3. The client and his/her parents provide psychosocial history information. (3)

3. Gather psychosocial history information that includes key developmental milestones and a family history of educational achievements and failures.

4. Cooperate with a hearing, vision, or medical examination. (4)

4. Refer the client for a hearing, vision, or medical examination to rule out possible hearing, visual, or health problems that are interfering with school performance.

5. Comply with the recommendations made by the multidisciplinary evaluation team at school regarding educational interventions. (5, 6)

5. Attend an individualized educational planning committee (IEPC) meeting with the parents, teachers, and school officials to determine the client's eligibility for special-education services, design education interventions, and establish educational goals.

6. Based on the IEPC goals and recommendations, arrange for the client to be moved to an appropriate classroom setting to maximize his/her learning.

6. Parents and teachers implement educational strategies that maximize the client's learning strengths and compensate for learning weaknesses. (7)

7. Consult with the client, parents, and school officials about designing effective learning programs for intervention strategies that build on his/her strengths and compensate for weaknesses.

7. Participate in outside tutoring to increase knowledge and skills in the area of academic weakness. (8, 9)

8. Recommend that the parents seek outside tutoring after school to boost the client's skills in the area of his/her academic weakness (e.g., reading, mathematics, written expression).

9. Refer the client to a private learning center for extra tutoring in the areas of academic weakness and assistance in improving study and test-taking skills.

8. Implement effective study skills to increase the frequency of completion of school assignments and improve academic performance. (10, 11)

10. Teach the client more effective study skills (e.g., remove distractions, study in quiet places, develop outlines, highlight important details, schedule breaks).

11. Consult with the teachers and parents about using a study buddy or peer tutor to assist the client in the area of academic weakness and improve study skills.

9. Implement effective test-taking strategies to decrease anxiety and improve test performance. (12, 13)

12. Teach the client more effective test-taking strategies (e.g., study over an extended period of time, review material regularly, read directions twice, recheck work).

13. Train the client in relaxation techniques or guided imagery to reduce his/her anxiety before or during the taking of tests.

10. Parents maintain regular (i.e., daily to weekly) communication with the teachers. (14)

14. Encourage the parents to maintain regular (i.e., daily or weekly) communication with the teachers to help the client remain organized and keep up with school assignments.

11. Use self-monitoring checklists, planners, or calendars to remain organized and help complete school assignments. (15, 16, 17)

15. Encourage the client to use self-monitoring checklists to increase completion of school assignments and improve academic performance.

16. Direct the client to use planners or calendars to record school or homework assignments and plan ahead for long-term projects.

17. Monitor the client's completion of school and homework assignments on a regular, consistent basis (or use the "Getting It Done" program in the *Child Psychotherapy Homework Planner,* 2nd ed. by Jongsma, Peterson, and McInnis).

12. Establish a regular routine that allows time to engage in play, to spend quality time with the family, and to complete homework assignments. (18)

18. Assist the client and his/her parents in developing a routine daily schedule at home that allows the client to achieve a healthy balance of completing school/homework assignments, engaging in independent play, and spending quality time with family and peers.

13. Parents and teachers increase the frequency of praise and positive reinforcement of the client's school performance. (19, 20)

19. Encourage the parents and teachers to give frequent praise and positive reinforcement for the client's effort and accomplishment on academic tasks.

20. Identify a variety of positive reinforcers or rewards to maintain the client's interest and motivation to complete school assignments.

14. Identify and resolve all emotional blocks or learning inhibitions that are within the client and/or the family system. (21, 22)

21. Teach the client positive coping mechanisms (e.g., relaxation techniques, positive self-talk, cognitive restructuring) to use when encountering anxiety, frustration, or difficulty with schoolwork.

22. Conduct family sessions that probe the client's family system to identify any emotional blocks or inhibitions to learning; assist the family in resolving identified family conflicts.

15. Parents increase the time spent being involved with the client's homework. (23, 24)

23. Encourage the parents to demonstrate and/or maintain regular interest and involvement in the client's homework (e.g., parents reading aloud to or alongside the client, using flashcards to improve math skills, rechecking spelling words).

24. Assist the parents and teachers in the development of systematic rewards for progress and accomplishment (e.g., charts with stars for goal attainment, praise for each success, some material reward for achievement).

16. Parents decrease the frequency and intensity of arguments with the client over issues related to school performance and homework. (25, 26)

25. Conduct family therapy sessions to assess whether the parents have developed unrealistic expectations or are placing excessive pressure on the client to perform; confront and challenge the parents about placing excessive pressure on the client.

26. Encourage the parents to set firm, consistent limits and use natural, logical consequences for the client's noncompliance or refusal to do homework; instruct the parents to avoid unhealthy power struggles or lengthy arguments over homework each night.

17. Parents verbally recognize that their pattern of overprotectiveness interferes with the client's academic growth and responsibility. (27)

27. Observe parent-child interactions to assess whether the parents' overprotectiveness or infantilization of the client contributes to his/her academic underachievement; assist the parents in developing realistic expectations of his/her learning potential.

18. Increase the frequency of on-task behavior at school, increasing the completion of

28. Consult with school officials about ways to improve the client's on-task behaviors (e.g., keep

school assignments without expressing frustration and the desire to give up. (28, 29)

him/her close to the teacher; keep him/her close to positive peer role models; call on him/her often; provide frequent feedback to him/her; structure the material into a series of small steps).

29. Assign the client to read material designed to improve his/her organization and study skills (e.g., *13 Steps to Better Grades* by Silverman); process the information gained from the reading.

19. Increase the frequency of positive statements about school experiences and confidence in the ability to succeed academically. (30, 31, 32)

30. Reinforce the client's successful school experiences and positive statements about school.

31. Confront the client's self-disparaging remarks and expressed desire to give up on school assignments.

32. Assign the client the task of making one positive self-statement daily about school and his/her ability and have him/her record it in a journal.

20. Decrease the frequency and severity of acting out behaviors when encountering frustrations with school assignments. (33, 34, 35, 36)

33. Help the client to identify which rewards would increase his/her motivation to improve academic performance; implement these suggestions into the academic program.

34. Conduct individual play therapy sessions to help the client work through and resolve painful emotions, core conflicts, or stressors that impede academic performance.

35. Help the client to realize the connection between negative or painful emotions and decrease in academic performance.

36. Teach the client positive coping and self-control strategies (e.g., cognitive restructuring; positive self-talk; "stop, look, listen, and think") to inhibit the impulse to act out or engage in negative attention-seeking behaviors when encountering frustrations with schoolwork.

21. Identify and verbalize how specific, responsible actions lead to improvements in academic performance. (37, 38)

37. Explore periods of time when the client completed schoolwork regularly and/or achieved academic success; identify and encourage him/her to use similar strategies to improve his/her current academic performance.

38. Examine coping strategies that the client has used to solve other problems; encourage him/her to use similar coping strategies to overcome problems associated with learning.

22. Develop a list of resource people within school setting to whom the client can turn for support, assistance, or instruction for learning problems. (39)

39. Identify a list of individuals within the school to whom the client can turn for support, assistance, or instruction when he/she encounters difficulty or frustration with learning.

23. Increase the time spent in independent reading. (40)

40. Encourage the parents to use a reward system to reinforce the client for engaging in independent reading (or use the "Reading Adventure" program in the *Child Psychotherapy Homework Planner*, 2nd ed. by Jongsma, Peterson, and McInnis).

24. Express feelings about school through artwork and mutual storytelling. (41, 42, 43)

41. Use mutual storytelling techniques whereby the therapist and client alternate telling stories through the use of puppets, dolls, or stuffed animals. The therapist first models appropriate ways

to manage frustration related to learning problems, then the client follows by creating a story with similar characters or themes.

42. Have the client create a variety of drawings on a posterboard or large sheet of paper that reflect how his/her personal and family life would be different if he/she completed homework regularly; process the content of these drawings.

43. Instruct the client to draw a picture of a school building, then have him/her create a story that tells what it is like to be a student at that school to assess possible stressors that may interfere with learning and academic progress.

__. _____   __. _____
  _____   _____
__. _____   __. _____
  _____   _____
__. _____   __. _____
  _____   _____

DIAGNOSTIC SUGGESTIONS

Axis I:	315.00	Reading Disorder
	315.1	Mathematics Disorder
	315.2	Disorder of Written Expression
	V62.3	Academic Problem
	314.01	Attention-Deficit/Hyperactivity Disorder, Combined Type
	314.00	Attention-Deficit/Hyperactivity Disorder, Predominantly Inattentive Type
	300.4	Dysthymic Disorder
	313.81	Oppositional Defiant Disorder
	312.9	Disruptive Behavior Disorder NOS

| _____ | _____ |
| _____ | _____ |

Axis II: 317   Mild Mental Retardation
                  V62.89   Borderline Intellectual Functioning
                  V71.09   No Diagnosis

| _____ | _____ |
| _____ | _____ |

ADOPTION

BEHAVIORAL DEFINITIONS

1. Adopted into the present family since infancy.
2. Adopted into the present family after the age of 2.
3. Adopted as an older special-needs child or as a set of siblings into the family.
4. Relates to significant others in a withdrawn, rejecting way, avoiding eye contact and keeping self at a distance from them.
5. Exhibits a pattern of hoarding or gorging food.
6. Displays numerous aggressive behaviors that are out of proportion for the presenting situations and seems to reflect a need to vent pent-up frustration.
7. Lies and steals often when it is not necessary to do so.
8. Displays an indiscriminate pattern of showing open affection to casual friends and strangers.
9. Parents experience excessive, unnecessary frustration with the adopted child's development and level of achievement.
10. Parents are anxious and fearful of the adopted child's questioning of his/her background (e.g., "Where did I come from?" "Who do I look like?").

___. _____
_____
_____

___. _____
_____
_____

___. _____
_____

LONG-TERM GOALS

1. Termination of self-defeating acting out behaviors and acceptance of self as loved and lovable within an adopted family.
2. Resolution of the key adoption issues of loss, abandonment, and rejection.
3. The establishment and maintenance of healthy family connections.
4. Removal of all barriers to enable the establishment of a healthy bond between parents and child(ren).
5. Develop a nurturing relationship with parents.
6. Build and maintain a healthy adoptive family.

—. _____
    _____
—. _____
    _____
—. _____
    _____

SHORT-TERM OBJECTIVES

1. Family members and the client develop a trusting relationship with the therapist that will allow for open expression of thoughts and feelings. (1)

2. Cooperate with and complete all assessments and evaluations. (2, 3)

THERAPEUTIC INTERVENTIONS

1. Actively build the level of trust with the client and his/her family members by using consistent eye contact, active listening, unconditional positive regard, and empathic responses to help promote the open expressions of their thoughts and feelings about the adoption.

2. Conduct or refer the parents and child(ren) for a psychosocial assessment to assess the parents' strength of marriage, parenting style, stress management/coping strengths, resolution of infertility issues, and to assess the child's developmental level, attachment capacity, behavioral issues, temperament, and strengths.

3. Comply with all recommendations of the evaluations or assessments. (4)

3. Conduct or arrange for a psychological evaluation to determine the client's level of behavioral functioning, cognitive style, and intelligence.

4. Summarize assessment date and present the findings and recommendations to the family. Encourage and monitor the family's follow-through on all the recommendations.

4. Parents acknowledge unresolved grief associated with their infertility. (5)

5. Assess the parents' unresolved grief around the issue of their infertility; refer them for further conjoint or individual treatment if necessary.

5. Family members attend family therapy sessions and report on their perception of the adjustment process. (6)

6. Establish a wellness plan whereby the family goes at 3-month intervals for a checkup with the therapist to evaluate how the assimilation and attachment process is proceeding. If all is well, checkups can be annual after the first year.

6. Parents commit to improving communication and affection expression within the marriage relationship. (7)

7. Refer the parents to a skills-based marital program such as "Prep" (see *Fighting for Your Marriage* by Markman, Stanley, and Blumberg) to strengthen their marital relationship by improving responsibility acceptance, communication, and conflict resolution.

7. Attend and actively take part in play therapy sessions to reduce acting out behaviors connected to unresolved rage, loss, and fear of abandonment. (8, 9, 10, 11)

8. Conduct filial therapy (i.e., parents' involvement in play therapy sessions), in which the client takes the lead in expressing anger and the parents respond empathically to the client's feelings (e.g., hurt, fear, sadness, helplessness) beneath the anger.

9. Employ psychoanalytic play therapy (e.g., explore and gain understanding of the etiology of unconscious conflicts, fixations, or arrests; interpret resistance, transference, or core anxieties) to help the client work through and resolve issues contributing to acting out behaviors.

10. Conduct individual play therapy sessions to provide the opportunity for expression of feelings surrounding past loss, neglect, and/or abandonment.

11. Employ the ACT model (see *Play Therapy: The Art of the Relationship* by Landreth) in play therapy sessions to *acknowledge* feelings, *communicate* limits, and *target* acceptable alternatives to acting out or aggressive behaviors.

8. Verbalize the connection between anger and/or withdrawal and the underlying feelings of fear, abandonment, and rejection. (12)

12. Assist the client in making connections between underlying painful emotions of loss, rejection, rage, abandonment, and acting out and/or aggressive behaviors.

9. Identify feelings that are held inside and rarely expressed. (13, 14, 15)

13. Use puppets, dolls, or stuffed toys to tell a story to the client about others who have experienced loss, rejection, or abandonment to show how they have resolved these issues. Then ask the client to create a similar story using puppets, dolls, or stuffed toys.

14. Ask the client to draw an outline of himself/herself on a sheet of paper, and then instruct him/her to fill the inside with pictures and objects that reflect what he/she has on the inside that fuels the acting out behaviors.

15. Use expressive art materials (e.g., Play-Doh, clay, finger paint) to create pictures and sculptures that aid the client in expressing and resolving his/her feelings of rage, rejection, and loss.

10. Identify and release feelings in socially acceptable, nondestructive ways. (16, 17, 18)

16. Read with the client, or have the parents read to him/her, *A Volcano in My Tummy* (Whittenhouse and Pudney) or *Don't Rant and Rave on Wednesday!* (Moser) to help him/her to recognize his/her anger and to present ways to handle angry feelings.

17. Play with the client, or have the parents play with him/her, The Talking, Feeling, Doing Game (Gardner) or The Anger Control Game (Berg) to assist him/her in identifying and expressing feelings and thoughts.

18. Use a feelings chart, felts, or cards to increase the client's ability to identify, understand, and express feelings.

11. Express feelings directly related to being an adopted child. (19, 20)

19. Ask the client to read *How It Feels to Be Adopted* (Krementz) and list two or three items from each age-appropriate vignette that he/she will process with the therapist.

20. Assign the client to read books on adoption to help him/her clarify issues and not feel alone (e.g., *I Feel Different* by Stinson; *Adoption Is for Always* by Welvoord-Girrard).

12. Parents verbalize an increased ability to understand and handle acting out behaviors. (21, 22, 23)

21. Affirm often with the parents the health of their family while they are working with the disturbed client to avoid triangulation and undermining of parental authority by him/her.

22. Refer the parents and/or the client to an adoption support group.

23. Work with the parents in conjoint sessions to frame the client's acting out behaviors as *opportunities to reparent the client.* Then strategize with them to come up with specific ways to intervene in the problem behaviors.

13. Parents affirm the client's identity as based in self, bioparents, and adoptive family. (24, 25, 26)

24. Ask the parents to read material to increase their knowledge and understanding of adoption (e.g., *Helping Children Cope with Separation and Loss* by Jennett-Jarratt; *Adoption Wisdom* by Russell; *The Whole Life Adoption Book* by Schouler; *Making Sense of Adoption* by Melina).

25. Refer the parents to reliable Internet sites that provide information and support to adoptive parents (e.g., www.adoption.com; www.adoption.about.com www.olderchildadoptions.com; www.adoptionsites.com).

26. Educate the parents on the importance of affirming the client's entire identity (i.e., self, bioparents, adoptive parents), and show them specific ways to reaffirm him/her (e.g., verbally identify talents, such as art or music, that are similar to those of the biological parents; recognize positive tasks that the client does that are similar to those of the adoptive mom or dad).

14. Express and preserve own history and its contribution to identity. (27)

27. Assign the parents to help the client create a *life book* that chronicles his/her life to this point in order to give him/her a visual perspective and knowledge of his/her own history and identity

(or assign the "Create a Memory Album" exercise in the *Child Psychotherapy Homework Planner,* 2nd ed. by Jongsma, Peterson, and McInnis).

15. Verbalize needs and wishes. (28)

28. Assist the client in clarifying and expressing his/her needs and desires (or assign the exercise "Three Wishes Game" from the *Child Psychotherapy Homework Planner,* 2nd ed. by Jongsma, Peterson, and McInnis).

16. Verbalize a feeling of increased confidence and self-acceptance. (26, 27, 29)

26. Educate the parents on the importance of affirming the client's entire identity (i.e., self, bioparents, adoptive parents), and show them specific ways to reaffirm him/her (e.g., verbally identify talents, such as art or music, that are similar to those of the biological parents; recognize positive tasks that the client does that are similar to those of adoptive mom or dad).

27. Assign the parents to help the client create a *life book* that chronicles his/her life to this point in order to give him/her a visual perspective and knowledge of his/her own history and identity (or assign the "Create a Memory Album" exercise in the *Child Psychotherapy Homework Planner,* 2nd ed. by Jongsma, Peterson, and McInnis).

29. Assign a self-esteem-building exercise to help the client develop self-knowledge, acceptance, and confidence (see *SEALS & Plus* by Korb-Khara, Azok, and Leutenberg).

17. Parents verbalize reasonable expectations for the client's behavior given his/her developmental stage and the process of adjustment to adoption. (30)

18. Parent spends one-on-one time with the client in active play. (31, 32)

19. Parents increase the frequency of expressing affection verbally and physically toward the client. (33)

20. Parents speak only positively regarding the client's bioparents. (34)

21. Parents feel free to ask questions regarding the details of adoption adjustment. (35)

30. Process the parents' expectations for the client's behavior and adjustment; confront and modify unrealistic expectations and foster realistic expectations considering his/her developmental stage and adjustment to the adoption process.

31. Use a *Theraplay* (Jernberg and Booth) attachment-based approach, in which the therapist takes charge by planning and structuring each session. The therapist uses his/her power to entice the client into the relationship and to keep the focus of therapy on the relationship, not on intrapsychic conflicts. Also, parents are actively involved and are trained to be cotherapists.

32. Assign each parent to spend time in daily one-on-one active play with the client.

33. Encourage the parents to provide large, genuine, daily doses of positive verbal reinforcement and physical affection; monitor and encourage them to continue this behavior and to reinforce positive attachment signs when they appear.

34. Encourage the parents to refrain from negative references about the bioparents.

35. Conduct sessions with the parents to give them opportunities to raise adoption-specific issues of concern to them (e.g., how to handle an open adoption, how much to share with the client about his/her bioparents) in order to give them direction and support.

22. Parents verbalize reasonable discipline and nurturance guidelines. (36, 37, 38)

36. Provide the parents with education about keeping discipline related to the offense reasonable and always respectful to reduce resentment and rebellion. (Recommend *How to Raise Responsible Children* by Glen and Nelson.)

37. Ask the parents to read *The Seven Habits of Highly Effective Families* (Covey) for suggestions on how to increase their family's health and connections.

38. Have the parents spend individual one-on-one time with the children who were part of the family prior to the adoption.

23. Family members express an acceptance of and trust in each other. (39, 40)

39. Refer the family to an initiatives weekend (e.g., high-and low-ropes course, tasks, and various group-oriented physical problem-solving activities) to increase trust, co-operation, and connections with each other.

40. In a family session, construct a genogram that includes all family members, showing how everyone is connected in order to demonstrate the client's origins and what he/she has become a part of.

__. _____
_____
__. _____
_____
__. _____
_____

__. _____
_____
__. _____
_____
__. _____
_____

DIAGNOSTIC SUGGESTIONS

Axis I: 309.0   Adjustment Disorder With Depressed Mood

309.4   Adjustment Disorder With Mixed Disturbance of
Emotions and Conduct

300.4   Dysthymic Disorder

314.01   Attention-Deficit/Hyperactivity Disorder,
Combined Type

309.81   Posttraumatic Stress Disorder

313.89   Reactive Attachment Disorder of Infancy or
Early Childhood

_____   _____

_____   _____

Axis II: V71.09   No Diagnosis

_____   _____

_____   _____

ANGER MANAGEMENT

BEHAVIORAL DEFINITIONS

1. Repeated angry outbursts that are out of proportion to the precipitating event.
2. Excessive yelling, swearing, crying, or use of verbally abusive language when efforts to meet desires are frustrated or limits are placed on behavior.
3. Frequent fighting, intimidation of others, and acts of cruelty or violence toward people or animals.
4. Verbal threats of harm to parents, adult authority figures, siblings, or peers.
5. Persistent pattern of destroying property or throwing objects when angry.
6. Consistent failure to accept responsibility for anger control problems accompanied by repeated pattern of blaming others for poor control of anger.
7. Repeated history of engaging in passive-aggressive behaviors (e.g., forgetting, pretending not to listen, dawdling, procrastinating) to frustrate or annoy others.
8. Strained interpersonal relationships with peers due to aggressiveness and anger control problems.
9. Underlying feelings of depression, anxiety, or insecurity that contribute to angry outbursts and aggressive behaviors.

—. _____
_____
—. _____
_____
—. _____
_____

LONG-TERM GOALS

1. Express anger through appropriate verbalizations and healthy physical outlets on a consistent basis.
2. Significantly reduce the frequency and intensity of temper outbursts.
3. Terminate all destruction of property, physical aggression, and acts of violence or cruelty toward people or animals.
4. Interact consistently with adults and peers in a mutually respectful manner.
5. Markedly reduce frequency of passive-aggressive behaviors by expressing anger and frustration through controlled, respectful, and direct verbalizations.
6. Resolve the core conflicts that contribute to the emergence of anger control problems.
7. Parents establish and maintain appropriate parent-child boundaries, setting firm, consistent limits when the client reacts in a verbally or physically aggressive or passive-aggressive manner.

—. _____
_____

—. _____
_____

—. _____
_____

SHORT-TERM OBJECTIVES

1. Identify situations, thoughts, and feelings that trigger angry feelings, problem behaviors, and the targets of those actions. (1)

2. Cooperate with a medical evaluation to assess possible organic contributors to poor anger control. (2)

THERAPEUTIC INTERVENTIONS

1. Thoroughly assess the various stimuli (e.g., situations, people, thoughts) that have triggered the client's anger and the thoughts, feelings, and actions that have characterized his/her anger responses.

2. Refer the client to a physician for a complete physical exam to rule out organic contributors (e.g., brain damage, tumor, elevated testosterone levels) to poor anger control.

3. Complete psychological testing. (3)

3. Conduct or arrange for psychological testing to help in assessing whether a comorbid condition (e.g., depression, Attention-Deficit/Hyperactivity Disorder [ADHD]) is contributing to anger control problems; follow-up accordingly with client and parents regarding treatment options.

▼ 4. Cooperate with a physician evaluation for possible treatment with psychotropic medications and take medications consistently, if prescribed. (4, 5)

4. Assess the client for the need for psychotropic medication to assist in anger and behavioral control, referring him/her, if indicated, to a physician for an evaluation for prescription medication. ▼

5. Monitor the client's prescription compliance, effectiveness, and side effects; provide feedback to the prescribing physician. ▼

▼ 5. Recognize and verbalize how feelings are connected to misbehavior. (6)

6. Actively build the level of trust with the client through consistent eye contact, active listening, unconditional positive regard, and warm acceptance to help increase his/her ability to identify and express feelings instead of acting them out; assist the client in making a connection between his/her feelings and reactive behaviors (or assign "Risk Factors Leading to Child Behavior Problems" in the *Child Psychotherapy Homework Planner*, 2nd ed. by Jongsma, Peterson, and McInnis). ▼

▼ 6. Increase the number of statements that reflect the acceptance of responsibility for misbehavior. (7, 8, 9)

7. Firmly confront the client's oppositional behavior and attitude, pointing out consequences for himself/herself and others. ▼

▼ indicates that the Objective/Intervention is consistent with those found in evidence-based treatments.

8. Confront statements in which the client lies and/or blames others for his/her misbehaviors and fails to accept responsibility for his/her actions. ▼

9. Explore and process the factors that contribute to the client's pattern of blaming others (e.g., harsh punishment experiences, family pattern of blaming others). ▼

▼ 7. Agree to learn alternative ways to think about and manage frustration, anger, and angry action. (10, 11)

10. Assist the client in reconceptualizing frustration and anger as involving different components (cognitive, physiological, affective, and behavioral) that go through predictable phases (e.g., demanding expectations not being met leading to increased arousal and anger leading to acting out) that can be managed. ▼

11. Assist the client in identifying the positive consequences of managing frustration and anger (e.g., respect from others and self, cooperation from others, improved physical health); ask the client to agree to learn new ways to conceptualize and manage anger and misbehavior (or assign "Anger Control" from the *Child Psychotherapy Homework Planner,* 2nd ed. by Jongsma, Peterson, and McInnis). ▼

▼ 8. Learn and implement calming strategies as part of a new way to manage reactions to frustration. (12)

12. Teach the client calming techniques (e.g., muscle relaxation, paced breathing, calming imagery) as part of a tailored strategy for responding appropriately to angry feelings when they occur. ▼

▼ 9. Identify, challenge, and replace self-talk that leads to frustration, anger, and angry actions with self-talk that facilitates more constructive reactions. (13)

13. Explore the client's self-talk that mediates his/her frustration and anger (e.g., demanding expectations reflected in should, must, or have to statements); identify and challenge biases, assisting him/her in generating appraisals and self-talk that corrects for the biases and facilitates a more flexible and temperate response to frustration. ▼

▼10. Learn and implement thought-stopping to manage intrusive unwanted thoughts that trigger anger and angry actions. (14)

14. Teach the client the "thought-stopping" technique and assign implementation on a daily basis between sessions; review implementation, reinforcing success and providing corrective feedback toward improvement. ▼

▼11. Verbalize feelings of frustration, disagreement, and anger in a controlled, assertive way. (15)

15. Use instruction, videotaped or live modeling, and/or role-playing to help develop the client's anger control skills, such as calming, self-statement, assertion skills; if indicated, refer him/her to an anger control group for further instruction. ▼

▼12. Implement problem-solving and/or conflict resolution skills to manage interpersonal problems constructively. (16)

16. Teach the client conflict resolution skills (e.g., empathy, active listening, "I messages," respectful communication, assertiveness without aggression, compromise); use modeling, role-playing, and behavior rehearsal to work through several current conflicts. ▼

▼13. Practice using new calming, communication, conflict resolution, and thinking skills. (17, 18)

17. Assist the client in constructing and consolidating a client-tailored strategy for managing anger that combines any of the somatic, cognitive, communication, problem-solving, and/or conflict resolution skills relevant to his/her needs. ▼

18. Use any of several techniques (e.g., relaxation, imagery, behavioral rehearsal, modeling, role-playing, feedback of videotaped practice) in increasingly challenging situations to help the client consolidate the use of his/her new anger management skills. ▼

▼14. Practice using new calming, communication, conflict resolution, and thinking skills in homework exercises. (19)

19. Assign the client homework exercises to help him/her practice newly learned calming, assertion, conflict resolution, or cognitive restructuring skills as needed; review and process toward the goal of consolidation. ▼

▼15. Decrease the number, intensity, and duration of angry outbursts, while increasing the use of new skills for managing anger. (20)

20. Monitor the client's reports of angry outbursts toward the goal of decreasing their frequency, intensity, and duration through the client's use of new anger management skills (or assign "Anger Control" or "Child Anger Checklist" in the *Child Psychotherapy Homework Planner,* 2nd ed. by Jongsma, Peterson, and McInnis); review progress, reinforcing success and providing corrective feedback toward improvement. ▼

▼16. Identify social supports that will help facilitate the implementation of new skills. (21)

21. Encourage the client to discuss and/or use his/her new anger management skills with trusted peers, family, or otherwise significant others who are likely to support his/her change. ▼

▼17. Parents learn and implement Parent Management Training skills to recognize and manage problem behavior of the client. (22, 23, 24, 25, 26)

22. Use a Parent Management Training approach beginning with teaching the parents how parent and child behavioral interactions can encourage or discourage positive or negative behavior and that changing key elements of those

interactions (e.g., prompting and reinforcing positive behaviors) can be used to promote positive change (e.g., *Parenting the Strong-Willed Child* by Forehand and Long; *Living with Children* by Patterson). ▼

23. Teach the parents how to specifically define and identify problem behaviors, identify their reactions to the behavior, determine whether the reaction encourages or discourages the behavior, and generate alternatives to the problem behavior. ▼

24. Teach parents how to implement key parenting practices consistently, including establishing realistic age-appropriate rules for acceptable and unacceptable behavior, prompting of positive behavior in the environment, use of positive reinforcement to encourage behavior (e.g., praise), use of clear and direct instruction, time out, and other loss-of-privilege practices for problem behavior. ▼

25. Assign the parents home exercises in which they implement and record results of implementation exercises (or assign "Clear Rules, Positive Reinforcement, Appropriate Consequences" in the *Adolescent Psychotherapy Homework Planner*, 2nd ed. by Jongsma, Peterson, and McInnis); review in session, providing corrective feedback toward improved, appropriate, and consistent use of skills. ▼

26. Ask the parents to read parent training manuals (e.g., *Living with Children* by Patterson) or watch videotapes demonstrating the techniques being learned in session (see Webster-Stratton, 1994). ▽

▼18. Parents and client participate in play sessions in which they use their new rules for appropriate conduct. (27, 28)

27. Conduct Parent-Child Interaction Therapy in which child-directed and parent-directed sessions focus on teaching appropriate child behavior, and parental behavioral management skills (e.g., clear commands, consistent consequences, positive reinforcement) are developed (see *Parent-Child Interaction Therapy* by Bell and Eyberg). ▽

28. Teach parents to use the time out technique as a consequence for inappropriate behavior; if possible, use a "signal seat" that has a battery-operated buzzer that serves as both a timer and an alert that the child is not staying in the seat (see Hamilton and Mac-Quiddy, 1984). ▽

▼19. Increase compliance with rules at home and school. (29)

29. Design a reward system and/or contingency contract for the client and meet with school officials to reinforce identified positive behaviors at home and school and deter impulsive or rebellious behaviors. ▽

▼20. Parents verbalize appropriate boundaries for discipline to prevent further occurrences of abuse and to ensure the safety of the client and his/her siblings. (30, 31)

30. Explore the client's family background for a history of neglect and physical or sexual abuse that may contribute to his/her behavioral problems; confront the client's parents to cease physically abusive or overly punitive methods of discipline. ▽

31. Implement the steps necessary to protect the client or siblings from further abuse (e.g., report abuse to the appropriate agencies; remove the client or perpetrator from the home). ▼

▼21. Increase the frequency of civil, respectful interactions with parents/adults. (32)

32. Establish with the client the basics of treating others respectfully. Teach the principle of reciprocity, asking him/her to agree to treat everyone in a respectful manner for a 1-week period to see if others will reciprocate by treating him/her with more respect. ▼

▼22. Demonstrate the ability to play by the rules in a cooperative fashion. (33)

33. Use puppets, dolls, or stuffed animals to create a story that models appropriate ways to manage anger and resolve conflict; ask the client to create a story with similar characters or themes; play games (e.g., checkers) toward the same goals. ▼

▼23. Increase the frequency of responsible and positive social behaviors. (34, 35)

34. Direct the client to engage in three altruistic or benevolent acts (e.g., read to a developmentally disabled student, mow grandmother's lawn) before the next session to increase his/her empathy and sensitivity to the needs of others. ▼

35. Place the client in charge of tasks at home (e.g., preparing and cooking a special dish for a family get-together, building shelves in the garage, changing oil in the car) to demonstrate confidence in his/her ability to act responsibly. ▼

24. Identify and verbally express feelings associated with past neglect, abuse, separation, or abandonment. (36)

36. Encourage and support the client in expressing feelings associated with neglect, abuse, separation, or abandonment and help process

(e.g., assign the task of writing a letter to an absent parent or use the empty-chair technique or assign "The Lesson of Salmon Rock . . . Fighting Leads to Loneliness" in the *Child Psychotherapy Homework Planner,* 2nd ed. by Jongsma, Peterson, and McInnis).

25. Parents participate in marital therapy. (37)

37. Assess the marital dyad for possible substance abuse, conflict, or triangulation that shifts the focus from marriage issues to the client's acting out behaviors; refer for appropriate treatment, if needed.

26. Identify and verbally acknowledge family dynamics that contribute to the emergence of anger control problems. (38, 39, 40)

38. Conduct family therapy sessions to explore the dynamics that contribute to the emergence of the client's anger control problems.

39. Assess the family dynamics by employing the family-sculpting technique, in which the client defines the roles and behaviors of each family member in a scene of his/her choosing.

40. Give a directive to uninvolved or disengaged parent(s) to spend more time with the client in leisure, school, or work activities; review progress, reinforcing success and redirecting failure.

___. _____
_____

___. _____
_____

___. _____
_____

___. _____
_____

___. _____
_____

___. _____
_____

DIAGNOSTIC SUGGESTIONS

Axis I:	312.81	Conduct Disorder, Childhood-Onset Type
	312.82	Conduct Disorder, Adolescent-Onset Type
	312.89	Conduct Disorder, Unspecified Onset
	313.81	Oppositional Defiant Disorder
	312.9	Disruptive Behavior Disorder NOS
	314.01	Attention-Deficit/Hyperactivity Disorder, Predominantly Hyperactive-Impulsive Type
	314.9	Attention-Deficit/Hyperactivity Disorder NOS
	312.34	Intermittent Explosive Disorder
	V71.02	Child Antisocial Behavior
	V61.20	Parent-Child Relational Problem
	_____	_____
	_____	_____
Axis II:	V71.09	No Diagnosis
	_____	_____
	_____	_____

ANXIETY

BEHAVIORAL DEFINITIONS

1. Excessive anxiety, worry, or fear that markedly exceeds the normal level for the client's stage of development.
2. High level of motor tension, such as restlessness, tiredness, shakiness, or muscle tension.
3. Autonomic hyperactivity (e.g., rapid heartbeat, shortness of breath, dizziness, dry mouth, nausea, diarrhea).
4. Hypervigilance, such as feeling constantly on edge, concentration difficulties, trouble falling or staying asleep, and a general state of irritability.
5. A specific fear that has become generalized to cover a wide area and has reached the point where it significantly interferes with the client's and the family's daily life.
6. Excessive anxiety or worry due to parent's threat of abandonment, overuse of guilt, denial of autonomy and status. friction between parents, or interference with physical activity.

___. _____

_____

___. _____

_____

___. _____

_____

LONG-TERM GOALS

1. Reduce overall frequency, intensity, and duration of the anxiety so that daily functioning is not impaired.
2. Stabilize anxiety level while increasing ability to function on a daily basis.

3. Resolve the core conflict that is the source of anxiety.
4. Enhance ability to effectively cope with the full variety of life's anxieties.

__. _____
_____
_____

__. _____
_____

__. _____
_____

SHORT-TERM OBJECTIVES

THERAPEUTIC INTERVENTIONS

1. Describe current and past experiences with specific fears, prominent worries, and anxiety symptoms including their impact on functioning and attempts to resolve it. (1, 2)

1. Actively build the level of trust with the client through consistent eye contact, active listening, unconditional positive regard, and warm acceptance to help increase his/her ability to identify and express concerns.

2. Assess the focus, excessiveness, and uncontrollability of the client's fears and worries and the type, frequency, intensity, and duration of his/her anxiety symptoms (e.g., *The Anxiety Disorders Interview Schedule for Children— Parent Version* or *Child Version* by Silverman and Albano; "Finding and Losing Your Anxiety" in the *Child Psychotherapy Homework Planner,* 2nd ed. by Jongsma, Peterson, and McInnis).

2. Complete questionnaires designed to assess fear, worry, and anxiety symptoms. (3)

3. Administer a patient-report measure to help assess the nature and degree of the client's fears, worries, and anxiety symptoms (e.g., *The Fear Survey Schedule for Children* by Ollendick).

▼ 3. Cooperate with an evaluation by a physician for antianxiety medication. (4, 5)

4. Refer the client to a physician for a psychotropic medication consultation. ▼

5. Monitor the client's psychotropic medication compliance, side effects, and effectiveness; confer regularly with the physician. ▼

▼ 4. Verbalize an understanding of how thoughts, physical feelings, and behavioral actions contribute to anxiety and its treatment. (6, 7, 8)

6. Discuss how fears and worries typically involve excessive concern about unrealistic threats; various bodily expressions of tension, overarousal, and hypervigilance; and avoidance of what is threatening, which interact to maintain the problem (see *Helping Your Anxious Child* by Rapee, Spence, Cobham, and Wignall). ▼

7. Discuss how treatment targets fear, worry, anxiety symptoms, and avoidance to help the client manage thoughts and overarousal effectively while overcoming unnecessary avoidance. ▼

8. Assign the parents to read psychoeducational sections of books or treatment manuals to emphasize key therapy concepts (e.g., *Helping Your Anxious Child* by Rapee, Spence, Cobham, and Wignall). ▼

▼ 5. Learn and implement calming skills to reduce overall anxiety and manage anxiety symptoms. (9, 10, 11, 12)

9. Teach the client calming skills (e.g., progressive muscle relaxation, guided imagery, slow diaphragmatic breathing) and how to discriminate better between relaxation and tension; teach the client how to apply these skills to his/her daily life. ▼

▼ indicates that the Objective/Intervention is consistent with those found in evidence-based treatments.

10. Assign the client homework each session in which he/she practices calming daily; review and reinforce success while providing corrective feedback toward improvement. ▼

11. Assign the parents to read and discuss with the client progressive muscle relaxation and other calming strategies in relevant books or treatment manuals (e.g., *New Directions in Progressive Relaxation Training* by Bernstein, Borkovec, and Hazlett-Stevens). ▼

12. Use biofeedback techniques to facilitate the client's success at learning relaxation skills. ▼

▼ 6. Verbalize an understanding of the role that fearful thinking plays in creating fears, excessive worry, and persistent anxiety symptoms. (13, 14, 15)

13. Discuss examples demonstrating that unrealistic fear or worry typically overestimates the probability of threats and underestimates the client's ability to manage realistic demands. ▼

14. Assist the client in challenging his/her fear or worry by examining the actual probability of the negative expectation occurring, the real consequences of it occurring, his/her ability to manage the likely outcome, the worst possible outcome, and his/her ability to accept it (see *Helping Your Anxious Child* by Rapee, Spence, Cobham, and Wignall). ▼

15. Help the client gain insight into the notion that fear and worry involve a form of avoidance of the problem, that this creates anxious arousal, and precludes resolution. ▼

▼ 7. Identify, challenge, and replace fearful self-talk with positive, realistic, and empowering self-talk. (16, 17, 18, 19)

16. Explore the client's schema and self-talk that mediate his/her fear response; challenge the biases; assist him/her in replacing the distorted messages with reality-based alternatives and positive self-talk that will increase his/her self-confidence in coping with irrational fears or worries. ▼

17. Assign the client a homework exercise in which he/she identifies fearful self-talk and creates reality-based alternatives (or assign "Tools for Anxiety" in the *Adolescent Psychotherapy Homework Planner II* by Jongsma, Peterson, and McInnis); review and reinforce success, providing corrective feedback toward improvement. ▼

18. Teach the client to implement a "thought-stopping" technique (thinking of a STOP sign and then a pleasant scene) for fears or worries that have been addressed but persist (or assign "Making Use of the Thought-Stopping Technique" in the *Adult Psychotherapy Homework Planner,* 2nd ed. by Jongsma); monitor and encourage the client's use of the technique in daily life between sessions. ▼

19. Assign parents to read and discuss with the client cognitive restructuring of fears or worries in relevant books or treatment manuals (e.g., *Helping Your Anxious Child* by Rapee, Spence, Cobham, and Wignall). ▼

▼ 8. Participate in live, or imaginal then live, exposure exercises in which worries and fears are gradually faced. (20, 21, 22, 23)

20. Direct and assist the client in constructing a hierarchy around two to three spheres of worry for use in exposure (e.g., fears of school

failure, worries about relationship problems). ▼

21. Select initial exposures that have a high likelihood of being a success experience for the client; develop a coping plan for managing the negative affect engendered by exposure; mentally rehearse the procedure. ▼

22. Ask the client to vividly imagine conducting the exposure, or conduct it live until anxiety associated with it weakens and a sense of safety and/or confidence strengthens; process the experience. ▼

23. Assign the client a homework exercise in which he/she does gradual exposure to identified fears and records responses (see *Phobic and Anxiety Disorders in Children and Adolescents* by Ollendick and March*)*; review, reinforce success, and provide corrective feedback toward improvement (or assign "Gradually Facing a Phobic Fear" in the *Adolescent Psychotherapy Homework Planner,* 2nd ed. by Jongsma, Peterson, and McInnis). ▼

▼ 9. Learn and implement new strategies for realistically addressing fears or worries. (24, 25)

24. Ask the client to develop a list of key conflicts that trigger fear or worry and process this list, teaching skills, toward resolution (e.g., problem-solving, assertiveness, acceptance, cognitive restructuring). ▼

25. Assign the client a homework exercise in which he/she works on solving a current problem (see *Helping Your Anxious Child* by Rapee, Spence, Cobham, and

Wignall; or "An Anxious Story" from the *Child Psychotherapy Homework Planner,* 2nd ed. by Jongsma, Peterson, and McIn-nis*)*; review, reinforce success, and provide corrective feedback toward improvement. ▼

▼10. Increase participation in daily social and academic activities. (26)

26. Encourage the client to strengthen his/her new nonavoidant ap-proach by using distraction from anxious thoughts through increas-ing daily social and academic activities and other potentially rewarding experiences. ▼

▼11. Parents verbalize an understand-ing of the client's treatment plan and a willingness to participate in it with the client. (27)

27. If acceptable to the client and if possible, involve the client's par-ents in the treatment, having them participate in selective activities. ▼

▼12. Parents learn and implement constructive ways to respond to the client's fear and avoidance. (28, 29)

28. Conduct Family Anxiety Man-agement sessions (see *FRIENDS Program for Children* series by Barrett, Lowry-Webster, and Turner) in which the family is taught how to prompt and reward courageous behavior, empatheti-cally ignore excessive complaining and other avoidant behaviors, manage their own anxieties, and model the behavior being taught in session. ▼

29. Teach family members problem-solving and communication skills to assist the client's progress through therapy. ▼

▼13. Parents learn and implement problem-solving strategies, assertive communication, and other constructive ways to respond to their own anxieties. (30)

30. Teach and encourage parents to use the same nonavoidant skills the client is learning to manage and approach their own fears and worries, including problem-solving conflicts and assertive communication (e.g., *Keys to Parenting Your Anxious Child* by Manassis). ▼

▼14. Learn and implement relapse prevention strategies for managing possible future fears or worries. (31, 32, 33, 34)

31. Discuss with the client the distinction between a lapse and relapse, associating a lapse with an initial and reversible return of a fear, worry, anxiety symptom, or urges to avoid and relapse with the decision to return to a fearful and avoidant manner of dealing with the fear or worry. ▼

32. Identify and rehearse with the client the management of future situations or circumstances in which lapses could occur. ▼

33. Instruct the client to routinely use his/her newly learned skills in relaxation, cognitive restructuring, exposure, and problem-solving exposures as needed to address emergent fears or worries, building them into his/her life as much as possible. ▼

34. Develop a "coping card" or other reminder on which coping strategies and other important information (e.g., "Breathe deeply and relax," "Challenge unrealistic worries," "Use problem-solving") are recorded for the client's later use. ▼

15. Verbalize an increased understanding of anxious feelings and their causes. (35, 36, 37)

35. Use child-centered play therapy approaches (e.g., provide unconditional positive regard; reflect feelings in a nonjudgmental manner; display trust in child's capacity to work through issues) to increase the client's ability to cope with anxious feelings.

36. Assign the client the task of drawing two or three situations that generally bring on anxious feelings.

16. Identify areas of conflict that underlie the anxiety. (38, 39)

17. Identify and use specific coping strategies for anxiety reduction. (40, 41, 42, 43)

37. Conduct psychoanalytical play therapy sessions (e.g., explore and gain an understanding of the etiology of unconscious conflicts, fixations, or arrests; interpret resistance or core anxieties) to help the client work through to resolutions of the issues that are the source of his/her anxiety.

38. Use puppets, felts, or a sand tray to enact situations that provoke anxiety in the client. Involve him/her in creating such scenarios, and model positive cognitive responses to the situations that bring on anxiety.

39. Play the therapeutic game, My Home and Places (Flood) with the client to help identify and talk about divorce, peers, alcohol abuse, or other situations that make him/her anxious.

40. Use a narrative approach (White) in which the client writes out the story of his/her anxiety or fear and then acts out the story with the therapist to externalize the issues. Work with the client to reach a resolution or develop an effective way to cope with the anxiety or fear (see "An Anxious Story" from the *Child Psychotherapy Homework Planner,* 2nd ed. by Jongsma, Peterson, and McInnis).

41. Conduct sessions with a focus on anxiety-producing situations in which techniques of storytelling, drawing pictures, and viewing photographs are used to assist the client in talking about and reducing the level of anxiety or fear.

42. Use a mutual storytelling technique (Gardner) in which the client tells a story about a central character who becomes anxious. The therapist then interprets the story for its underlying meaning and retells the client's story while weaving in healthier adaptations to fear or anxiety and resolution of conflicts.

43. Prescribe a Predication Task (Shuzer) for anxiety management. (The client predicts the night before whether the anxiety will bother him/her the next day. The therapist directs the client to be a good detective and bring back key elements that contributed to it being a "good day" so the therapist then can reinforce or construct a solution to increasing the frequency of "good days.")

18. Parents verbalize constructive ways to respond to the client's anxiety. (44, 45, 46)

44. Work with the parents in family sessions to develop their skills in effectively responding to the client's fears and anxieties with calm confidence rather than fearful reactivity (e.g., parents remind the client of a time when he/she handled a fearful situation effectively; express confidence in the client's ability to face the fearful situation).

45. Educate the client's parents to increase their awareness and understanding of which fears and anxieties are normal for various stages of child development.

46. Assign the client's parents to read books related to child development and parenting (e.g., *Between Parent and Child* by Ginott; *How to Talk So Kids Will Listen and Listen So Kids Will Talk* by Faber and Mazlish).

19. Participate in family therapy sessions that identify and resolve conflicts between family members. (47, 48)

47. Conduct a family session in which the system is probed to determine the level of fear or anxiety that is present or to bring to the surface underlying conflicts.

48. Work in family sessions to resolve conflicts and to increase the family's level of healthy functioning.

__. _____

_____

__. _____

_____

__. _____

_____

__. _____

_____

__. _____

_____

__. _____

_____

DIAGNOSTIC SUGGESTIONS

Axis I: 300.02   Generalized Anxiety Disorder
           300.00   Anxiety Disorder NOS
           314.01   Attention-Deficit/Hyperactivity Disorder, Combined Type

_____   _____

_____   _____

Axis II: V71.09   No Diagnosis

_____   _____

_____   _____

ATTACHMENT DISORDER

BEHAVIORAL DEFINITIONS

1. Brought into family through adoption after coming from an abusive, neglectful biological family.
2. Consistent pattern of failing to initiate or respond to social interactions in an age-appropriate way (e.g., withdrawing and rejecting behavior toward primary caregivers, a general detached manner toward everyone).
3. Pattern of becoming friendly too quickly and/or showing indiscriminate affection to strangers.
4. Three years old or older and has no significant bond with any caregiver.
5. Resists accepting care from others, usually being very insistent that he/she does not need help from anyone.
6. Hoarding or gorging food.
7. Aggressive behaviors toward peers, siblings, and caregivers.
8. Frequent lying without remorse.
9. Stealing petty items without need for them.
10. By age 7, little or no sign of conscience development is evident (e.g., shows no guilt or remorse when confronted with his/her misbehavior).
11. Excessive clinginess to primary caregiver, becoming emotionally distraught when out of caregiver's immediate presence.
12. Has experienced persistent disregard for his/her emotional and/or physical needs.
13. Has been subjected to frequent changes in primary caregiver.

—. _____
_____
—. _____
_____
—. _____
_____

LONG-TERM GOALS

1. Establishment and maintenance of a bond with primary caregivers.
2. Resolution of all barriers to forming healthy connections with others.
3. Capable of forming warm physical and emotional bonds with the parents.
4. Has a desire for and initiates connections with others.
5. Keeps appropriate distance from strangers.
6. Tolerates reasonable absence from presence of parent or primary caregiver without panic.

—. _____
_____

—. _____
_____

—. _____
_____

SHORT-TERM OBJECTIVES

1. Openly express thoughts and feelings. (1, 2, 3)

THERAPEUTIC INTERVENTIONS

1. Actively build the level of trust with the client through consistent eye contact, active listening, unconditional positive regard, and empathic responses to help promote the open expressions of his/her thoughts and feelings.

2. Conduct a celebrity-style interview with the client to elicit information (e.g., school likes/dislikes, favorite food, music, best birthday, hopes, wishes, dreams, "if I had a million dollars") in order to build a relationship and help him/her learn more about himself/herself.

3. Conduct all sessions in a consistent and predictable manner so that all is clear for the client and he/she can start to take a risk and trust the therapist.

2. Cooperate with and complete all assessments and testing. (4, 5)

4. Conduct or refer the parents and the client for psychosocial evaluation to assess the strength of the parent's marriage, parenting style, stress management/coping strengths, resolutions of the infertility issue, and to assess the client's developmental level, attachment capacity, behavior issues, temperament, and strengths.

5. Conduct or arrange for psychological evaluation to determine level of behavioral functioning, cognitive style, and intelligence.

3. Comply with all recommendations of assessments and evaluations. (6)

6. Summarize assessment data and present findings and recommendations to the family; monitor and encourage their follow-through on all the recommendations on each evaluation and assessment.

4. Parents commit to improving the communication and affection within the marriage relationship. (7)

7. Refer the parents to a skills-based marital program such as PREP (e.g., *Fighting for Your Marriage* by Markman, Stanley, and Blumberg) to strengthen their marital relationship by improving personal responsibility, communication, and conflict resolution.

5. Parents acknowledge unresolved grief associated with infertility. (8)

8. Assess the parents' unresolved grief around the issue of their infertility; refer them for further conjoint or individual treatment if necessary.

6. Parent(s) make a verbal commitment to take an active role in the client's treatment and in developing skills to work with the client and his/her issues. (9, 10, 11)

9. Elicit from the parents a firm commitment to be an active part of the client's treatment by participating in sessions and being cotherapists in the home.

10. Work with the parents in conjoint sessions to frame the client's acting out behaviors as opportunities to reparent the client. Then

strategize with them to come up with specific ways to intervene in the problem behaviors.

11. Train and empower the parents as cotherapists (e.g., being patient, showing unconditional positive regard, setting limits firmly but without hostility, verbalizing love and expectations clearly, seeking to understand messages of pain and fear beneath the acting out behavior) in the process of developing the client's capacity to form healthy bonds/connections.

7. Parents verbalize an understanding of the dynamics of attachment and trauma. (12)

12. Provide education to the parents on the nature of attachment and the overall effect of trauma on children and families.

8. Parents verbalize reasonable expectations regarding progress. (13, 14)

13. Process with the parents the issue of expectations for the client's behavior and adjustment; confront and modify unrealistic expectations regarding their child's emotional attachment progress and foster more realistic expectations considering the client's history.

14. Explore with the parents the reality that "strong relationships involve love, understanding, trust, time, money, sharing, giving, stimulating, and inspiring; they seldom come automatically, and love may be the last thing on the list rather than the first" (see *Anxiously Awaiting Attachment* by Paddock).

9. Attend and actively take part in play therapy sessions. (15, 16, 17)

15. Use the *Theraplay* (Jernberg and Booth) attachment-based approach, in which the therapist takes charge by planning and structuring each session. The

therapist uses his/her power to entice the client into a relationship and to keep the focus of therapy on the relationship, not on intrapsychic conflicts. Also, the parents are actively involved and are trained to be cotherapists.

16. Employ the ACT Model (Landreth) in play therapy sessions to acknowledge feelings, communicate limits, and target acceptable alternatives to acting out or aggressive behaviors.

17. Conduct filial therapy (i.e., parent involvement in play therapy sessions), whereby the client takes the lead in expressing anger and the parent responds empathically to the client's feelings (e.g., hurt, fear, sadness, helplessness) beneath the anger.

10. Parents acknowledge their frustrations regarding living with a detached child and state their commitment to keep trying. (18, 19)

18. Suggest to the parents that they read books to increase their understanding and give encouragement in continuing to work with their child (e.g., *The Difficult Child* by Turecki; *The Challenging Child* by Greenspan).

19. Empathize with the parents' frustrations regarding living with a detached child; allow them to share their pain and disappointment while reinforcing their commitment to keep trying.

11. Share fears attached to new situations. (20)

20. Encourage the client to share his/her fears in order to gain self-acceptance (or assign the exercise "Dixie Overcomes Her Fears" from the *Child Psychotherapy Homework Planner*, 2nd ed. by Jongsma, Peterson, and McInnis).

12. Identify specific positive talents, traits, and accomplishments about self. (21)

13. Verbalize memories of the past that have shaped current identity and emotional reactions. (22, 23)

14. Parents acknowledge the client's history and affirm him/her as an individual. (23)

15. Parents spend one-on-one time with the client in active play. (24)

16. Parents gradually increase the frequency of expressing affection verbally and physically toward the client. (25)

17. Report an increased ability to trust, giving examples of trust. (26, 27)

21. Assign a self-esteem-building exercise from *SEALS & Plus* (Korb-Khalsa, Azok, and Leutenberg) to help develop self-knowledge, acceptance, and confidence.

22. Assign the parents to help the client create a *life book* that chronicles his/her life to this point in order to give a visual perspective and knowledge of his/her history and identity (or assign the exercise "Create a Memory Album" in the *Child Psychotherapy Homework Planner,* 2nd ed. by Jongsma, Peterson, and McInnis).

23. Educate the parents on the importance of affirming the client's entire identity (i.e., self, bioparents, adoptive parents), and show them specific ways to reaffirm him/her.

23. Educate the parents on the importance of affirming the client's entire identity (i.e., self, bioparents, adoptive parents), and show them specific ways to reaffirm him/her.

24. Assign the parents to each spend specific time in daily one-on-one active play with the client.

25. Encourage the parents to provide large, genuine, daily doses of positive verbal reinforcement and physical affection. Monitor and encourage the parents to continue this behavior and to identify positive attachment signs when they appear.

26. Have the client attend an initiative or adventure-based summer camp to build his/her self-esteem, trust

in self and others, conflict resolution skills, and relationship skills.

27. Conduct a family session in which the parents, client, and therapist take part in a trust walk. (One person is blindfolded and led around by a guide through a number of tasks. Then roles are reversed and the process is repeated.) The object is to increase the client's awareness of his/her trust issues and to expand his/her sense of trust. Process and repeat at intervals over the course of treatment as a way to measure the client's progress in building trust.

18. Recognize and express angry feelings without becoming emotionally out of control. (28, 29)

28. Train the client in meditation and focused breathing as self-calming techniques to use when tension, anger, or frustration is building.

29. Read and process with the client *Don't Rant and Rave on Wednesdays!* (Moser) to assist him/her in finding ways to handle angry feelings in a controlled, effective way.

19. Parents demonstrate firm boundaries on the client's expressions of anger. (18, 30, 31)

18. Suggest to the parents that they read books to increase their understanding and give encouragement in continuing to work with their child (e.g., *The Difficult Child* by Turecki; *The Challenging Child* by Greenspan).

30. Help the parents to design preventive safety measures (i.e., supervision and environmental controls) if the client's behavior becomes dangerous or frightening.

31. Direct the parents to give constant feedback, structure, and repeated emphasis of expectations to the client in order to reassure

him/her that they are firmly in control and that they will not allow his/her intense feelings to get out of hand.

20. Family engages in social/recreational activities together. (32)

32. Encourage the parents to engage the client and family in many "cohesive shared experiences" (see James in *Handbook for Treatment of Attachment-Trauma Problems in Children*), such as attending church, singing together at home, attending sports events, building and work projects, and helping others.

21. Accept physical contact with family members without withdrawal. (33)

33. Assign the family the homework exercise of 10 minutes of physical touching twice daily for 2 weeks (see James in *Handbook for Treatment of Attachment-Trauma Problems in Children*) to decrease the client's barriers to others. (This can take the form of snuggling with the parent while watching television, feet or shoulder massage, being held in a rocking chair, or physical recreational games.) Process the experience with the therapist at the end of 2 weeks.

22. Parents use respite care to protect selves from burnout. (34, 35)

34. Assist the parents in finding care providers, then encourage and monitor the parents' use of respite care on a scheduled basis to avoid burnout and to keep their energy level high, as well as to build trust with the client through the natural process of leaving and returning.

35. Meet with the parents conjointly on a regular basis to allow them to vent their concerns and frustrations in dealing day in and day out with the client. Also, provide the parents with specific suggestions to handle difficult situations when they feel stuck.

23. Parents respond calmly but firmly to the client's detachment behavior. (36, 37)

36. Educate the parents to understand the psychological meaning and purpose for the client's detachment, and train them to implement appropriate interventions to deal day to day with the behavior in a therapeutic way (e.g., calmly reflecting on the client's feelings, ignoring negative behavior as much as is reasonably possible, rewarding any approximation of prosocial behavior, practicing unconditional positive regard).

37. Monitor the parents' implementation of interventions for detachment behavior and evaluate the effectiveness of their interventions; assist in making adjustments to interventions so that the client's feelings do not get out of hand.

24. Parents give the client choices and allow him/her to make own decisions. (38)

38. Ask the parents to give the client as many choices as is reasonable and possible to impart a sense of control and empowerment to him/her.

25. Complete a psychotropic medication evaluation and comply with all recommendations. (39)

39. Arrange for the client to have a psychiatric evaluation for medication, and if psychotropic medication is prescribed, monitor the client for compliance, side effects, and overall effectiveness of the medication.

26. Report a completion to the process of mourning losses in life. (40)

40. Assist, guide, and support the client in working through each stage of the grief process (see Grief/Loss Unresolved chapter in this *Planner*).

__·_____

_____

__·_____

_____

—. ———————————————————   —. ———————————————————
    ———————————————————   ———————————————————
—. ———————————————————   —. ———————————————————
    ———————————————————   ———————————————————

DIAGNOSTIC SUGGESTIONS

Axis I:	313.89	Reactive Attachment Disorder of Infancy and Early Childhood
	314.9	Attention-Deficit/Hyperactivity Disorder NOS
	296.3x	Major Depressive Disorder, Recurrent
	300.4	Dysthymic Disorder
	309.4	Adjustment Disorder With Mixed Disturbance of Emotions and Conduct
	309.81	Posttraumatic Stress Disorder
	300.3	Obsessive-Compulsive Disorder
	313.81	Oppositional Defiant Disorder
	————————————	
	————————————	
Axis II:	V71.09	No Diagnosis
	————————————	
	————————————	

ATTENTION-DEFICIT/HYPERACTIVITY DISORDER (ADHD)

BEHAVIORAL DEFINITIONS

✓ 1. Short attention span; difficulty sustaining attention on a consistent basis.
2. Susceptibility to distraction by extraneous stimuli and internal thoughts.
✓ 3. Gives impression that he/she is not listening well.
4. Repeated failure to follow through on instructions or complete school assignments or chores in a timely manner.
✓ 5. Poor organizational skills as demonstrated by forgetfulness, inattention to details, and losing things necessary for tasks.
6. Hyperactivity as evidenced by a high energy level, restlessness, difficulty sitting still, or loud or excessive talking.
7. Impulsivity as evidenced by difficulty awaiting turn in group situations, blurting out answers to questions before the questions have been completed, and frequent intrusions into others' personal business.
8. Frequent disruptive, aggressive, or negative attention-seeking behaviors.
9. Tendency to engage in carelessness or potentially dangerous activities.
10. Difficulty accepting responsibility for actions, projecting blame for problems onto others, and failing to learn from experience.
✓ 11. Low self-esteem and poor social skills.

___. _____

_____

___. _____

_____

___. _____

_____

LONG-TERM GOALS

1. Sustain attention and concentration for consistently longer periods of ✓ time.
2. Increase the frequency of on-task behaviors. ✓
3. Demonstrate marked improvement in impulse control.
4. Regularly take medication as prescribed to decrease impulsivity, hyperactiv- ✓ ity, and distractibility.
5. Parents and/or teachers successfully utilize a reward system, contingency contract, or token economy to reinforce positive behaviors and deter nega- tive behaviors.
6. Parents set firm, consistent limits and maintain appropriate parent-child ✓ boundaries.
7. Develop positive social skills to help maintain lasting peer friendships.

—. _____

_____

—. _____

_____

—. _____

_____

SHORT-TERM OBJECTIVES

THERAPEUTIC INTERVENTIONS

1. Complete psychological test- ing to confirm the diagnosis of ADHD and/or rule out emo- tional factors. (1)

1. Arrange for psychological test- ing to confirm the presence of ✓ ADHD and/or rule out emotional problems that may be contribut- ing to the client's inattentiveness, impulsivity, and hyperactivity; give feedback to the client and his/her parents regarding the test- ing results.

▼ 2. Take prescribed medication as directed by the physician. (2, 3)

2. Arrange for a medication evalua- ✓ tion for the client. ▼

___

▼ indicates that the Objective/Intervention is consistent with those found in evidence-based treatments.

3.   Monitor the client for psychotropic medication prescription
compliance, side effects, and
effectiveness; consult with the
prescribing physician at regular
intervals. ▼

▼ 3. Parents and the client demonstrate increased knowledge
about ADHD symptoms.
(4, 5, 6)

4.   Educate the client's parents and
siblings about the symptoms of
ADHD. ▼

5.   Assign the parents readings to
increase their knowledge about
symptoms of ADHD (e.g., *Taking
Charge of ADHD* by Barkley;
Your Hyperactive Child by Ingersoll; *Dr. Larry Silver's Advice
to Parents on Attention Deficit
Hyperactivity Disorder* by Silver).
▼

6.   Assign the client readings to
increase his/her knowledge
about ADHD and ways to manage symptoms (e.g., *Putting on
the Brakes* by Quinn and Stern;
*Sometimes I Drive My Mom
Crazy, but I Know She's Crazy
about Me* by Shapiro). ▼

▼ 4. Parents develop and utilize an
organized system to keep track
of the client's school assignments, chores, and household
responsibilities. (7, 8)

7.   Assist the parents in developing
and implementing an organizational system to increase the
client's on-task behaviors and
completion of school assignments, chores, or household
responsibilities (e.g., using calendars, charts, notebooks, and class
syllabi). ▼

8.   Assist the parents in developing
a routine schedule to increase the
client's compliance with school,
household, or work-related responsibilities. ▼

▼ 5. Parents maintain communication with the school to increase the client's compliance with completion of school assignments. (9)

▼ 6. Utilize effective study skills on a regular basis to improve academic performance. (10, 11)

▼ 7. Increase frequency of completion of school assignments, chores, and household responsibilities. (8, 12, 13)

9. Encourage the parents and teachers to maintain regular communication about the client's academic, behavioral, emotional, and social progress (or assign "Getting It Done" in the *Child Psychotherapy Homework Planner,* 2nd ed. by Jongsma, Peterson, and McInnis). ▼

10. Teach the client more effective study skills (e.g., clearing away distractions, studying in quiet places, scheduling breaks in studying). ▼

11. Assign the client to read *13 Steps to Better Grades* (Silverman) to improve organizational and study skills (or assign "Establish a Homework Routine" in the *Child Psychotherapy Homework Planner,* 2nd ed. by Jongsma, Peterson, and McInnis). ▼

8. Assist the parents in developing a routine schedule to increase the client's compliance with school, household, or work-related responsibilities. ▼

12. Consult with the client's teachers to implement strategies to improve school performance, such as sitting in the front row during class, using a prearranged signal to redirect the client back to task, scheduling breaks from tasks, providing frequent feedback, calling on the client often, arranging for a listening buddy, implementing a daily behavioral report card. ▼

13. Encourage the parents and teachers to use a behavioral classroom intervention (e.g., a school contract and reward system) to

reinforce appropriate behavior and completion of his/her assignments (or employ the "Getting It Done" program in the *Child Psychotherapy Homework Planner,* 2nd ed. by Jongsma, Peterson, and McInnis). ▼

▼ 8. Implement effective test-taking strategies on a consistent basis to improve academic performance. (14)

14. Teach the client more effective test-taking strategies (e.g., reviewing material regularly, reading directions twice, rechecking work). ▼

▼ 9. Delay instant gratification in favor of achieving meaningful long-term goals. (15, 16)

15. Teach the client mediational and self-control strategies (e.g., "stop, look, listen, and think") to delay the need for instant gratification and inhibit impulses to achieve more meaningful, longer-term goals. ▼

16. Assist the parents in increasing structure to help the client learn to delay gratification for longer-term goals (e.g., completing homework or chores before playing). ▼

▼ 10. Parents implement Parent Management Training approach in which parents utilize a reward/punishment system, contingency contract, and/or token economy. (17, 18, 19, 20, 21)

17. Teach the parents a Parent Management Training approach (e.g., a reward/punishment system, contingency contract, token economy), explaining how parent and child behavioral interactions can reduce the frequency of impulsive, disruptive, and negative attention-seeking behaviors and increase desired behavior (e.g., prompting and reinforcing positive behaviors; see *Parenting the Strong-Willed Child* by Forehand and Long; *Living with Children* by Patterson). ▼

18. Teach the parents how to specifically define and identify problem

behaviors, identify their reactions to the behavior, determine whether the reaction encourages or discourages the behavior, and generate alternatives to the problem behavior. ▽

19. Teach parents how to implement key parenting practices consistently, including establishing realistic age-appropriate rules for acceptable and unacceptable behavior, prompting of positive behavior in the environment, use of positive reinforcement to encourage behavior (e.g., praise), use of clear direct instruction, time out, and other loss-of-privilege practices for problem behavior. ▽

20. Assign the parents home exercises in which they implement and record results of implementation exercises (or assign "Clear Rules, Positive Reinforcement, Appropriate Consequences" in the *Adolescent Psychotherapy Homework Planner,* 2nd ed. by Jongsma, Peterson, and McInnis); review in session, providing corrective feedback toward improved, appropriate, and consistent use of skills. ▽

21. Ask the parents to read parent training manuals (e.g., *Living with Children* by Patterson) or watch videotapes demonstrating the techniques being learned in session (see Webster-Stratton, 1994). ▽

▽11. Learn and implement social skills to reduce anxiety and build confidence in social interactions. (22, 23)

22. Use instruction, modeling, and role-playing to build the client's general and developmentally appropriate social and/or communication skills. ▽

23. Assign the client to read about general social and/or communication skills in books or treatment manuals on building social skills (e.g., or assign the "Social Skills Exercise" in the *Child Psychotherapy Homework Planner,* 2nd ed. by Jongsma, Peterson, and McInnis). ▼

▼12. Identify and implement effective problem-solving strategies. (24, 25)

24. Teach older clients effective problem-solving skills (e.g., identifying the problem, brainstorming alternative solutions, selecting an option, implementing a course of action, evaluating). ▼

25. Utilize role-playing and modeling to teach the older child how to implement effective problem-solving techniques in his/her daily life (or assign "Stop, Think, and Act" in the *Child Psychotherapy Homework Planner,* 2nd ed. by Jongsma, Peterson, and McInnis, or use the therapeutic game, Stop, Relax and Think by Bridges [available from Childswork/Childsplay]). ▼

▼13. Increase the frequency of positive interactions with parents. (26, 27, 28)

26. Explore for periods of time when the client demonstrated good impulse control and engaged in fewer disruptive behaviors; process his/her responses and reinforce positive coping mechanisms that he/she used to deter impulsive or disruptive behaviors. ▼

27. Instruct the parents to observe and record three to five positive behaviors by the client in between therapy sessions; reinforce positive behaviors and encourage him/her to continue to exhibit these behaviors. ▼

14. Increase the frequency of socially appropriate behaviors with siblings and peers. (29, 30)

15. Increase verbalizations of acceptance of responsibility for misbehavior. (31, 32)

16. Identify stressors or painful emotions that trigger increase in hyperactivity and impulsivity. (33, 34)

28. Encourage the parents to spend 10 to 15 minutes daily of one-on-one time with the client to create a closer parent-child bond. Allow the client to take the lead in selecting the activity or task. ▽

29. Give homework assignments where the client identifies 5 to 10 strengths or interests; review the list in the following session and encourage him/her to utilize strengths or interests to establish friendships.

30. Assign the client the task of showing empathy, kindness, or sensitivity to the needs of others (e.g., allowing sibling or peer to take first turn in a video game, helping with a school fundraiser).

31. Firmly confront the client's impulsive behaviors, pointing out consequences for himself/herself and others.

32. Confront statements in which the client blames others for his/her annoying or impulsive behaviors and fails to accept responsibility for his/her actions.

33. Explore and identify stressful events or factors that contribute to an increase in impulsivity, hyperactivity, and distractibility. Help the client and parents develop positive coping strategies (e.g., "stop, look, listen, and think," relaxation techniques, positive self-talk) to manage stress more effectively.

34. Explore possible stressors, roadblocks, or hurdles that might cause impulsive and acting out behaviors to increase in the future.

Identify coping strategies (e.g., "stop, look, listen, and think," guided imagery, utilizing "I messages" to communicate needs) that the client and his/her family can use to cope with or overcome stressors, roadblocks, or hurdles.

17. Parents and the client regularly attend and actively participate in group therapy. (35)

35. Encourage the client's parents to participate in an ADHD support group.

18. Identify and list constructive ways to utilize energy. (36)

36. Give a homework assignment where the client lists the positive and negative aspects of his/her high energy level; review the list in the following session and encourage him/her to channel energy into healthy physical outlets and positive social activities.

19. Express feelings through artwork. (37)

37. Instruct the client to draw a picture reflecting what it feels like to have ADHD; process content of the drawing with the therapist.

__. _____   __. _____
    _____   _____
__. _____   __. _____
    _____   _____
__. _____   __. _____
    _____   _____

DIAGNOSTIC SUGGESTIONS

Axis I:	314.01	Attention-Deficit/Hyperactivity Disorder, Combined Type
	314.00	Attention-Deficit/Hyperactivity Disorder, Predominantly Inattentive Type
	314.01	Attention-Deficit/Hyperactivity Disorder, Predominantly Hyperactive-Impulsive Type
	314.9	Attention-Deficit/Hyperactivity Disorder NOS
	312.81	Conduct Disorder, Childhood-Onset Type

312.82	Conduct Disorder, Adolescent-Onset Type
313.81	Oppositional Defiant Disorder
312.9	Disruptive Behavior Disorder NOS
296.xx	Bipolar I Disorder

_____   _____

_____   _____

Axis II: V71.09   No Diagnosis

_____   _____

_____   _____

AUTISM/PERVASIVE DEVELOPMENTAL DISORDER

BEHAVIORAL DEFINITIONS

1. Shows a pervasive lack of interest in or responsiveness to other people.
2. Demonstrates a chronic failure to develop social relationships appropriate to the developmental level.
3. Lacks spontaneity and emotional or social reciprocity.
4. Exhibits a significant delay in or total lack of spoken language development.
5. Is impaired in sustaining or initiating conversation.
6. Demonstrates oddities in speech and language such as echolalia, pronominal reversal, or metaphorical language.
7. Rigidly adheres to repetition of nonfunctional rituals or stereotyped motor mannerisms.
8. Shows persistent preoccupation with objects, part of objects, or restricted areas of interest.
9. Exhibits a marked impairment or extreme variability in intellectual and cognitive functioning.
10. Demonstrates extreme resistance or overreaction to minor changes in routines or environment.
11. Exhibits emotional constriction or blunted affect.
12. Demonstrates a recurrent pattern of self-abusive behaviors (e.g., head banging, biting, burning himself/herself).

__. _____
   _____
__. _____
   _____
__. _____
   _____

LONG-TERM GOALS

1. Develop basic language skills and the ability to communicate simply with others.
2. Establish and maintain a basic emotional bond with primary attachment figures.
3. Family members develop acceptance of the client's overall capabilities and place realistic expectations on his/her behavior.
4. Engage in reciprocal and cooperative interactions with others on a regular basis.
5. Stabilize mood and tolerate changes in routine or environment.
6. Eliminate all self-abusive behaviors.
7. Attain and maintain the highest realistic level of independent functioning.

—. _____
_____
—. _____
_____
—. _____
_____

SHORT-TERM OBJECTIVES

1. Complete an intellectual and cognitive evaluation. (1)

2. Complete vision, hearing, or medical examination. (2, 3)

THERAPEUTIC INTERVENTIONS

1. Arrange for an intellectual and cognitive assessment to gain greater insights into the client's strengths and weaknesses; provide feedback to the parents.

2. Refer the client in early childhood years for vision and/or hearing examination to rule out vision or hearing problems that may be interfering with his/her social and speech/language development.

3. Refer the client for medical examination to rule out health problems that may be interfering with speech/language development.

3. Complete a speech/language evaluation. (4)

4. Refer the client for speech/language evaluation; consult with speech/language pathologist about evaluation findings.

4. Attend speech and language therapy sessions. (5)

5. Refer the client to a speech/language pathologist for ongoing services to improve his/her speech and language abilities.

5. Complete a neurological evaluation and/or neuropsychological testing. (6)

6. Arrange for neurological evaluation or neuropsychological testing of the client to rule out organic factors.

6. Comply fully with the recommendations offered by the assessment(s) and individualized educational planning committee (IEPC). (7, 8)

7. Attend an IEPC review to establish the client's eligibility for special education services, to update and revise educational interventions, and to establish new behavioral and educational goals.

8. Consult with the parents, teachers, and other appropriate school officials about designing effective learning programs, classroom assignments, or interventions that build on the client's strengths and compensate for weaknesses.

7. Comply with the move to an appropriate alternative residential placement setting. (9)

9. Consult with parents, school officials, and mental health professionals about the need to place the client in an alternative residential setting (e.g., foster care, group home, residential program).

▽ 8. Participate in a psychiatric evaluation regarding the need for psychotropic medication. (10)

10. Arrange for psychiatric evaluation of the client to assess the need for psychotropic medication. ▽

▽ 9. Increase the frequency of appropriate, self-initiated verbalizations toward the therapist, family members, and others. (11, 12, 13, 14)

11. Actively build the level of trust with the client through consistent eye contact, frequent attention and interest, unconditional positive regard, and warm acceptance to facilitate increased communication. ▽

▽ indicates that the Objective/Intervention is consistent with those found in evidence-based treatments.

12. Teach the parents behavior management techniques (e.g., prompting behavior, reinforcement and reinforcement schedules, use of ignoring for off-task behavior). ▼

13. Teach the parents a Pivotal Response Intervention (see *Pivotal Response Training for Autism* by Koegel and Koegel) in which they are taught how to use behavioral management skills to increase their child's motivation to respond to and to self-initiate social interactions in the context of play; urge them to use natural reinforcers and child-selected stimulus materials; provide feedback toward improvement. ▼

14. Have parents and client practice Pivotal Response techniques until parents reach an 80% correct use criterion. ▼

▼10. Decrease the frequency and severity of temper outbursts and aggressive behaviors. (15, 16, 17)

15. Teach the parents to apply behavior management techniques (e.g., prompting behavior, reinforcement and reinforcement schedules, use of ignoring for off-task behavior) to decrease the client's temper outbursts and self-abusive behaviors (or assign "Clear Rules, Positive Reinforcement, Appropriate Consequences" in the *Adolescent Psychotherapy Homework Planner*, 2nd ed. by Jongsma, Peterson, and McInnis). ▼

16. Design a token economy for use in the home, classroom, or residential program to improve the client's social skills, anger management, impulse control, and speech/language abilities. ▼

▼11. Decrease the frequency and severity of self-abusive behaviors. (18)

17. Develop a contingency contract to improve the client's social skills and anger control. ▼

18. Teach the parents to apply behavior management techniques (e.g., prompting behavior, reinforcement and reinforcement schedules, use of ignoring for off-task behavior) to decrease the client's self-abusive behaviors such as scratching or hitting self (or assign "Clear Rules, Positive Reinforcement, Appropriate Consequences" in the *Adolescent Psychotherapy Homework Planner,* 2nd ed. by Jongsma, Peterson, and McInnis or "Reaction to Change and Excessive Stimulation" in the *Child Psychotherapy Homework Planner,* 2nd ed. by Jongsma, Peterson, and McInnis). ▼

▼12. Parents verbalize increased knowledge and understanding of autism and pervasive developmental disorders. (19, 20)

19. Educate the client's parents and family members about the maturation process in individuals with autism or pervasive developmental disorders and the challenges that this process presents. ▼

20. Assign the parents to view the videotape, *Straight Talk about Autism with Parents and Kids* (available from the A.D.D. Warehouse) to increase their knowledge about autism. ▼

▼13. Demonstrate essential self-care and independent living skills. (21, 22, 23, 24)

21. Counsel the parents about teaching the client essential self-care skills (e.g., combing hair, bathing, brushing teeth). ▼

22. Monitor and provide frequent feedback to the client regarding his/her progress toward developing self-care skills. ▼

23. Use modeling and operant conditioning principles and response-shaping techniques to help the client develop self-help skills (e.g., dressing self, making bed, fixing sandwich) and improve personal hygiene. ▽

24. Encourage the parents to use the "Activities of Daily Living Program" in the *Child Psychotherapy Homework Planner,* 2nd ed. (Jongsma, Peterson, and McInnis) to improve the client's personal hygiene and self-help skills. ▽

14. Parents increase social support network. (25, 26, 27)

25. Direct the parents to join an autism group or organization (e.g., Autism Society of America) to expand their social network, to gain additional knowledge of the disorder, and to give them support and encouragement (or assign "Initial Reaction to Diagnosis of Autism" in the *Child Psychotherapy Homework Planner,* 2nd ed. by Jongsma, Peterson, and McInnis).

26. Refer the client's parents to a support group for parents of autistic children.

27. Refer the parents to, and encourage them to use, respite care on a periodic basis.

15. Parents and siblings report feeling a closer bond with the client. (28, 29, 30)

28. Conduct family therapy sessions to provide the parents and siblings with the opportunity to share and work through their feelings pertaining to the client's autism or pervasive developmental disorder.

29. To facilitate a closer parent-child bond, use filial play therapy approaches (i.e., parental involvement in session) with a higher-functioning client to

increase the parents' awareness of the client's thoughts, feelings, and needs.

30. Assign the client and his/her parents a task (e.g., swimming, riding a bike) that will help build trust and mutual dependence.

16. Increase the frequency of positive interactions with parents and siblings. (31, 32, 33)

31. Encourage the family members to regularly include the client in structured work or play activities for 20 minutes each day.

32. Instruct the parents to sing songs (e.g., nursery rhymes, lullabies, popular hits, songs related to client's interests) with the client to help establish a closer parent-child bond and increase verbalizations in home environment.

33. Encourage detached parents to increase their involvement in the client's daily life, leisure activities, or schoolwork.

17. Identify and express basic emotions. (34, 35)

34. Use art therapy (e.g., drawing, painting, sculpting) with the higher-functioning client to help him/her express basic needs or emotions and facilitate a closer relationship with the parents, caretakers, and therapist.

35. Use Feelings Poster (available from Childswork/Childsplay) to help the higher-functioning client identify and express basic emotions.

18. Increase the frequency of social contacts with peers. (36)

36. Consult with the client's parents and teachers about increasing the frequency of his/her social contacts with peers (working with student aide in class, attending Sunday school, participating in Special Olympics, refer to summer camp).

—. _____   —. _____
      _____   _____

—. _____   —. _____
      _____   _____

—. _____   —. _____
      _____   _____

DIAGNOSTIC SUGGESTIONS

Axis I:

299.00	Autistic Disorder
299.80	Pervasive Developmental Disorder NOS
299.80	Rett's Disorder
299.10	Childhood Disintegrative Disorder
299.80	Asperger's Disorder
313.89	Reactive Attachment Disorder of Infancy or Early Childhood
307.3	Stereotypic Movement Disorder
295.xx	Schizophrenia

_____   _____

_____   _____

Axis II:

317	Mild Mental Retardation
319	Mental Retardation, Severity Unspecified
V71.09	No Diagnosis

_____   _____

_____   _____

BLENDED FAMILY

BEHAVIORAL DEFINITIONS

1. Children from a previous union are united into a single family unit, resulting in interpersonal conflict, anger, and frustration.
2. Resistance and defiance toward the new stepparent.
3. Open conflict between siblings from different parents now residing in the same family system.
4. Defiance, either overt or covert in nature, from one or several siblings toward the stepparent.
5. Verbal threats to the biological parent of going to live with the other parent or report abuse.
6. Interference from former spouse in the daily life of the new family system.
7. Anxiety and concern by both new partners regarding bringing their two families together.
8. No clear lines of communication or responsibilities assigned within the blended family, making for confusion, frustration, and unhappiness.

—. _____
   _____
—. _____
   _____
—. _____
   _____

LONG-TERM GOALS

1. Achieve a reasonable level of family connectedness and harmony whereby members support, help, and are concerned for each other.

2. Become an integrated, blended family system that is functional and bonded to each other.
3. Attain a level of peaceful coexistence whereby daily issues can be negotiated without becoming ongoing conflicts.
4. Accept stepparent and/or stepsiblings and treat them with respect, kindness, and cordiality.
5. Establish a new family identity in which each member feels he/she belongs and is valued.
6. Accept the new blended family system as not inferior to the nuclear family, just different.
7. Establish a strong bond between the couple as a parenting team that is free from triangulation and able to stabilize the family.

__. _____
_____
__. _____
_____
__. _____
_____

SHORT-TERM OBJECTIVES

THERAPEUTIC INTERVENTIONS

1. Each family member openly shares thoughts and feelings regarding the blended family. (1, 2, 3)

1. Within family therapy sessions, actively build the level of trust with each family member through consistent eye contact, active listening, unconditional positive regard, and acceptance to allow each to identify and express openly his/her thoughts and feelings regarding the blended family.

2. In a family session, use a set of markers and a large sheet of drawing paper for the following exercise: The therapist begins a drawing by making a scribble line on the paper, then each family member adds to the line using a colored marker of his/her choice. When the drawing is complete,

the family can be given the choice to either each interpret the drawing or to develop a mutual story based on the drawing (see Lowe in *101 Favorite Play Therapy Techniques*).

3. Conduct family, sibling, and marital sessions to address the issues of loss, conflict negotiation, parenting, stepfamily psychoeducation, joining, rituals, and relationship building.

2. Attend and freely participate in play therapy sessions with the therapist. (4, 5, 6)

4. Use child-centered play therapy approaches (e.g., providing unconditional positive regard, reflecting feelings in a nonjudgmental manner, displaying trust in the child's capacity to resolve issues) to assist the client in adjusting to changes, grieving losses, and cooperating with the new stepfamily.

5. Conduct individual play therapy sessions to provide the client an opportunity to express feelings about losses and changes in his/her life.

6. Seize opportunities in play therapy (especially when the client is playing with groups of animals, army figures, dollhouse, puppets), as well as in sibling and family sessions, to emphasize the need for everyone within the family to respect and cooperate with each other.

3. Family members verbalize realistic expectations and rejection of myths regarding stepfamilies. (7, 8, 9)

7. In a family session, ask the members to list their expectations for the new family; ask the members to share and process their lists with the whole family and the therapist.

8. Remind family members that instant love of new family members is a myth. It is unrealistic to expect children to immediately like (much less love) the partner who is serving in the new-parent role.

9. Help family members accept the position that siblings from different biological families need not like or love one another, but that they should be mutually respectful and kind.

4. Identify losses/changes in each of their lives. (10, 11)

10. Instruct the family to read *Changing Families: An Interactive Guide for Kids and Grownups* (Fassler, Lash, and Ives) to help them identify the changes within the family and give them ways to adjust and thrive.

11. Assign sibling members in a session to complete a list of losses and changes that each has experienced over the last year and then for all years. Give empathic confirmation while they share the list in the session, and help them to see the similarities of their experiences to those of their siblings.

5. Family members demonstrate increased skills in recognizing and expressing feelings. (12, 13, 14)

12. Have family or siblings play The Ungame (available from The Ungame Company) or The Talking, Feeling, Doing Game (available from Childswork/Childsplay) to promote each family member's awareness of self and his/her feelings.

13. Using feelings charts, a feelings felt board, or a feelings card, educate the family on identifying, labeling, and expressing feelings appropriately.

14. In a family session, help the family to practice identifying and expressing feelings by doing a feelings exercise (e.g., "I feel sad when _____," "I feel excited when _____"). The therapist should affirm and acknowledge each member as they share during the exercise.

6. Family members verbalize expanded knowledge of step-families. (15, 16)

15. Assign parents or teens to read material to expand their knowledge of stepfamilies and their development (e.g., *Stepfamily Realities* by Newman; *How to Win as a Stepfamily* by Visher and Visher; *Stepfamilies Stepping Ahead* by Stepfamily Association of America); process key concepts that they gathered from the reading.

16. Refer the parents to the Stepfamily Association of America (1-800-735-0329) to obtain additional information and resources on stepfamilies.

7. Family members demonstrate increased negotiating skills. (17, 18, 19)

17. Conduct the following exercise in a sibling session: Place several phone books and/or Sunday papers in the center of a room and instruct the clients to tear the paper into small pieces and throw the shredded paper into the air. The only two rules are that the paper must be thrown *up*, not at anyone, and that the participants must clean up afterward. Process the experience around releasing energy and emotion. Give positive feedback for following through and cooperating in cleaning up (see Daves in *101 Favorite Play Therapy Techniques*).

18. Train family members in building negotiating skills (e.g., identifying problems, brainstorming solutions, evaluating pros and cons, compromising, agreeing on a solution, making an implementation plan), and have them practice these skills on issues that present in family sessions.

19. Assign siblings to write a list of their conflicts and suggest solutions (or assign the exercise "Negotiating a Peace Treaty" from the *Child Psychotherapy Homework Planner,* 2nd ed. by Jongsma, Peterson, and McInnis).

8. Family members report a reduced level of tension between all members. (20, 21, 22)

20. Inject humor whenever appropriate in a family or sibling session to decrease tensions/conflict and to model balance and perspective. Give positive feedback to members who create appropriate humor.

21. Hold a family sibling session in which each child focuses on listing and developing an appreciation of each sibling's differences/uniqueness (or assign the exercise "Cloning the Perfect Sibling" from the *Child Psychotherapy Homework Planner,* 2nd ed. by Jongsma, Peterson, and McInnis).

22. In a brief, solution-focused intervention, reframe or normalize the conflictual situation to show the clients that it's a stage the family needs to get through. Identify the next stage as the coming-together stage, and talk about when they might be ready to move there and how they could begin (see O'Hanlon and Beadle in *A Guide to Possibility Land*).

9. Family members report increased trust of each other. (23, 24)

23. Read and process with the family the story of *Stone Soup* (Brown), focusing on the issues of risk, mistrust, and cooperation.

24. In a family session, read Dr. Seuss's *The Sneetches* to show members the folly of top dog–wunderdog, one-upmanship, and insider-outsider attitudes.

10. Each parent takes the primary role of disciplining own children. (25)

25. Encourage each parent to take the primary role in disciplining his/her own children, and have each refrain from all negative references to former spouses.

11. Parents attend a stepparenting didactic group to increase parenting skills. (26)

26. Refer the parents to a parenting group for stepparents.

12. Family members attend weekly family meetings in the home to express feelings. (27)

27. Assist the parents in implementing a once-a-week family meeting in which issues can be raised and resolved and members are encouraged to share their thoughts, complaints, and compliments.

13. Parents create and institute new family rituals. (28, 29, 30)

28. Assist the parents in creating and implementing daily rituals (e.g., mealtimes, bedtime stories, household chores, time alone with parents, times together) in order to give structure and connection to the system.

29. Conduct a family session in which rituals from both former families are examined. Then encourage the family to retain the rituals that are appropriate and will work in the new system and combine them with new rituals.

30. Give the family the assignment to create birthday rituals for the new blended unit.

14. Parents identify and eliminate triangulation within the system. (31)

31. Educate the parents on patterns of interactions within families by creating a genogram that denotes the family's patterns of interactions and focuses on the pattern of triangulation and its dysfunctional aspects.

15. Parents report a strengthening of their marital bond. (32, 33, 34)

32. Refer the couple to skills-based marital therapy based on strengthening avenues of responsibilities, communication, and conflict resolution (see Prep, *Fighting for Your Marriage* by Markman, Stanley, and Blumberg).

33. Work with the dyad in conjoint sessions to deal with issues of having time away alone, privacy, and individual space; develop specific ways for these things to occur regularly.

34. Hold conjoint session(s) with the couple to process the issue of showing affection toward each other. Help the couple to develop appropriate boundaries and ways of showing affection that do not give rise to unnecessary anger in their children.

16. Family members report an increased sense of loyalty and connectedness. (35, 36, 37)

35. Conduct family sessions in which a genogram is developed for the entire new family system to show how everyone is interconnected.

36. Refer the family to an initiatives camp weekend to increase cooperation, conflict resolution, and sense of trust. Process the experiences with the family in the next family session.

37. In a family session, assign the family to design on poster board a

coat of arms for the family that reflects where they came from and where they are now. Process this experience when completed and have the family display it in their home.

17. Parents spend one-on-one time with each child. (38)

38. Assist the parents in scheduling one-on-one time with each child and stepchild in order to give them undivided attention and to build/maintain relationships.

18. Report the development of a bond between each member. (38, 39)

38. Assist the parents in scheduling one-on-one time with each child and stepchild in order to give them undivided attention and to build/maintain relationships.

39. Emphasize and model in family, sibling, and couple sessions the need for the family to build their new relationships slowly, allowing everyone time and space to adjust and develop a level of trust with each other.

___. _____   ___. _____
   _____   _____

___. _____   ___. _____
   _____   _____

___. _____   ___. _____
   _____   _____

DIAGNOSTIC SUGGESTIONS

Axis I:	309.0	Adjustment Disorder With Depressed Mood
	309.3	Adjustment Disorder With Disturbance of Conduct
	309.24	Adjustment Disorder With Anxiety
	309.81	Posttraumatic Stress Disorder
	300.4	Dysthymic Disorder

V62.81   Relational Problem NOS

_____ _____

_____ _____

Axis II: V71.09   No Diagnosis

_____ _____

_____ _____

BULLYING/INTIMIDATION PERPETRATOR

BEHAVIORAL DEFINITIONS

1. Makes verbal threats to younger or weaker peers.
2. Engages in intimidating behavior only when reinforced by friends.
3. Engages in intimidating behavior even when alone and not reinforced by friends.
4. Uses mild, physically aggressive behavior to reinforce the verbal intimidation (e.g., pushing, grabbing and holding, throwing things at the victim).
5. Breaks or takes objects belonging to the victim of the bullying.
6. Has fits of rage in front of peers that include screaming, shouting, threatening, or name-calling.
7. Family of origin has provided models of threatening, intimidating, aggressive behavior.

—. _____

_____

—. _____

_____

—. _____

_____

LONG-TERM GOALS

1. Terminate intimidating behavior and treat others with respect and kindness.
2. Develop empathy and compassion for others.
3. Parents/caregivers terminate the use of aggressive means of control and implement positive parenting methods.

—. _____

_____

—. _____

_____

—. _____

_____

SHORT-TERM OBJECTIVES

THERAPEUTIC INTERVENTIONS

1. Describe the type of behavioral interaction that occurs with peers when the goal is to get own way or control the other peer. (1)

2. Parents/caregivers and teachers describe the client's pattern of bullying or intimidating his/her peers. (2)

3. Acknowledge, without denial, that bullying has been used against peers. (1, 3, 4)

1. Gather data from the client regarding his/her pattern of interaction with peers, especially when he/she is trying to control the situation or intimidate others.

2. Meet with the client's parents/caregivers and school teachers to ask for their input regarding his/her pattern of bullying or intimidating peers.

1. Gather data from the client regarding his/her pattern of interaction with peers, especially when he/she is trying to control the situation or intimidate others.

3. Confront the client with facts reported by others that indicate that he/she does engage in intimidating behavior toward peers.

4. Role-play several social interactions with peers in which the therapist, playing the role of the client, uses bullying behavior to intimidate others; ask the client to acknowledge that he/she does behave in this manner.

4. Verbalize an understanding of the feelings of the victim of intimidating behavior. (5, 6, 7, 8)

5. Teach the client empathy for the victim of his/her intimidating behavior by asking him/her to

list the feelings generated in the victim due to the client's bullying (e.g., fear, rejection, anger, helplessness, social withdrawal).

6. Engage the client in a role-playing session in which he/she is the victim of bullying from a peer (played by the therapist); stop the role-playing periodically to explore and identify the victim's feelings.

7. Assign the client to be alert to observing instances of bullying perpetrated by others and to note the feelings of the victim; process these experiences.

8. Explore the client's capacity for empathy; assess whether cruelty toward animals or other indicators of Conduct Disorder are present (see Conduct Disorder chapter in this *Planner*).

5. Identify feelings toward self. (9, 10)

9. Ask the client to write a list of words that are self-descriptive; assess his/her perception of himself/herself (e.g., low self-esteem, aggressive, isolated, unloved).

10. Administer or refer the client for psychological testing to determine his/her self-perception, emotional state, and relationship style; provide feedback of the test results to the client and his/her parents.

6. Identify the goal or intent of bullying or intimidating behavior. (11, 12, 13)

11. Assist the client in exploring his/her goal when he/she engages in intimidation of others (e.g., impress peers to gain acceptance; seek to control others; resolve a conflict using aggression).

12. Role-play social interactions in which the client is the bully; stop the action periodically to have

him/her verbalize his/her goal or intent.

13. Read book passages or view videos with the client in which bullying is taking place; ask him/her to identify the goal of the intimidator and the feelings of the victim.

7. Implement prosocial assertiveness to attain social interaction goals and to resolve disputes. (14, 15)

14. Assist the client in identifying prosocial means of attaining healthy social interaction goals (e.g., attain respect by being kind, honest, and trustworthy; attain leadership through assertiveness and respect, not aggression; use effective problem-solving techniques, rather than intimidation).

15. Role-play peer conflict situations with the client in which bullying is used first, then where assertiveness and problem-solving techniques are used.

8. Family members acknowledge the presence of intimidation in family interactions. (16, 17)

16. In a family therapy session, assign the family the task of resolving a conflict; assess for the use of effective and respectful problem-solving techniques versus authoritarianism and aggression.

17. Explore with the family members whether aggression, intimidation, and threats are often a part of family interaction, especially during times of conflict.

9. Family members demonstrate respect for each other's rights and feelings during conflict resolution. (18, 19)

18. Teach the family respectful conflict resolution techniques in which the parents' authority is recognized but not flaunted without regard to the feelings of others.

19. During a role-playing session, guide the family in the use of prosocial problem-solving techniques that respect each person's rights and feelings.

10. Attend a social skills training group. (20, 21)

11. Increase socially appropriate behavior with peers and siblings. (22, 23)

12. Attend and freely participate in play therapy sessions. (24, 25, 26, 27)

20. Refer the client to a social skills training group that emphasizes demonstrating respect and compassion for peers.

21. Review and process what the client has learned in attending the social skills training group.

22. Play The Social Conflict Game (Berg) with the client to assist him/her in developing behavioral skills to decrease interpersonal antisocialism with others.

23. Use The Anger Control Game (Shore) or a similar game to expand the client's ways to manage aggressive feelings.

24. Employ the ACT model (Landreth) in play therapy sessions to *acknowledge* the client's feelings, to *communicate* limits, and to *target* more appropriate alternatives to ongoing conflicts and aggression with peers and/or siblings.

25. Employ psychoanalytic play therapy approaches (e.g., explore and gain an understanding of the etiology of unconscious conflicts, fixations, or arrests; interpret resistance, transference, or core anxieties) to help the client work through and resolve peer conflicts.

26. Interpret the client's feelings expressed in play therapy and relate them to anger and aggressive behaviors toward peers.

27. Create scenarios with puppets, dolls, or stuffed animals that model and/or suggest constructive ways for the client to handle/manage conflicts with peers.

13. Read books and play therapeutic games to increase sensitivity to the causes and effects of bullying. (28)

28. Read books and play games with the client that focus on bullying to teach its causes and effects (e.g., *Sometimes I Like to Fight, but I Don't Do It Much Anymore* by Shapiro; *The Very Angry Day that Amy Didn't Have* by Shapiro; No More Bullies Game [available from Courage to Change]; The Anti-Bullying Game by Searle and Streng); process the application of principles learned to the client's daily life.

14. Identify family issues that contribute to bullying/intimidating behavior. (29)

29. Conduct family therapy sessions to explore the dynamics (e.g., parental modeling of aggressive behavior; sexual, verbal, or physical abuse of family members; substance abuse in the home; neglect) that contribute to the emergence of the client's bullying/intimidating behavior.

15. Identify and verbally express feelings that are associated with past neglect, abuse, separation, or abandonment. (30, 31)

30. Encourage and support the client in expressing his/her feelings associated with neglect, abuse, separation, or abandonment (see Attachment Disorder, Sexual Abuse Victim, and Physical/Emotional Abuse Victim chapters in this *Planner*).

31. Give the client permission to cry about past losses, separation, or abandonment; educate him/her about the healing nature of crying (i.e., provides an opportunity to express sadness, takes the edge off anger, helps to induce calmness after crying subsides).

__. _____

_____

__. _____

_____

__. _____   __. _____

_____   _____

__. _____   __. _____

_____   _____

DIAGNOSTIC SUGGESTIONS

Axis I: 313.81   Oppositional Defiant Disorder
312.xx   Conduct Disorder
312.9   Disruptive Behavior Disorder NOS
314.01   Attention-Deficit/Hyperactivity Disorder,
          Predominantly Hyperactive-Impulsive Type
314.9   Attention-Deficit/Hyperactivity Disorder NOS
V62.81   Relational Problem NOS
V71.02   Child or Adolescent Antisocial Behavior

_____ _____

_____ _____

Axis II: V71.09   No Diagnosis

_____ _____

_____ _____

CONDUCT DISORDER/DELINQUENCY

BEHAVIORAL DEFINITIONS

1. Persistent refusal to comply with rules or expectations in the home, school, or community.
2. Excessive fighting, intimidation of others, cruelty or violence toward people or animals, and destruction of property.
3. History of stealing at home, at school, or in the community.
4. School adjustment characterized by disrespectful attitude toward authority figures, frequent disruptive behaviors, and detentions or suspensions for misbehavior.
5. Repeated conflict with authority figures at home, at school, or in the community.
6. Impulsivity as manifested by poor judgment, taking inappropriate risks, and failing to stop and think about consequences of actions.
7. Numerous attempts to deceive others through lying, conning, or manipulating.
8. Consistent failure to accept responsibility for misbehavior accompanied by a pattern of blaming others.
9. Little or no remorse for misbehavior.
10. Lack of sensitivity to the thoughts, feelings, and needs of other people.

__. _____

_____

__. _____

_____

__. _____

_____

LONG-TERM GOALS

1. Comply with rules and expectations in the home, school, and community consistently.
2. Eliminate all illegal and antisocial behavior.
3. Terminate all acts of violence or cruelty toward people or animals and the destruction of property.
4. Express anger in a controlled, respectful manner on a consistent basis.
5. Parents establish and maintain appropriate parent-child boundaries, setting firm, consistent limits when the client acts out in an aggressive or rebellious manner.
6. Demonstrate empathy, concern, and sensitivity for the thoughts, feelings, and needs of others on a regular basis.
7. Parents learn and implement good child behavioral management skills.

—. _____
    _____
—. _____
    _____
—. _____
    _____

SHORT-TERM OBJECTIVES	THERAPEUTIC INTERVENTIONS
1. Identify situations, thoughts, and feelings that trigger angry feelings, problem behaviors, and the targets of those actions. (1)	1. Thoroughly assess the various stimuli (e.g., situations, people, thoughts) that have triggered the client's anger and the thoughts, feelings, and actions that have characterized his/her anger responses.
2. Cooperate with a medical evaluation to assess possible organic contributors to poor anger control. (2)	2. Refer the client to a physician for a complete physical exam to rule out organic contributors (e.g., brain damage, tumor, elevated testosterone levels) to poor anger control.
3. Complete psychological testing. (3)	3. Conduct or arrange for psychological testing to help in assessing whether a comorbid condition

4. Cooperate with the recommendations or requirements mandated by the criminal justice system. (4, 5, 6)

▼ 5. Cooperate with a physician evaluation for possible treatment with psychotropic medications and take medications consistently, if prescribed. (7, 8)

▼ 6. Recognize and verbalize how feelings are connected to misbehavior. (9)

(e.g., depression, attention-deficit/hyperactivity disorder [ADHD]) is contributing to anger control problems; follow-up accordingly with client and parents regarding treatment options.

4. Consult with criminal justice officials about the appropriate consequences for the client's destructive or aggressive behaviors (e.g., pay restitution, community service, probation, intensive surveillance).

5. Consult with parents, school officials, and criminal justice officials about the need to place the client in an alternative setting (e.g., foster home, group home, residential program, juvenile detention facility).

6. Encourage and challenge the parents not to protect the client from the natural or legal consequences of his/her destructive or aggressive behaviors.

7. Assess the client for the need for psychotropic medication to assist in anger and behavioral control, referring him/her, if indicated, to a physician for an evaluation for prescription medication. ▼

8. Monitor the client's prescription compliance, effectiveness, and side effects; provide feedback to the prescribing physician. ▼

9. Actively build the level of trust with the client through consistent eye contact, active listening, unconditional positive regard, and

---

▼ indicates that the Objective/Intervention is consistent with those found in evidence-based treatments.

warm acceptance to help increase his/her ability to identify and express feelings instead of acting them out; assist the client in making a connection between his/her feelings and reactive behaviors (or assign "Risk Factors Leading to Child Behavior Problems" in the *Child Psychotherapy Homework Planner,* 2nd ed. by Jongsma, Peterson, and McInnis). ▼

▼ 7. Increase the number of statements that reflect the acceptance of responsibility for misbehavior. (10, 11, 12)

10. Firmly confront the client's antisocial behavior and attitude, pointing out consequences for himself/herself and others. ▼

11. Confront statements in which the client lies and/or blames others for his/her misbehaviors and fails to accept responsibility for his/her actions. ▼

12. Explore and process the factors that contribute to the client's pattern of blaming others (e.g., harsh punishment experiences, family pattern of blaming others). ▼

▼ 8. Agree to learn alternative ways to think about and manage anger and misbehavior. (13, 14)

13. Assist the client in reconceptualizing anger as involving different components (cognitive, physiological, affective, and behavioral) that go through predictable phases (e.g., demanding expectations not being met leading to increased arousal and anger leading to acting out) that can be managed. ▼

14. Assist the client in identifying the positive consequences of managing anger and misbehavior (e.g., respect from others and self, cooperation from others, improved physical health); ask the client to agree to learn new ways to conceptualize and manage anger and misbehavior. ▼

▼ 9. Learn and implement calming strategies as part of a new way to manage reactions to frustration. (15)

▼ 10. Identify, challenge, and replace self-talk that leads to anger and misbehavior with self-talk that facilitates more constructive reactions. (16)

▼ 11. Learn and implement thought-stopping to manage intrusive unwanted thoughts that trigger anger and acting out. (17)

▼ 12. Verbalize feelings of frustration, disagreement, and anger in a controlled, assertive way. (18)

▼ 13. Implement problem-solving and/or conflict resolution skills to manage interpersonal problems constructively. (19)

15. Teach the client calming techniques (e.g., muscle relaxation, paced breathing, calming imagery) as part of a tailored strategy for responding appropriately to angry feelings when they occur. ▼

16. Explore the client's self-talk that mediates his/her angry feelings and actions (e.g., demanding expectations reflected in should, must, or have to statements); identify and challenge biases, assisting him/her in generating appraisals and self-talk that corrects for the biases and facilitates a more flexible and temperate response to frustration. ▼

17. Teach the client the "thought-stopping" technique and assign implementation on a daily basis between sessions; review implementation, reinforcing success and providing corrective feedback toward improvement. ▼

18. Use instruction, videotaped or live modeling, and/or role-playing to help develop the client's anger control skills, such as calming, self-statement, assertion skills; if indicated, refer him/her to an anger control group for further instruction. ▼

19. Teach the client conflict resolution skills (e.g., empathy, active listening, "I messages," respectful communication, assertiveness without aggression, compromise); use modeling, role-playing, and behavior rehearsal to work through several current conflicts. ▼

▽14. Practice using new calming, communication, conflict resolution, and thinking skills in group or individual therapy. (20, 21)

20. Assist the client in constructing and consolidating a client-tailored strategy for managing anger that combines any of the somatic, cognitive, communication, problem-solving, and/or conflict resolution skills relevant to his/her needs. ▽

21. Use any of several techniques (e.g., relaxation, imagery, behavioral rehearsal, modeling, role-playing, feedback of videotaped practice) in increasingly challenging situations to help the client consolidate the use of his/her new anger management skills. ▽

▽15. Practice using new calming, communication, conflict resolution, and thinking skills in homework exercises. (22)

22. Assign the client homework exercises to help him/her practice newly learned calming, assertion, conflict resolution, or cognitive restructuring skills as needed; review and process toward the goal of consolidation. ▽

▽16. Decrease the number, intensity, and duration of angry outbursts, while increasing the use of new skills for managing anger. (23)

23. Monitor the client's reports of angry outbursts toward the goal of decreasing their frequency, intensity, and duration through the client's use of new anger management skills (or assign "Anger Control" or "Anger Checklist" in the *Child Psychotherapy Homework Planner*, 2nd ed. by Jongsma, Peterson, and McInnis); review progress, reinforcing success and providing corrective feedback toward improvement. ▽

▽17. Identify social supports that will help facilitate the implementation of new skills. (24)

24. Encourage the client to discuss and/or use his/her new anger and conduct management skills with trusted peers, family, or otherwise significant others who are likely to support his/her change. ▽

▼18. Parents learn and implement Parent Management Training skills to recognize and manage problem behavior of the client. (25, 26, 27, 28, 29)

25. Use a Parent Management Training approach beginning with teaching the parents how parent and child behavioral interactions can encourage or discourage positive or negative behavior and that changing key elements of those interactions (e.g., prompting and reinforcing positive behaviors) can be used to promote positive change (e.g., *Parenting the Strong-Willed Child* by Forehand and Long; *Living with Children* by Patterson). ▼

26. Teach the parents how to specifically define and identify problem behaviors, identify their reactions to the behavior, determine whether the reaction encourages or discourages the behavior, and generate alternatives to the problem behavior. ▼

27. Teach parents how to implement key parenting practices consistently, including establishing realistic age-appropriate rules for acceptable and unacceptable behavior, prompting of positive behavior in the environment, use of positive reinforcement to encourage behavior (e.g., praise), use of clear direct instruction, time out, and other loss-of-privilege practices for problem behavior. ▼

28. Assign the parents home exercises in which they implement and record results of implementation exercises (or assign "Clear Rules, Positive Reinforcement, Appropriate Consequences" in the *Adolescent Psychotherapy Homework Planner,* 2nd ed. by Jongsma, Peterson, and McInnis); review in session,

providing corrective feedback to-ward improved, appropriate, and consistent use of skills. ▽

▽19. Parents and client participate in play sessions in which they use their new rules for appropriate conduct (30, 31)

29. Use Webster-Stratton videotapes to teach parenting techniques (see Webster-Stratton, 1994, 1996). ▽

30. Conduct Parent-Child Interaction Therapy in which child-directed and parent-directed sessions focus on teaching appropriate child behavior, and parental behavioral management skills (e.g., clear commands, consistent conse-quences, positive reinforcement) are developed (see *Parent-Child Interaction Therapy* by Bell and Eyberg). ▽

31. Teach parents to use the time out technique as a consequence for inappropriate behavior; if pos-sible, use a "signal seat" that has a battery-operated buzzer that serves as both a timer and an alert that the child is not staying in the seat (see Hamilton and Mac-Quiddy, 1984). ▽

▽20. Increase compliance with rules at home and school. (32)

32. Design a reward system and/or contingency contract for the client and meet with school officials to reinforce identified positive behav-iors at home and school and deter impulsive or rebellious behaviors. ▽

▽21. Parents verbalize appropriate boundaries for discipline to prevent further occurrences of abuse and to ensure the safety of the client and his/her sib-lings. (33, 34)

33. Explore the client's family back-ground for a history of neglect and physical or sexual abuse that may contribute to his/her be-havioral problems; confront the client's parents to cease physically abusive or overly punitive meth-ods of discipline. ▽

34. Implement the steps necessary to protect the client and siblings from further abuse (e.g., report abuse to the appropriate agencies; remove the client or perpetrator from the home). ▼

▼22. Increase verbalizations of empathy and concern for other people. (35)

35. Use role-playing and role reversal techniques to help the client develop sensitivity to the feelings of others in reaction to his/her antisocial behaviors (or assign "Apology Letter for Bullying" in the *Child Psychotherapy Homework Planner,* 2nd ed. by Jongsma, Peterson, and McInnis). ▼

▼23. Increase the frequency of responsible and positive social behaviors. (36, 37, 38)

36. Direct the client to engage in three altruistic or benevolent acts (e.g., read to a developmentally disabled student, mow grandmother's lawn) before the next session to increase his/her empathy and sensitivity to the needs of others. ▼

37. Assign homework designed to increase the client's empathy and sensitivity toward the thoughts, feelings, and needs of others. ▼

38. Place the client in charge of tasks at home (e.g., preparing and cooking a special dish for a family get-together, building shelves in the garage, changing oil in the car) to demonstrate confidence in his/her ability to act responsibly. ▼

24. Identify and verbally express feelings associated with past neglect, abuse, separation, or abandonment. (39)

39. Encourage and support the client in expressing feelings associated with neglect, abuse, separation, or abandonment and help process (e.g., assign the task of writing a letter to an absent parent, use the empty-chair technique, assign

"The Lesson of Salmon Rock . . . Fighting Leads to Loneliness" in the *Child Psychotherapy Homework Planner,* 2nd ed. by Jongsma, Peterson, and McInnis).

25. Parents participate in marital therapy. (40)

40. Assess the marital dyad for possible substance abuse, conflict, or triangulation that shifts the focus from marriage issues to the client's acting out behaviors; refer for appropriate treatment, if needed.

__. _____   __. _____
   _____   _____

__. _____   __. _____
   _____   _____

__. _____   __. _____
   _____   _____

DIAGNOSTIC SUGGESTIONS

Axis I:	312.81	Conduct Disorder, Childhood-Onset Type
	312.82	Conduct Disorder, Adolescent-Onset Type
	313.81	Oppositional Defiant Disorder
	312.9	Disruptive Behavior Disorder NOS
	314.01	Attention-Deficit/Hyperactivity Disorder, Predominantly Hyperactive-Impulsive Type
	314.9	Attention-Deficit/Hyperactivity Disorder NOS
	312.34	Intermittent Explosive Disorder
	V71.02	Child Antisocial Behavior
	V61.20	Parent-Child Relational Problem

_____   _____

_____   _____

| Axis II: | V71.09 | No Diagnosis |

_____   _____

_____   _____

DEPRESSION

BEHAVIORAL DEFINITIONS

1. Demonstrates sad or flat affect.
2. Reports a preoccupation with the subject of death.
3. Reports suicidal thoughts and/or actions.
4. Exhibits moody irritability.
5. Isolates self from family and/or peers.
6. Deterioration in academic performance.
7. Lacks interest in previously enjoyed activities.
8. Refuses to communicate openly.
9. Demonstrates low energy.
10. Makes little or no eye contact.
11. Frequently expresses statements reflecting low self-esteem.
12. Exhibits a reduced appetite.
13. Demonstrates an increased need for sleep.
14. Exhibits poor concentration and indecision.
15. Expresses feelings of hopelessness, worthlessness, or inappropriate guilt.
16. Reports unresolved feelings of grief.
17. Uses street drugs to elevate mood.

—. _____
   _____
—. _____
   _____
—. _____
   _____

LONG-TERM GOALS

1. Elevate mood and show evidence of usual energy, activities, and socialization level.
2. Renew typical interest in academic achievement, social involvement, and eating patterns as well as occasional expressions of joy and zest for life.
3. Reduce irritability and increase normal social interaction with family and friends.
4. Acknowledge the depression verbally and resolve its causes, leading to normalization of the emotional state.
5. Develop healthy cognitive patterns and beliefs about self and the world that lead to alleviation and help prevent the relapse of depression symptoms.
6. Develop healthy interpersonal relationships that lead to alleviation and help prevent the relapse of depression symptoms.
7. Appropriately grieve the loss in order to normalize mood and to return to previous adaptive level of functioning.

__. _____
   _____
__. _____
   _____
__. _____
   _____

SHORT-TERM OBJECTIVES	THERAPEUTIC INTERVENTIONS
1. Describe current and past experiences with depression complete with its impact on function and attempts to resolve it. (1)	1. Assess current and past mood episodes including their features, frequency, intensity, and duration (e.g., Clinical Interview supplemented by the *Inventory to Diagnose Depression* by Zimmerman, Coryell, Corenthal, and Wilson).
2. Verbally identify, if possible, the source of depressed mood. (2, 3)	2. Ask the client to make a list of what he/she is depressed about (or assign the "Childhood Depression Survey" in the *Child Psychotherapy Homework Planner,* 2nd ed. by Jongsma, Peterson, and McInnis); process the list content.

3. Complete psychological testing to assess the depth of
depression, the need for antidepressant medication, and
suicide prevention measures. (4)

4. Verbalize any history of suicide attempts and any current
suicidal urges. (5)

5. State no longer having thoughts
of self-harm. (6, 7)

▼ 6. Take prescribed psychotropic
medications responsibly at
times ordered by physician.
(8, 9)

▼ 7. Identify and replace depressive
thinking that leads to depression. (10, 11, 12, 13)

3. Encourage the client to share
his/her feelings of depression in
order to clarify them and gain
insight as to causes.

4. Arrange for the administration
of an objective assessment instru-
ment for evaluating the client's
depression and suicide risk (e.g.,
Beck Depression Inventory for
Youth); evaluate results and give
feedback to the client.

5. Explore the client's history and
current state of suicidal urges and
behavior.

6. Assess and monitor the client's
suicide potential.

7. Arrange for hospitalization,
as necessary, when the client is
judged to be harmful to self.

8. Evaluate the client's possible need
for psychotropic medication and
arrange for a physician to give
him/her a physical examination
to rule out organic causes for
depression, assess need for antidepressant medication, and order
a prescription, if appropriate. ▼

9. Monitor and evaluate the client's
psychotropic medication compliance, effectiveness, and side
effects; communicate with prescribing physician. ▼

10. Assist the client in developing an
awareness of his/her automatic
thoughts that reflect a depres-
sogenic schemata; challenge
depressive thinking patterns and
replace them with reality-based
thoughts ▼

▼ indicates that the Objective/Intervention is consistent with those found in evidence-based
treatments.

11. Assign the client to keep a daily journal of automatic thoughts associated with depressive feelings (e.g., "Daily Record of Dysfunctional Thoughts" in *Cognitive Therapy of Depression* by Beck, Rush, Shaw, and Emery); process the journal material to challenge depressive thinking patterns and replace them with reality-based thoughts. ▼

12. Do "behavioral experiments" in which depressive automatic thoughts are treated as hypotheses/predictions, reality-based alternative hypotheses/predictions are generated, and both are tested against the client's past, present, and/or future experiences. ▼

13. Reinforce the client's positive, reality-based cognitive messages that enhance self-confidence and increase adaptive action (or assign "Recognizing Your Abilities, Traits, and Accomplishments" in the *Adolescent Psychotherapy Homework Planner II* by Jongsma, Peterson, and McInnis). ▼

▼ 8. Learn new ways to overcome depression through activity. (14, 15)

14. Assist the client in developing age-appropriate coping strategies for managing feelings of depression (e.g., more physical exercise, less internal focus, increased social involvement, more assertiveness, greater need sharing, constructive anger expression); reinforce success. ▼

15. Engage the client in "behavioral activation" by scheduling activities that have a high likelihood for pleasure and mastery; use rehearsal, role-playing, role reversal,

W 9. Learn and implement social skills to reduce anxiety and build confidence in social interactions. (16)

W 10. Learn and implement problem-solving and/or conflict resolution skills to resolve interpersonal problems. (17)

11. Initiate and respond actively to social communication with family and peers. (18, 19)

12. Verbalize any unresolved grief issues that may be contributing to depression. (20)

13. Implement a routine of physical exercise. (21)

14. Learn and implement relapse prevention skills. (22)

as needed, to assist adoption in the client's daily life; reinforce success. W

16. Use instruction, modeling, and role-playing to build the client's general social and/or communication skills (see *Social Effectiveness Therapy for Children and Adolescents* by Turner, Beidel, Turner, and Morris). W

17. Teach the client age-appropriate conflict resolution skills (e.g., empathy, active listening, "I messages," respectful communication, assertiveness without aggression, compromise) to help alleviate depression; use modeling, role-playing, and behavior rehearsal to work through several current conflicts. W

18. Encourage the client to participate in social/recreational activities that enrich his/her life (or assign "Greeting Peers" or "Show Your Strengths" in the *Child Psychotherapy Homework Planner,* 2nd ed. by Jongsma, Peterson, and McInnis).

19. Use therapeutic feelings games (e.g., The Talking, Feeling, and Doing Game) to assist the client in being more verbal.

20. Explore the role of unresolved grief issues as they contribute to the client's current depression (see Grief/Loss Unresolved chapter in this *Planner*).

21. Develop and reinforce a routine of physical exercise for the client.

22. Build the client's relapse prevention skills by helping him/her identify early warning signs of

relapse, reviewing skills learned during therapy, and developing a plan for managing challenges.

15. State the connection between rebellion, self-destruction, or withdrawal and the underlying depression. (23, 24, 25)

23. Assess the client's level of self-understanding about self-defeating behaviors linked to the depression.

24. Interpret and confront the client's acting out behaviors as avoidance of the real conflict involving his/her unmet emotional needs and reflection of the depression.

25. Teach the client the connection between angry, irritable behaviors and feelings of hurt and sadness (or assign the exercise "Surface Behavior/Inner Feelings" in the *Child Psychotherapy Homework Planner,* 2nd ed. by Jongsma, Peterson, and McInnis).

16. Specify what is missing from life to cause the unhappiness. (26, 27)

26. Explore the client's fears regarding abandonment or loss of love from others.

27. Ask the client what is missing from his/her life that contributes to the unhappiness (or assign "Three Wishes Game" in the *Child Psychotherapy Homework Planner,* 2nd ed. by Jongsma, Peterson, and McInnis).

17. Specify what in the past or present life contributes to sadness. (28, 29)

28. Explore the emotional pain from the client's past that contributes to the feelings of hopelessness and low self-esteem.

29. Assist the client in identifying his/her current unmet emotional needs and specifying ways to meet those needs (or assign the exercise "Unmet Emotional Needs—Identification and Satisfaction" from the *Adolescent Psychotherapy Homework Planner,* 2nd ed. by Jongsma, Peterson, and McInnis).

18. Express negative feelings through artistic modalities. (30, 31)

30. Use art therapy (e.g., drawing, coloring, painting, collage, sculpture) to help the client express depressive feelings; use his/her artistic products as a springboard for further elaboration of emotions and their causes.

31. Ask the client to produce a family drawing to help assess the factors contributing to his/her depression.

19. Express emotional needs to significant others. (32)

32. Hold family therapy sessions to facilitate the client's expression of conflict with family members while teaching family members and significant others to encourage, support, and tolerate the client's respectful expression of his/her thoughts and feelings.

20. Improve academic performance as evidenced by better grades and positive teacher reports. (33)

33. Challenge and encourage the client's academic effort; arrange for a tutor, if needed, to increase the client's sense of academic mastery.

21. Adjust sleep hours to those typical of the developmental stage. (34)

34. Monitor the client's sleep patterns and the restfulness of sleep.

22. Eat nutritional meals regularly without strong urging from others. (35)

35. Monitor and encourage the client's food consumption.

23. Express feelings of sadness, hurt, and anger in play therapy sessions. (36, 37)

36. Arrange for a play therapy session that allows for the client to express feelings toward himself/herself and others.

37. Interpret the feelings expressed in play therapy as those of the client toward real life circumstances.

24. Verbalize the life changes that would result in a reduction of sadness and an increase in hope. (27, 38)

27. Ask the client what is missing from his/her life that contributes to the unhappiness (or assign "Three Wishes Game" in the *Child*

Psychotherapy Homework Planner, 2nd ed. by Jongsma, Peterson, and McInnis).

38. Assign the client the homework of writing three ways he/she would like to change the world to bring increased feelings of joy, peace, and security (or assign the exercise "Three Ways to Change the World" in the *Child Psychotherapy Homework Planner,* 2nd ed. by Jongsma, Peterson, and McInnis).

__. _____   __. _____
   _____   _____
__. _____   __. _____
   _____   _____
__. _____   __. _____

DIAGNOSTIC SUGGESTIONS

Axis I: 309.0   Adjustment Disorder With Depressed Mood
            296.xx Bipolar I Disorder
            296.89 Bipolar II Disorder
            300.4   Dysthymic Disorder
            296.2x Major Depressive Disorder, Single Episode
            296.3x Major Depressive Disorder, Recurrent
            V62.82 Bereavement

            _____ _____
            _____ _____

Axis II: V71.09 No Diagnosis

            _____ _____
            _____ _____

DISRUPTIVE/ATTENTION-SEEKING

BEHAVIORAL DEFINITIONS

1. Repeated attempts to draw attention to self through silly, immature, or regressive behaviors, loud talking, and making inappropriate noises or gestures.
2. Frequent disruptions in the classroom by interrupting the teacher and/or interfering with classmates' attention and concentration by talking excessively, blurting out remarks, speaking without permission, and laughing or making noises at inappropriate times.
3. Strained sibling and peer relationships due to annoying or antagonistic behaviors (e.g., teasing, mocking, name-calling, picking on others).
4. Fails to follow agreed-upon rules in play or game activities, refusing to share or cooperate, and demanding that others do things his/her way.
5. Obstinate refusal to comply with reasonable requests by authority figures in home or school settings.
6. Unwillingness to back down or bend during an argument with family members, peers, or adult authority figures.
7. Lack of sensitivity to or awareness of how attention-seeking behaviors impact other people.
8. Lack of awareness of important social cues and/or failure to follow expected social norms.
9. Numerous complaints by siblings or peers of inappropriate touching or contact and intrusions into personal space.

—. _____
   _____
—. _____
   _____
—. _____
   _____

LONG-TERM GOALS

1. Terminate disruptive attention-seeking behaviors, and increase cooperative, prosocial interactions.
2. Gain attention, approval, and acceptance from other people through appropriate verbalizations and positive social behaviors.
3. Establish and maintain positive sibling relationships and lasting peer friendships.
4. Comply with rules and expectations in home and school settings on a regular basis.
5. Resolve core conflicts that contribute to the emergence of disruptive, antagonistic, annoying, or negative attention-seeking behaviors.
6. React appropriately to important social cues and follow expected rules of engagement in play, classroom, extracurricular, or social activities.
7. Parents set firm, consistent limits on the client's disruptive or negative attention-seeking behaviors and maintain appropriate parent-child boundaries.

__. _____

_____

__. _____

_____

__. _____

_____

SHORT-TERM OBJECTIVES	THERAPEUTIC INTERVENTIONS
1. Cooperate with a psychological assessment to rule out diagnosable conditions contributing to disruptive behavior. (1, 2)	1. Arrange for psychological testing of the client to assess whether emotional factors or Attention-Deficit/Hyperactivity Disorder (ADHD) are contributing to his/her disruptive, antagonistic, annoying, or negative attention-seeking behaviors; provide feedback to the client and his/her parents.
	2. Assess the client for the presence of symptom patterns that indicate the presence of Oppositional

Defiant Disorder or Conduct Disorder and treat appropriately if positive for either of these conditions (see chapters on Conduct Disorder/Delinquency and Oppositional Defiant in this *Planner*).

2. Complete a psychoeducational evaluation. (3)

3. Arrange for a psychoeducational evaluation of the client to rule out the presence of a learning disability that may be contributing to his/her disruptive and negative attention-seeking behaviors in the school setting; provide feedback to the client's parents or school officials.

3. Parents and teachers establish appropriate boundaries, develop clear rules, and follow through consistently with consequences for the client's disruptive or annoying behaviors. (4, 5, 6, 7, 8)

4. Assist the parents in establishing clearly defined boundaries and consequences for the client's disruptive, antagonistic, annoying, and negative attention-seeking behaviors.

5. Establish clear rules for the client in home and school; ask him/her to repeat the rules to demonstrate an understanding of the expectations.

6. Consult with the parents about increasing structure in the home to help the client delay gratification for longer-term goals (e.g., completing homework or chores before playing video games or socializing with peers).

7. Consult with the parents, teachers, and school officials to design and implement interventions (e.g., sitting in the front row during class, providing frequent feedback, calling on the client often, using a teacher's aide to assist with learning problems) to deter

the client's impulsivity, improve academic performance, and increase positive behaviors in the classroom.

8. Assign the parents readings to increase their knowledge about effective disciplinary techniques (e.g., *1-2-3 Magic: Training Your Preschoolers and Preteens to Do What You Want* by Phelan; *Family Rules* by Kaye; *Assertive Discipline for Parents* by Canter and Canter).

4. Parents increase the frequency of praise and positive reinforcement to the client. (9, 10)

9. Encourage the parents to provide frequent praise and positive reinforcement for the client's positive social behaviors and good impulse control.

10. Design a reward system and/or contingency contract for the client to reinforce identified positive behaviors, completion of school and homework assignments, and to reduce the frequency of disruptive and negative attention-seeking behaviors.

5. Reduce the frequency and severity of disruptive or negative attention-seeking behaviors at home and/or school. (11, 12, 13, 14)

11. Design and implement a token economy to increase the client's positive social behaviors and deter disruptive and negative attention-seeking behaviors.

12. Teach mediational and self-control strategies (e.g., relaxation; "stop, look, listen, and think") to help the client to delay the impulse to act out and engage in negative attention-seeking behaviors.

13. Encourage the client to use self-monitoring checklists at home or school to improve impulse control and social skills.

14. Assign the client to read material that will help him/her learn to improve impulse control and attain the ability to stop and think about possible consequences of negative social behaviors (see *How I Learned to Think Things Through* by Shapiro).

6. Verbalize an awareness of how disruptive behaviors negatively affect self and others. (15, 16, 17)

15. Firmly confront the client's annoying and disruptive behaviors, pointing out consequences for himself/herself and others.

16. Help the client develop an awareness of how disruptive behaviors lead to negative consequences for himself/herself and others (or assign the "Stop, Think, and Act" exercise in the *Child Psychotherapy Homework Planner,* 2nd ed. by Jongsma, Peterson, and McInnis).

17. Confront statements in which the client blames others for his/her annoying or disruptive behaviors and fails to accept responsibility for his/her actions.

7. Recognize and verbalize how unpleasant or negative emotions are connected to disruptive, antagonistic, or negative, attention-seeking behaviors. (18)

18. Help the client to make a connection between unpleasant or negative emotions and annoying or disruptive behaviors.

8. Identify and implement appropriate ways to elicit attention from family members, authority figures, or peers. (19, 20, 21, 22)

19. Teach effective communication and assertiveness skills to help the client to meet his/her needs for attention and approval through appropriate verbalizations and positive social behaviors.

20. Instruct the parents and teachers to observe and record positive behaviors by the client in between

therapy sessions; reinforce and encourage the client to continue to engage in the positive behaviors.

21. Assess periods of time during which the client displays positive social behaviors; reinforce any strengths or resources used to gain approval and acceptance from peers.

22. Introduce the idea that the client can change the pattern of engaging in disruptive or negative attention-seeking behaviors by asking the following question: "What will you be doing when you stop getting into trouble?" Process the client's responses and help him/her develop an action plan to accomplish goals or desired behavior changes.

9. Identify and list stressors that contribute to the emergence of disruptive and negative, attention-seeking behaviors. (23, 24)

23. Explore with the client possible stressors or frustrations (e.g., lengthy separation from parent, learning problems, failure experiences) that might cause negative behaviors to reappear in the future; help him/her and family members identify how to manage stressors or frustrations.

24. Conduct family therapy sessions to explore the dynamics that contribute to the emergence of the client's disruptive and negative attention-seeking behaviors.

10. Increase parental time spent with the client in positive and rewarding activities. (25, 26, 27)

25. Conduct filial play therapy sessions (i.e., parental involvement in session) to help improve the quality of the parent-child relationship and increase the parent's awareness of the factors contributing to the client's disruptive or annoying behaviors.

26. Give a directive to uninvolved or disengaged parent(s) to spend more time with the client in leisure, school, or household activities.

27. Prescribe a symptom by directing the client to engage in annoying or disruptive behaviors for a specific length of time or at a set time each day to help disrupt established patterns of negative behaviors. (This intervention seeks to diffuse the client's power of gaining negative attention through the annoying and disruptive behaviors.)

11. Identify and verbally express feelings associated with past neglect, abuse, separation, or abandonment. (28, 29, 30, 31)

28. Explore the client's family background for a history of physical, sexual, or substance abuse, which may contribute to his/her disruptive behaviors.

29. Encourage and support the client in expressing feelings associated with neglect, abuse, separation, or abandonment.

30. Use child-centered play therapy approaches (e.g., provide unconditional, positive regard, offer nonjudgmental reflection of feelings, display trust in child's capacity to act responsibly) to help the client express and work through feelings surrounding past neglect, abuse, separation, or abandonment.

31. Use the empty-chair technique to assist the client in expressing and working through feelings of anger and sadness about past neglect, abuse, separation, or abandonment.

12. Increase the frequency of socially appropriate behaviors with siblings and peers. (32, 33, 34)

32. Encourage the client to participate in extracurricular or positive peer group activities to provide a healthy outlet for anger, improve social skills, and increase self-esteem.

33. Refer the client for group therapy to improve his/her social judgment and interpersonal skills.

34. Play the game, You & Me: A Game of Social Skills (Shapiro) to help the client develop positive social skills.

13. Increase verbalizations of empathy and concern for other people. (35)

35. Assign the client the task of showing empathy, kindness, or sensitivity to the needs of others (e.g., reading a bedtime story to a sibling, helping a classmate with reading or math problems).

14. Express feelings in therapeutic games or individual play therapy sessions. (36, 37, 38)

36. Play the game, The Helping, Sharing, and Caring Game (Gardner) with the client to promote his/her greater expression of empathy and concern for other people.

37. Interpret the feelings expressed in individual play therapy sessions, and relate them to the client's negative attention-seeking behaviors.

38. Employ psychoanalytic play therapy principles (e.g., explore and gain an understanding of the etiology of unconscious conflicts, fixations, or arrests; interpret resistance, transference, or core anxieties) to help the client work through and resolve issues contributing to disruptive behaviors.

15. Express feelings through art therapy and mutual storytelling. (39, 40)

39. Use puppets, dolls, or stuffed animals to create a story that models appropriate ways to gain approval

and acceptance from peers; then ask the client to create a story with similar characters or themes.

40. Use the Color Your Life technique (O'Connor) to improve the client's ability to identify and verbalize feelings instead of acting them out: Ask the client to match colors to different emotions (e.g., red-anger, blue-sad, black-very sad, yellow-happy), and then fill up a blank page with colors that reflect his/her feelings about different life events.

16. Take medication as prescribed by the physician. (41)

41. Arrange for a medication evaluation to improve the client's impulse control and stabilize his/her moods.

—. _____
_____
—. _____
_____
—. _____
_____

—. _____
_____
—. _____
_____
—. _____
_____

DIAGNOSTIC SUGGESTIONS

Axis I:	312.9	Disruptive Behavior Disorder NOS
	314.01	Attention-Deficit/Hyperactivity Disorder, Predominantly Hyperactive-Impulsive Type
	314.01	Attention-Deficit/Hyperactivity Disorder, Combined Type
	312.81	Conduct Disorder, Childhood-Onset Type
	313.81	Oppositional Defiant Disorder
	309.3	Adjustment Disorder With Disturbance of Conduct
	309.4	Adjustment Disorder With Mixed Disturbance of Emotions and Conduct

	V71.02	Child Antisocial Behavior
	V61.20	Parent-Child Relational Problem
	_____	_____
	_____	_____

Axis II: V71.09   No Diagnosis

           _____   _____

           _____   _____

DIVORCE REACTION

BEHAVIORAL DEFINITIONS

1. Infrequent contact or loss of contact with a parental figure due to separation or divorce.
2. Intense emotional reaction (e.g., crying, begging, pleading, temper outbursts) associated with separation of parental figures and/or when making the transfer from one parent's home to another.
3. Persistent fears and worries about being abandoned or separated from a parent.
4. Strong feelings of grief and sadness combined with feelings of low self-worth, lack of confidence, social withdrawal, and loss of interest in activities that normally bring pleasure.
5. Feelings of guilt accompanied by unreasonable belief regarding behaving in some manner to cause parents' divorce and/or failing to prevent their divorce from occurring.
6. Marked increase in frequency and severity of acting out, oppositional, and aggressive behaviors since the onset of parents' marital problems, separation, or divorce.
7. Significant decline in school performance and lack of interest or motivation in school-related activities.
8. Appearance of regressive behaviors (e.g., thumb sucking, baby talk, rocking, bed-wetting).
9. Pseudomaturity as manifested by denying or suppressing painful emotions about parents' divorce and often assuming parental roles or responsibilities.
10. Numerous psychosomatic complaints in response to anticipated separations, stress, or frustration.
11. Loss of contact with positive support network due to geographic move.

__. _____
   _____
__. _____

—. _____
   _____
   _____

LONG-TERM GOALS

1. Accept parents' separation or divorce with understanding and control of feelings and behavior.
2. Alleviate fear of abandonment and establish loving, secure relationship with the parents.
3. Eliminate feelings of guilt and statements that reflect self-blame for parents' divorce.
4. Elevate and stabilize mood.
5. Parents establish and maintain consistent visitation arrangement that meets the client's emotional needs.
6. Parents establish and maintain appropriate parent-child boundaries in discipline and assignment of responsibilities.
7. Parents consistently demonstrate mutual respect for one another, especially in front of the children.
8. Create a strong, supportive social network outside of the immediate family to offset loss of nurturance or support from within family.

—. _____
   _____

—. _____
   _____

—. _____
   _____

SHORT-TERM OBJECTIVES	THERAPEUTIC INTERVENTIONS
1. Tell the story of parents' separation or divorce. (1, 2)	1. Actively build the level of trust with the client through consistent eye contact, active listening, unconditional positive regard, and warm acceptance to improve his/her ability to identify and express feelings connected to parents' separation or divorce.

2. Identify and express feelings related to parents' separation or divorce. (2, 3, 4, 5, 6)

2. Explore, encourage, and support the client in verbally expressing and clarifying his/her feelings associated with the separation or divorce.

2. Explore, encourage, and support the client in verbally expressing and clarifying his/her feelings associated with the separation or divorce.

3. Read books with the client to assist him/her in expressing his/her feelings about the parents' divorce and changes in the family system (e.g., *Dinosaur's Divorce: A Guide for Changing Families* by Brown, Tolon Brown, and Krasney Brown; *Divorce Workbook: A Guide for Kids and Families* by Ives, Fassler, and Lash).

4. Create a photo album by first instructing the client to gather a diverse collection of photographs covering many aspects of his/her life; then place the pictures in a photo album during a session while allowing him/her to verbalize his/her feelings about changes in the family system.

5. Use the Color Your Life technique (O'Connor) to improve the client's ability to identify and verbalize feelings: Ask the client to match colors with different emotions (e.g., red-anger, purple-rage, yellow-happy, blue-sad, black-very sad), and then instruct him/her to fill a blank page with colors that reflect his/her feelings about his/her parents' separation or divorce.

6. Ask the client to first draw pictures of different emotions on

blank faces and then share time when he/she experienced those emotions about parent's separation or divorce (or assign the "Feelings and Faces" exercise from the *Child Psychotherapy Homework Planner,* 2nd ed. by Jongsma, Peterson, and McInnis).

3. Describe how parents' separation or divorce has impacted his/her personal and family life. (7)

7. Use the empty-chair technique to help the client express mixed emotions he/she feels toward both parents about changes in personal or family life due to separation or divorce.

4. Express thoughts and feelings within the family system regarding parental separation or divorce. (8, 9)

8. Hold family therapy sessions to allow the client and siblings to express feelings about separation or divorce in presence of parents.

9. Encourage the parents to provide opportunities (e.g., family meetings) at home to allow the client and siblings to express feelings about separation/divorce and subsequent changes in family system.

5. Recognize and affirm self as not being responsible for parents' separation or divorce. (10, 11)

10. Explore the factors contributing to the client's feelings of guilt and self-blame about parents' separation/divorce; assist him/her in realizing that his/her negative behaviors did not cause parents' divorce to occur.

11. Assist the client in realizing that he/she does not have the power or control to bring parents back together.

6. Parents verbalize an acceptance of the responsibility for dissolution of the marriage. (12, 13)

12. Conduct family therapy sessions where the parents affirm the client and siblings as not being responsible for separation or divorce.

13. Challenge and confront statements by the parents that place blame or responsibility for separation or divorce on the children.

7. Identify positive and negative aspects of parents' separation or divorce. (14)

8. Identify and verbalize unmet need to parents. (15, 16)

9. Reduce the frequency and severity of angry, depressed, and anxious moods. (17, 18)

10. Express feelings of anger about the parents' separation or divorce through controlled, respectful verbalizations and healthy physical outlets. (19, 20)

14. Give homework assignment in which the client lists both positive and negative aspects of parents' divorce; process this list in the next session and allow him/her to express different emotions.

15. Give parents the directive of spending 10 to 15 minutes of one-on-one time with the client and siblings on a regular daily basis to identify and meet the children's needs.

16. Consult with the client and his/her parents about establishing routine or ritual (e.g., snuggling and reading books together, playing board games, watching a favorite video) to help decrease his/her emotional distress around periods of separation or transfer from one parent's home to another.

17. Empower the client by reinforcing his/her ability to cope with divorce and make healthy adjustments.

18. Assist the client in making a connection between underlying painful emotions about divorce and angry outbursts or aggressive behaviors.

19. Identify appropriate and inappropriate ways for the client to express anger about the parents' separation or divorce.

20. Use the Angry Tower technique (Saxe) to help the client identify and express feelings of anger about divorce: Build a tower out of plastic containers; place a small object (representing anger) on top of the tower; instruct the client to throw a small fabric ball

11. Parents verbally recognize how their guilt and failure to follow through with limits contributes to the client's acting out or aggressive behaviors. (21, 22)

12. Reduce the frequency and severity of acting out, oppositional, and aggressive behaviors. (23, 24, 25)

13. Complete school and homework assignments on a regular basis. (26, 27)

at the tower while verbalizing feelings of anger connected to the divorce.

21. Encourage and challenge the parents not to allow guilt feelings about divorce to interfere with the need to impose consequences for acting out or oppositional behaviors.

22. Assist the parents in establishing clearly defined rules, boundaries, and consequences for acting out, oppositional, or aggressive behaviors.

23. Help the client to recognize how an increase in acting out behaviors is connected to emotional pain surrounding the parents' divorce (or assign the "Surface Behavior/Inner Feelings" exercise in the *Child Psychotherapy Homework Planner,* 2nd ed. by Jongsma, Peterson, and McInnis).

24. Assign the parents to read a book to learn to manage the client's increased acting out, oppositional, and aggressive behaviors (e.g., *1-2-3 Magic: Training Your Preschoolers and Preteens to Do What You Want* by Phelan); process the reading with the therapist.

25. Design a reward system and/or contingency contract with the client to reinforce good anger control and deter acting out, oppositional, or aggressive behaviors.

26. Assist the parents in establishing a new study routine to help the client complete school or homework assignments.

14. Decrease the frequency of somatic complaints. (28)

15. Noncustodial parent verbally recognizes pattern of over-indulgence and begins to set limits on money spending and/or time spent in leisure or recreational activities. (29)

16. Noncustodial parent begins to assign household responsibilities and/or require the client to complete homework during visits. (30)

17. Reduce the frequency of regressive, immature, and ir-responsible behaviors. (31, 32)

18. Parents cease making unneces-sary, hostile, or overly critical remarks about the other par-ent in the presence of their child(ren). (33)

19. Parents recognize and agree to cease the pattern of soliciting information and/or sending messages to the other parent through the child(ren). (34, 35)

27. Design and implement a reward system and/or contingency con-tract to reinforce completion of school and homework assignments or good academic performance.

28. Refocus the client's discussion from physical complaints to emo-tional conflicts and the expression of feelings.

29. Encourage the noncustodial par-ent to set limits on the client's misbehavior and refrain from overindulging the client during visits.

30. Give a directive to the non-custodial parent to assign a chore of having the client complete a school or homework assignment during a visit.

31. Teach how enmeshed or overly protective parents reinforce the client's regressive, immature, or irresponsible behaviors by failing to set necessary limits.

32. Have the client and his/her parents identify age-appropriate ways for him/her to meet needs for attention, affection, and ac-ceptance; process the list and encourage him/her to engage in age-appropriate behaviors.

33. Challenge and confront the par-ents to cease making unnecessary hostile or overly critical remarks about the other parent in the pres-ence of the child(ren).

34. Counsel the parents about not placing the child(ren) in the middle by soliciting information about the other parent or sending messages through the child(ren) to the other parent about adult matters.

20. Disengaged or uninvolved parent follows through with recommendations to spend greater quality time with the client. (36, 37, 38)

21. Identify and express feelings through mutual story-telling and artwork. (39, 40, 41)

35. Challenge and confront the client about playing one parent against the other to meet needs, obtain material goods, or avoid responsibility.

36. Hold individual and/or family therapy session to challenge and encourage noncustodial parent to maintain regular visitation and involvement in the client's life.

37. Give a directive to the disengaged or distant parent to spend more time or perform a specific task with the client (e.g., going on an outing to the zoo, assisting the client with homework, working on a project around the home).

38. Use family theraplay principles (e.g., active involvement by the parent in the session, with him/her responding empathically to the client's feelings or needs) to strengthen or facilitate a closer parent-child relationship.

39. Use a mutual storytelling technique whereby the therapist and client alternate telling stories through the use of puppets, dolls, or stuffed animals: The therapist first models appropriate ways to express emotions related to the parents' separation or divorce; the client then follows by creating a story with similar characters or themes.

40. Have the client draw a variety of pictures reflecting his/her feelings about his/her parents' divorce or how divorce has impacted his/her life; place these pictures in a notebook that is given to him/her at the end of therapy as a keepsake.

22. Increase participation in a positive peer group and extra-curricular or school-related activities. (42)

23. Participate in a support group with other children of divorce. (43)

24. Increase contacts with adults and build a support network outside the family. (44)

41. Instruct the client to draw pictures of both his/her mother's and father's homes, and then have him/her share what it is like to live in or visit each home to assess the quality of his/her relationship with each parent.

42. Encourage the client to participate in school, extracurricular, or positive peer group activities to offset the loss of time spent with his/her parents.

43. Refer the client to a children-of-divorce group to assist him/her in expressing feelings and to help him/her understand that he/she is not alone in going through the divorce process.

44. Identify a list of adult individuals (e.g., school counselor, neighbor, uncle or aunt, Big Brother or Big Sister, member of clergy) outside of the family to whom the client can turn for support, guidance, and nurturance to help him/her cope with divorce, family move, or change in schools.

__. _____

__. _____

__. _____

__. _____

__. _____

__. _____

DIAGNOSTIC SUGGESTIONS

Axis I: 309.0   Adjustment Disorder With Depressed Mood
                309.24   Adjustment Disorder With Anxiety

309.28	Adjustment Disorder With Mixed Anxiety and Depressed Mood
309.3	Adjustment Disorder With Disturbance of Conduct
309.4	Adjustment Disorder With Mixed Disturbance of Emotions and Conduct
300.4	Dysthymic Disorder
300.02	Generalized Anxiety Disorder
309.21	Separation Anxiety Disorder
313.81	Oppositional Defiant Disorder
300.81	Undifferentiated Somatoform Disorder

_____   _____

_____   _____

Axis II: V71.09   No Diagnosis

_____   _____

_____   _____

ENURESIS/ENCOPRESIS

BEHAVIORAL DEFINITIONS

1. Repeated pattern of voluntary or involuntary voiding of urine into bed or clothes during the day or at night after age 5, when continence is expected.
2. Repeated passage of feces, whether voluntary or involuntary, in inappropriate places (e.g., clothing, floor) after age 5, when continence is expected.
3. Feelings of shame associated with Enuresis or Encopresis that cause the avoidance of situations (e.g., overnight visits with friends) that might lead to further embarrassment.
4. Social ridicule, isolation, or ostracism by peers because of Enuresis or Encopresis.
5. Frequent attempts to hide feces or soiled clothing because of shame or fear of further ridicule, criticism, or punishment.
6. Excessive anger, rejection, or punishment by the parents or caretakers centered on toilet-training practices, which contributes to low self-esteem.
7. Strong feelings of fear or hostility, which are channeled into acts of Enuresis and Encopresis.
8. Poor impulse control, which contributes to lack of responsibility with toilet-training practices.
9. Deliberate smearing of feces.

—. _____
_____
_____

—. _____
_____
_____

—. _____
_____

LONG-TERM GOALS

1. Eliminate all diurnal and/or nocturnal episodes of Enuresis.
2. Terminate all episodes of Encopresis, whether voluntary or involuntary.
3. Resolve the underlying core conflicts contributing to the emergence of Enuresis or Encopresis.
4. Parents eliminate rigid or coercive toilet-training practices.
5. Cease all incidents of smearing feces.
6. Increase self-esteem and successfully work through feelings of shame or humiliation associated with past Enuresis or Encopresis.

__. _____

_____

__. _____

_____

__. _____

_____

SHORT-TERM OBJECTIVES

1. Comply with a physician's orders for medical tests and evaluations. (1, 2)

2. Complete psychological testing. (3)

▼ 3. Take prescribed medication as directed by the physician. (4)

THERAPEUTIC INTERVENTIONS

1. Refer the client for a medical examination to rule out organic or physical causes of the Enuresis or Encopresis.

2. Arrange for a medication evaluation of the client.

3. Conduct psychological testing to rule out the presence of Attention-Deficit/Hyperactivity Disorder (ADHD), impulse-control disorder, or serious underlying emotional problems; provide feedback from the testing to the client and his/her parents.

4. Monitor the client for medication compliance, side effects, and effectiveness; consult with the

---

▼ indicates that the Objective/Intervention is consistent with those found in evidence-based treatments.

prescribing physician at regular intervals and be alert for Enuresis relapse after discontinuation. ▽

▽ 4. Parents consistently comply with the use of bell-and-pad conditioning procedures to treat nocturnal Enuresis. (5, 6)

5. Train the client and his/her parents to treat Enuresis by using bell-and-pad conditioning procedures in which a urine-sensitive pad causes an alarm to sound when involuntary wetting occurs. ▽

6. Employ overlearning method (e.g., require the client to drink a gradually increasing, but small, amount of fluid shortly before bedtime) along with the use of bell-and-pad conditioning procedures in latter states of treatment to help prevent the client's relapse of nocturnal Enuresis. ▽

▽ 5. Reduce the frequency of enuretic behavior. (7, 8, 9, 10, 11)

7. Design and counsel the parents on the use of positive reinforcement procedures to increase the client's bladder control. ▽

8. Teach the client and his/her parents an effective urine-retention training technique that increases the client's awareness of the sensation or need to urinate by having the client hold urine for increasingly longer periods of time before voiding (or assign "Bladder Retention Training Program" in the *Child Psychotherapy Homework Planner,* 2nd ed. by Jongsma, Peterson, and McInnis); reward successful retention. ▽

9. Train the client's parents or caretakers in the use of staggered-awakening procedures, using a variable-interval schedule, to control nocturnal Enuresis. ▽

10. Design and implement dry-bed techniques, training the parents and the client in response inhibition, positive reinforcement, rapid awakening, gradual increase of fluid intake, self-correction of accidents, and decreased critical comments about toilet-training behavior. ▽

11. Teach the client to assume greater responsibility in managing nocturnal Enuresis (or assign the "Dry Bed Training Program" in the *Child Psychotherapy Homework Planner,* 2nd ed. by Jongsma, Peterson, and McInnis). ▽

6. Reduce the frequency of encopretic behavior. (12, 13)

12. Train the client and his/her parents how to implement a systematic operant conditioning program that combines positive reinforcement techniques with the use of glycerin suppositories or enemas if the client does not defecate voluntarily every day.

13. Teach the client to assume greater responsibility in developing bowel control and recognizing negative consequences that result from encopretic incidents (or assign the "Bowel Control Training Program" in the *Child Psychotherapy Homework Planner,* 2nd ed. by Jongsma, Peterson, and McInnis).

7. Increase the client's role in implementing the toilet-training practices and interventions. (14, 15, 16, 17)

14. Encourage and challenge the client to assume active responsibility for achieving mastery of bladder and/or bowel control (e.g., keeping a record of wet and dry days, setting an alarm clock for voiding times, cleaning soiled underwear or linens).

15. Challenge and confront the client's and/or parents' lack of motivation or compliance in following through with the recommended therapeutic interventions.

16. Inquire into what the client does differently on days when he/she demonstrates good bladder/bowel control and does not have any enuretic or encopretic incidents; process his/her responses and reinforce any effective strategies that are used to gain bladder/bowel control.

17. Assign the client and his/her parents to read material to educate them about bed-wetting and help the client assume an active role in overcoming nocturnal enuresis (e.g., *Dry All Night: The Picture Book Technique that Stops Bed Wetting* by Mack and Wilensky).

8. Verbalize how anxiety or fears associated with toilet-training practices are unrealistic or irrational. (18, 19)

18. Explore the client's irrational cognitive messages that produce fear or anxiety associated with toilet training; replace the irrational messages with realistic messages.

19. Assist the client in realizing how his/her anxiety or fears associated with toilet training are irrational or unrealistic.

9. Identify the negative social consequences that may occur from peers if Enuresis or Encopresis continues. (20)

20. Identify and discuss negative social consequences that the client may experience from peers in order to increase his/her motivation to master bladder/bowel control.

10. Parent(s) verbally recognize how rigid toilet-training practices or hostile, critical remarks contribute to the client's Enuresis or Encopresis. (21, 22, 23)

21. Counsel the client's parents on effective, nonabusive toilet-training practices.

22. Conduct family therapy sessions to assess the dynamics that contribute to the emergence or

reinforcement of the client's Enuresis, Encopresis, or smearing of feces.

23. Explore parent-child interactions to assess whether the parents' toilet-training practices are excessively rigid or whether the parents make frequent hostile, critical remarks about the client.

11. Decrease the frequency and severity of hostile, critical remarks by the parents regarding the client's toilet training. (24, 25)

24. Confront and challenge the parents about making overly critical or hostile remarks that contribute to the client's low self-esteem, shame and embarrassment, and anger.

25. Assess parent-child interactions for the presence of a hostile-dependent cycle whereby the client's wetting or soiling angers the parents, the parents respond in an overly critical or hostile manner, the client seeks to punish the parents for their strong display or anger, and so on.

12. Understand and verbally recognize the secondary gain that results from Enuresis or Encopresis. (26, 27, 28)

26. Assist the client and his/her parents in developing an insight into the secondary gain (e.g., parental attention; avoidance of separation from the parents; physician or counselor attention) received from Enuresis or Encopresis.

27. Use a strategic family therapy approach in which the therapist does not talk about Enuresis or Encopresis but discusses what might surface if this problem were resolved (i.e., camouflaged problems may be revealed).

28. Use Ericksonian therapy intervention of prescribing the symptom, whereby the client is instructed to pick out a specific night of the

week when he/she will deliberately wet the bed. (Paradoxical intervention allows the client to control Enuresis by making the unconscious behavior a conscious maneuver.)

13. Strengthen the relationship with the disengaged parent as demonstrated by increased time spent with the client. (29, 30, 31)

29. Assign the disengaged parent the responsibility of overseeing or teaching the client effective toilet-training practices (e.g., keeping a record of wet and dry days, gently awakening the client for bladder voiding, reminding or teaching the client how to clean soiled underwear or linens).

30. Give a directive to the disengaged parent to spend quality time with the client (e.g., working on homework together, going to the park, engaging in a sporting activity).

31. Encourage the client and parents to engage in "free play" during family play therapy sessions to assess the quality of the parent-child relationships and gain an understanding of the family dynamics that contribute to the development of Enuresis or Encopresis.

14. Identify and express feelings associated with past separation, loss, trauma, or rejection experiences and how they are connected to current Encopresis/Enuresis. (32, 33, 34)

32. Determine whether the client's Enuresis, Encopresis, or smearing of feces is associated with past separation, loss, traumatization, or rejection experiences.

33. Explore, encourage, and support the client in verbally expressing and clarifying feelings associated with past separation, loss, trauma, or rejection experiences.

34. Employ psychoanalytic play therapy approaches (e.g., explore and gain understanding of the etiology of unconscious conflicts,

15. Express feelings through art-work and mutual storytelling. (35)

16. Increase the frequency of posi-tive self-descriptive statements that reflect improved self-esteem. (36, 37)

17. Appropriately express anger verbally and physically rather than channeling anger through Enuresis, Encopresis, or smear-ing of feces. (38, 39)

18. Increase the parents' empa-thetic responses to the client's thoughts, feelings, and needs. (40)

—. _____

_____

—. _____

_____

fixations, or arrests; interpret resistance, transference, or core anxieties) to help the client work through and resolve issues con-tributing to bladder/bowel control problems.

35. Instruct the client to draw a pic-ture that reflects how enuretic or encopretic incidents affect self-esteem.

36. Assist the client in identifying and listing his/her positive charac-teristics to help decrease feelings of shame and embarrassment; reinforce his/her positive self-statements.

37. Assign the client to make one positive self-statement daily and record that in a journal.

38. Teach the client effective commu-nication and assertiveness skills to improve his/her ability to express thoughts and feelings through ap-propriate verbalizations.

39. Teach the client appropriate physical outlets that allow the expression of anger in a construc-tive manner, rather than through inappropriate wetting or soiling.

40. Direct the parents to use the Once Upon a Time Potty Book and Doll Set (Weinstock; available from Childswork/Childsplay) to increase the preschool child's mo-tivation to develop bladder/bowel control.

—. _____

_____

—. _____

_____

—. _____   —. _____

_____   _____

DIAGNOSTIC SUGGESTIONS

Axis I: 307.6   Enuresis (Not Due to a General Medical
                           Condition)
                787.6   Encopresis, With Constipation and Overflow
                           Incontinence
                307.7   Encopresis, Without Constipation and Overflow
                           Incontinence
                300.4   Dysthymic Disorder
                296.xx   Major Depressive Disorder
                299.80   Pervasive Developmental Disorder NOS
                309.81   Posttraumatic Stress Disorder
                313.81   Oppositional Defiant Disorder
                314.01   Attention-Deficit/Hyperactivity Disorder,
                           Combined Type

                _____   _____

                _____   _____

Axis II: V71.09   No Diagnosis

                _____   _____

                _____   _____

FIRE SETTING

BEHAVIORAL DEFINITIONS

1. Has set one or more fires in the last 6 months.
2. Has been regularly observed playing with fire, fireworks, or combustible substances.
3. Is around fire whenever possible.
4. Consistently has matches, lighters, candles, and so forth in his/her possession.
5. Has an easily discernible fascination and/or preoccupation with fire.
6. Does not experience tension or sexual arousal prior to fire-setting behavior, or gratification or relief when witnessing the fire.

—. _____
_____
_____
—. _____
_____
—. _____
_____

LONG-TERM GOALS

1. Establish safety of self, the family, and the community.
2. Terminate the fascination and preoccupation with fire.
3. Redirect or rechannel fascination with fire into constructive arenas.
4. Establish the existence of a psychotic process or major affective disorder and procure placement in an appropriate treatment program.
5. Parents responsibly monitor and supervise the client's behaviors and whereabouts.

—. _____

—. _____

—. _____

SHORT-TERM OBJECTIVES

1. Parents consistently guide and supervise the client's behavior, including monitoring him/her for possessing articles connected with fire (e.g., matches, lighters). (1, 2, 3)

2. Identify the constructive and destructive aspects of fires. (4, 5)

THERAPEUTIC INTERVENTIONS

1. Teach the parents to consistently structure and supervise the client's behavior.

2. Monitor the parents' efforts to structure, set limits on, and supervise the client, giving support, encouragement, and redirection as appropriate.

3. Assist the client and parents in developing ways to increase his/her impulse control through use of positive reinforcement at times of apparent control.

4. Assign and work with the client and parents to create two collages, one that emphasizes fire's positive aspects and one that focuses on fire's destructive aspects. Discuss with the client as the collage is presented.

5. Construct with the client and his/her parents a list of questions for the client to ask a firefighter or a nurse in a local burn unit. Then help arrange an interview with one of these individuals. Afterward, process the experience and information gathered.

3. Report a decrease in the impulse to set fires. (6, 7)

6. Assign the family an operant-based intervention in which the parent allows the client to strike matches under supervision, noting a need for caution. A sum of money will be placed next to the pack and the client will receive a predetermined sum as well as warm praise for each match left unstruck. Monitor intervention and give redirection and feedback as needed.

7. Assign an intervention of stimulus satiation in which the client is given a box of matches with his/her parent(s) instructing the client how to safely strike. Allow the client to strike as many as he/she would like. Monitor intervention and redirect as needed.

4. Demonstrate steps necessary to prevent destruction from fire. (8, 9)

8. Assist and coach parents in implementing steps necessary to prevent destruction from fire such as teaching a safe way to build a fire and an effective way to put it out or giving a monetary reward to the client for turning in any fire-setting material (or assign the exercise "Fire-Proofing Your Home and Family" from the *Child Psychotherapy Homework Planner,* 2nd ed. by Jongsma, Peterson, and McInnis). Process the assignment in the next family session.

9. Ask the father (or male father figure) to teach the client how to safely build a fire. The father is to emphasize the need for strict control of and respect for the power of fire. Therapist will provide materials for a fire in session (matches, sticks, coffee can). Therapist will monitor and process the assignment.

5. Increase the frequency of positive interactions and connectedness between family members. (10, 11, 12)

10. Use a family-system approach to address fire-setting behavior; require the entire family to attend an agreed-upon number of sessions during which the family's roles, ways of communicating, and conflicts will be explored and confronted.

11. Assign each family member to list the positive or supportive and negative or conflictual aspects of the family (or assign the exercise "When a Fire Has No Fuel" from the *Child Psychotherapy Homework Planner,* 2nd ed. by Jongsma, Peterson, and McInnis). Process the assignment in the next family sessions.

12. Assist the family members in learning to identify, express, and tolerate their own feelings and those of other family members.

6. The client and his/her family demonstrate the ability to identify, express, and tolerate unpleasant feelings. (12, 13)

12. Assist the family members in learning to identify, express, and tolerate their own feelings and those of other family members.

13. Gently probe the client's emotions in order to help him/her become better able to identify and express his/her feelings.

7. Parents and caregivers identify and implement ways of satisfying the client's unmet emotional needs. (14, 15)

14. Assess the client's unmet needs for attention, nurturance, and affirmation. Assist all caregivers (parents, siblings, teachers, baby-sitters, and extended family) in identifying actions (e.g., loud talk, acts of showing off, making up stories) in which they can engage to help satisfy the client's emotional needs.

15. Assess the degree of chaos and/or violence in family leading to the

8. Increase positive time spent with the father or another significant male figure in his/her life. (16, 17)

9. Verbalize feelings of rejection and anger. (18)

10. Identify instances of physical or sexual abuse. (19)

11. Cooperate with an evaluation for psychotropic medication or Attention-Deficit/Hyperactivity Disorder (ADHD). (20, 21)

12. Comply with all recommendations of the psychiatric or ADHD evaluation. (22, 23)

client's desire for power or control over his/her environment. Encourage more structure, predictability, and respect within the family.

16. Ask father to identify three things he could do to relate more to the client. Then assign him to implement two of the three, and monitor the results.

17. Assist the mother or other caregiving person to obtain an older companion for the client through the Big Brother or Big Sister program.

18. Probe the client's feelings of hurt and anger over relationship rejection with peers and/or family. Interpret fire setting as an expression of rage.

19. Assess whether the client's fire setting is associated with his/her being a victim of sexual and/or physical abuse.

20. Assess whether the client's fire setting is associated with a psychotic process or major affective disorder that may need psychotropic medication treatment; refer him/her to a physician for evaluation, if necessary.

21. Assess the client for the presence of ADHD.

22. Assist and monitor the family's follow-through with all the recommendations from the psychiatric or ADHD evaluations.

23. Assist the family in placing the client in a residential treatment program for intense treatment of serious psychiatric disturbance, if indicated.

—. _____   —. _____
_____   _____
—. _____   —. _____
_____   _____
—. _____   —. _____
_____   _____

DIAGNOSTIC SUGGESTIONS

Axis I: 312.xx   Conduct Disorder
314.9   Attention-Deficit/Hyperactivity Disorder NOS
309.3   Adjustment Disorder With Disturbance of
Conduct
309.4   Adjustment Disorder With Mixed Disturbance of
Emotions and Conduct
312.30   Impulse-Control Disorder NOS
298.9   Psychotic Disorder NOS
296.xx   Major Depressive Disorder

_____   _____
_____   _____

Axis II: V71.09   No Diagnosis

_____   _____
_____   _____

GENDER IDENTITY DISORDER

BEHAVIORAL DEFINITIONS

1. Repeatedly states the desire to be, or feels that he/she is, the opposite sex.
2. Preference for dressing in clothes typically worn by the other sex.
3. Prefers the roles of the opposite sex in make-believe play or fantasies.
4. Insists on participating in games and pastimes that are typical of the other sex.
5. Prefers playmates of the opposite sex.
6. Frequently passes as the opposite sex.
7. Insists that he/she was born the wrong sex.
8. Verbalizes a disgust with or rejection of his/her sexual anatomy.

—. _____
   _____
   _____
—. _____
   _____
   _____
—. _____
   _____

LONG-TERM GOALS

1. Terminate the confusion regarding sexual identity and accept own gender and sexual anatomy.
2. Stop dressing as and playing like the opposite sex.
3. Accept the genitalia as a normal part of the body, and terminate the repulsion of or desire to change it.
4. Establish and maintain lasting (i.e., 6 months or longer) same-sex peer friendship.

—. _____
   _____
—. _____
   _____
—. _____
   _____

SHORT-TERM OBJECTIVES

1. Openly express feelings regarding sexual identity and identify the causes for rejection of gender identity. (1, 2, 3)

2. Identify and replace negative, distorted cognitive messages regarding gender identity. (4, 5)

3. Express comfort with or even pride in sexual identity. (6, 7, 8, 9)

THERAPEUTIC INTERVENTIONS

1. Actively build the level of trust with the client through consistent eye contact, active listening, unconditional positive regard, and warm acceptance to help him/her increase the ability to identify and express feelings.

2. Explore the client's reasons for attraction to an opposite-sex identity.

3. Use play therapy techniques to explore the client's sexual attitudes and causes for the rejection of gender identity.

4. Use cognitive therapy techniques to identify negative messages the client gives to himself/herself about sexual identity.

5. Assist the client in identifying positive, realistic self-talk that can replace negative cognitions regarding gender identity.

6. Confront and reframe the client's self-disparaging comments about gender identity and sexual anatomy.

7. Assist the client in identifying positive aspects of his/her own sexual identity.

4. Parents explore their subtle and direct messages to the client that reinforce gender identity confusion. (10, 11)

5. Demonstrate an increased self-esteem as evidenced by positive statements made about talents, traits, and appearance. (7, 12)

6. Same-sex parent (or parent substitute) and the client agree to increase time spent together in activities. (13, 14, 15, 16)

8. Assign a mirror exercise in which the client talks positively to himself/herself regarding sexual identity.

9. Reinforce the client's positive self-descriptive statements.

10. Hold family therapy sessions to explore the dynamics that may reinforce the client's gender confusion.

11. Meet with the parents to explore their attitudes and behaviors that may contribute to the client's sexual identity confusion.

7. Assist the client in identifying positive aspects of his/her own sexual identity.

12. Assist the client in developing a list of his/her positive traits, talents, and physical characteristics.

13. Explore the client's feelings of hurt, anger, or distrust of the same-sex parent or parent substitute and the causes for these negative feelings.

14. Assign the same-sex parent to increase time and contact with the client in play and work activities while urging the opposite-sex parent to support the client in appropriate gender identification.

15. Assign homework designed to structure the client's time spent with the same-sex adult (e.g., assign "One-on-One" in the *Child Psychotherapy Homework Planner,* 2nd ed. by Jongsma, Peterson, and McInnis).

16. Help the client to obtain the volunteer services of a same-sex Big Brother or Big Sister.

7. Verbalize the desire to be with the same-sex parent or other significant same-sex adult in quiet and active times. (17, 18)

17. Conduct a family therapy session in which the client can explore and express his/her feelings toward the same-sex parent; work toward resolution of any negativity in these feelings.

18. Encourage and reinforce the client for spending time with the same-sex parent or parent substitute.

8. Opposite-sex parent encourage and reinforce gender-appropriate dress, play, and peer-group identification as well as a strong relationship between the client and the same-sex parent. (14, 19)

14. Assign the same-sex parent to increase time and contact with the client in play and work activities while urging the opposite-sex parent to support the client in appropriate gender identification.

19. Encourage the parents in positively reinforcing appropriate gender identity, dress, and social behavior in the client.

9. Increase time spent in socialization with same-sex peers. (20, 21)

20. Assign the client to initiate social (play) activities with same-sex peers.

21. Monitor and give positive feedback when the client's dress, socialization, and peer identity are appropriate.

10. Dress consistently in clothes that are typical of same-sex peers without objection. (21, 22)

21. Monitor and give positive feedback when the client's dress, socialization, and peer identity are appropriate.

22. Review whether the client's desire to cross-dress is related to times of high stress in the family or occurs when the client is feeling ignored.

11. List some positive role models for own sexual identity, and tell why they are respected. (23, 24)

23. Assign the client to list some positive, same-sex role models, and process the reasons for respecting these individuals.

24. Assign the client homework designed to structure role-model

identification (or assign "I Want to Be Like . . ." in the *Child Psychotherapy Homework Planner,* 2nd ed. by Jongsma, Peterson, and McInnis).

12. Disclose any physical or sexual abuse. (3, 25)

3. Use play therapy techniques to explore the client's sexual attitudes and causes for the rejection of gender identity.

25. Explore the possibility that the client was physically or sexually abused (see Physical/Emotional Abuse Victim and Sexual Abuse Victim chapters in this *Planner*).

—. _____   —. _____
    _____   _____

—. _____   —. _____
    _____   _____

—. _____   —. _____
    _____   _____

DIAGNOSTIC SUGGESTIONS

Axis I: 302.6   Gender Identity Disorder in Children
                 302.6   Gender Identity Disorder NOS

                 _____   _____

                 _____   _____

Axis II: V71.09   No Diagnosis

                 _____   _____

                 _____   _____

GRIEF/LOSS UNRESOLVED

BEHAVIORAL DEFINITIONS

1. Loss of contact with a parent due to the parent's death.
2. Loss of contact with a parent figure due to termination of parental rights.
3. Loss of contact with a parent due to the parent's incarceration.
4. Loss of contact with a positive support network due to a geographic move.
5. Loss of meaningful contact with a parent figure due to the parent's emotional abandonment.
6. Strong emotional response experienced when the loss is mentioned.
7. Lack of appetite, nightmares, restlessness, inability to concentrate, irritability, tearfulness, or social withdrawal that began subsequent to a loss.
8. Marked drop in school grades, and an increase in angry outbursts, hyperactivity, or clinginess when separating from parents.
9. Feelings of guilt associated with the unreasonable belief in having done something to cause the loss or not having prevented it.
10. Avoidance of talking at length or in any depth about the loss.

___. _____

_____

___. _____

_____

___. _____

_____

LONG-TERM GOALS

1. Begin a healthy grieving process around the loss.
2. Complete the process of letting go of the lost significant other.
3. Work through the grieving and letting-go process and reach the point of emotionally reinvesting in life.
4. Successfully grieve the loss within a supportive emotional environment.
5. Resolve the loss and begin reinvesting in relationships with others and in age-appropriate activities.
6. Resolve feelings of guilt, depression, or anger that are associated with the loss and return to the previous level of functioning.

___. _____

_____

___. _____

_____

___. _____

_____

SHORT-TERM OBJECTIVES

1. Develop a trusting relationship with the therapist as evidenced by the open communication of feelings and thoughts associated with the loss. (1, 2, 3)

THERAPEUTIC INTERVENTIONS

1. Actively build the level of trust with the client through consistent eye contact, active listening, unconditional positive regard, and warm acceptance while asking him/her to identify and express feelings associated with the loss.

2. Read with the client a story about loss (e.g., *Where is Daddy?* by Gof; *Emma Says Goodbye* by Nystrom), and afterward discuss the story.

3. Educate the client and his/her parents about the stages of the grieving process, and teach the parents how to answer any of his/her questions.

2. Attend and freely participate in art and play therapy sessions. (4, 5, 6)

4. Using child-centered play therapy approaches (e.g., providing unconditional positive regard, reflecting feelings in a nonjudgmental manner, displaying trust in the child's capacity to act responsibly), assist the client in working through his/her loss.

5. Conduct individual play therapy sessions with the client to provide the environment for expressing and working through feelings connected to his/her loss.

6. Use various art therapy techniques with Play-Doh, clay, finger paints, and/or markers to help the client creatively express his/her feelings connected to his/her loss; ask him/her to give an explanation of his/her creation.

3. Tell the story of the loss. (7, 8, 9)

7. Use a mutual storytelling technique (Gardner) in which the client tells his/her story. The therapist interprets the story for its underlying meaning and then tells a story using the same characters in a similar setting, but weaves into the story a healthy way to adapt to and resolve the loss.

8. Use a before-and-after drawing technique (see the "Before and After Drawing Technique" by Cangelasi in *101 Favorite Play Therapy Techniques* by Kaduson and Schaefer) to help guide the client in telling the story, through drawings, of how he/she was before and after the loss; work through the connected feelings.

9. Suggest that the client act out or tell about the loss by using puppets or felt figures on a board.

4. Identify feelings connected with the loss. (10, 11, 12)

10. Assist the client in identifying his/her feelings by using the Five Faces technique (see *Helping Children Cope with Separation and Loss* by Jewett).

11. Play either the Goodbye Game (available from Childswork/Childsplay) or The Good Mourning Game (Bisenius and Norris) with the client to assist him/her in exploring grief.

12. Ask the client to write a letter to the lost person describing his/her feelings and read this letter to the therapist.

5. Verbalize and experience feelings connected with the loss. (13, 14, 15)

13. Conduct a play therapy session around the use of "Art or Verbal Metaphor for Children Experiencing Loss" (see Short in *101 Favorite Play Therapy Techniques* by Kaduson and Schaefer), in which the client is asked to talk about what his/her life was like prior to and after the loss using stories and drawings. Mirror, acknowledge, and validate the client's feelings.

14. Assist the client in identifying, labeling, and expressing feelings connected with the loss.

15. Assign the client to keep a daily grief journal of drawings representing thoughts and feelings associated with the loss; review the journal in therapy sessions.

6. Attend a grief support group. (16)

16. Refer the client to a grief support group for children.

7. Verbalize questions about the loss, and work to obtain answers for each. (17, 18)

17. Expand the client's understanding of death by reading to him/her *Lifetimes* (Mellonie and Ingpen), and discuss all questions that arise from the reading.

18. Assist the client in developing a list of questions about a specific loss; then try to direct him/her to resources (e.g., books, member of clergy, parent, counselor) for possible answers for each question.

8. Verbalize an increase in understanding the process of grieving and letting go. (19, 20)

19. Use *The Empty Place: A Child's Guide Through Grief* (Temes) to work the client through his/her grief process.

20. Read to the client *Don't Despair on Thursdays!* (Moser), and process the various suggestions given to handle the feelings connected to his/her grief.

9. Decrease the expression of feelings of guilt and blame for the loss. (21, 22, 23)

21. Explore the client's thoughts and feelings of guilt and blame surrounding the loss, replacing irrational thoughts with realistic thoughts.

22. Use a Despart Fable (see *Helping Children Cope with Separation and Loss* by Jewett) or a similar variation to help the client communicate blame for the loss (e.g., the therapist states, "A child says softly to himself, 'Oh, I did wrong.' What do you suppose the child believes he/she did wrong?").

23. Help the client lift the self-imposed curse that he/she believes to be the cause for the loss by asking the person who is perceived as having imposed the curse to take it back or by using a pretend phone conversation in which the client apologizes for the behavior that he/she believes is the cause for the curse.

10. Identify positive things about the deceased loved one and/or the lost relationship and how these things may be remembered. (24, 25)

11. Verbalize and resolve feelings of anger or guilt focused on self, on God, or on the deceased loved one that block the grief process. (26, 27)

12. Say good-bye to the lost loved one. (28, 29)

13. Parents verbalize an increase in their understanding of the grief process. (3, 30, 31)

24. Ask the client to list positive things about the deceased and how he/she plans to remember each, then process the list.

25. Ask the client to bring to a session pictures or mementos connected with the loss and to talk about them with the therapist.

26. Encourage and support the client in sessions to look angry, then to act angry, and finally to verbalize the anger.

27. Use behavioral techniques (e.g., kneading clay, kicking a paper bag stuffed with newsprint, using foam bats to hit objects without damage) in order to encourage the client to release repressed feelings of anger; explore the target causes for anger.

28. Assign the client to write a good-bye letter to a significant other or to make a good-bye drawing, and then process the letter or drawing within the session (or assign the "Grief Letter" exercise in the *Child Psychotherapy Homework Planner*, 2nd ed. by Jongsma, Peterson, and McInnis.)

29. Assign the client to visit the grave of the loved one with an adult to communicate feelings and say good-bye, perhaps by leaving a letter or drawing; process the experience.

3. Educate the client and his/her parents about the stages of the grieving process, and teach the parents how to answer any of his/her questions.

30. Teach the parents specific ways to provide comfort, consolation, love, companionship, and support to the client in grief (e.g., bringing up the loss occasionally for discussion, encouraging the client to talk freely of the loss, suggesting photographs of the loved one be displayed, spending one-on-one time with the client in quiet activities that may foster sharing of feelings, spending time with the client in diversion activities).

31. Assign the parents to read books on grief to help them become familiar with the grieving process (e.g., *Learning to Say Good-bye* by LeShan; *Helping Children Cope with Separation and Loss* by Jewett).

14. Parents increase their verbal openness about the loss. (32, 33)

32. Conduct family sessions in which each member of the client's family talks about his/her experience related to the loss.

33. Refer the client's parents to a grief/loss support group.

15. Participate in memorial services, funeral services, or other grieving rituals. (34)

34. Encourage the parents to allow the client to participate in the rituals and customs of grieving if he/she is willing to be involved.

16. Parents and the client attend and participate in a formal session to say good-bye to the parents whose parental rights are being terminated. (35, 36)

35. Conduct a session with the parents who are losing custody of the client to prepare them to say good-bye to him/her in a healthy, affirming way.

36. Facilitate a good-bye session with the client and the parents who are losing custody to give the client permission to move on with his/her life. If the parents who are

17. Verbalize positive memories of the past and hopeful statements about the future. (37, 38, 39)

losing custody or the current parents are not available, ask them to write a letter than can be read at the session, or conduct a role-playing session in which the client says good-bye to each parent.

37. Assist the client in making a record of his/her life in a book format to help visualize past, present, and future life. When it is completed, have the client keep a copy and give another to the current parents.

38. Assign the client to collect pictures and other memorabilia of the lost loved one into an album (or assign the exercise "Create a Memory Album" from the *Child Psychotherapy Homework Planner*, 2nd ed. by Jongsma, Peterson, and McInnis).

39. Encourage the client to express positive memories of the lost loved one (or assign "Petey's Journey through Sadness" in the *Child Psychotherapy Homework Planner*, 2nd ed. by Jongsma, Peterson, and McInnis).

__. _____   __. _____

_____   _____

__. _____   __. _____

_____   _____

__. _____   __. _____

_____   _____

DIAGNOSTIC SUGGESTIONS

| Axis I: | 296.2x | Major Depressive Disorder, Single Episode |
| | 296.3x | Major Depressive Disorder, Recurrent |

V62.82	Bereavement
309.0	Adjustment Disorder With Depressed Mood
309.4	Adjustment Disorder With Mixed Disturbance of Emotions and Conduct
300.4	Dysthymic Disorder
_____	_____
_____	_____

Axis II:

V71.09	No Diagnosis
_____	_____
_____	_____

LOW SELF-ESTEEM

BEHAVIORAL DEFINITIONS

1. Verbalizes self-disparaging remarks, seeing self as unattractive, worthless, stupid, a loser, a burden, unimportant, and so on.
2. Takes blame easily.
3. Inability to accept compliments.
4. Refuses to take risks associated with new experiences, as she/he expects failure.
5. Avoids social contact with adults and peers.
6. Seeks excessively to please or receive attention/praise of adults and/or peers.
7. Unable to identify or accept positive traits or talents about self.
8. Fears rejection from others, especially peer group.
9. Acts out in negative, attention-seeking ways.
10. Difficulty saying no to others; fears not being liked by others.

__. _____
   _____
   _____
__. _____
   _____
   _____
__. _____
   _____

LONG-TERM GOALS

1. Elevate self-esteem.
2. Increase social interaction, assertiveness, confidence in self, and reasonable risk taking.
3. Build a consistently positive self-image.
4. Demonstrate improved self-esteem by accepting compliments, by identifying

positive characteristics about self, by being able to say no to others, and by eliminating self-disparaging remarks.

5. See self as lovable and capable.
6. Increase social skill level.

__. _____
     _____
     _____
__. _____
     _____
     _____
__. _____
     _____

SHORT-TERM OBJECTIVES

1. Attend and actively partici-
    pate in play therapy sessions.
    (1, 2, 3)

THERAPEUTIC INTERVENTIONS

1. Employ psychoanalytic play
    therapy approaches (e.g., allow
    the client to take the lead with the
    therapist in exploring the source
    of unconscious conflicts, fixations,
    or developmental arrests) to assist
    the client in developing trust in
    the therapist and in letting go of
    negative thought patterns/beliefs
    or fears that impact his/her level
    of self-esteem.

2. Use puppets in a directed or
    nondirected way to allow the
    client to play out scenes involv-
    ing self-esteem (e.g., making
    friends, stating conversations,
    trying something new, working
    out a conflict, expressing feelings,
    asking for something that he/she
    needs).

3. Conduct a session using an
    expressive clay technique, either
    directed (see *Clayscaper* by Had-
    ley) or nondirected, to assist the
    client's expression and communi-
    cation of significant issues and to
    facilitate increased self-esteem.

2. Verbalize an increased awareness of self-disparaging
   statements. (4, 5)

4. Confront and reframe the client's
   self-disparaging comments.

5. Assist the client in becoming
   aware of how he/she expresses or
   acts out (e.g., lack of eye contact,
   social withdrawal, expectation of
   failure or rejection) negative feelings about self.

3. Decrease frequency of negative
   self-statements. (6, 7)

6. Refer the client to a group therapy
   that is focused on ways to build
   self-esteem.

7. Probe the parents' interactions
   with the client in family sessions,
   and redirect or rechannel any
   patterns of discipline that are
   negative or critical of the client.

4. Decrease verbalized fear of
   rejection while increasing statements of self-acceptance. (8, 9)

8. Ask the client to make one
   positive statement about him-
   self/herself daily, and record it on
   a chart or in a journal.

9. Assist the client in developing
   positive self-talk as a way of
   boosting his/her confidence and
   positive self-image.

5. Identify positive traits and
   talents about self. (10, 11, 12)

10. Develop with the client a list
    of positive affirmations about
    himself/herself, and ask that it be
    read three times daily.

11. Use the Positive Attitude Ball
    (available from Childswork/Childs-
    play) or a similar aid to identify
    and affirm with the client positive
    things about him/her for the first
    5 minutes of each session.

12. Reinforce verbally the client's use
    of positive statements of confi-
    dence or identification of positive
    attributes about himself/herself.

6. Identify and verbalize feelings.
   (13, 14, 15)

13. Use a therapeutic game (e.g.,
    The Talking, Feeling, and Doing
    Game, available from Creative

Therapeutics; *Let's See About Me,* available from Childswork/Childsplay; *The Ungame,* available from The Ungame Company) to promote the client becoming more aware of himself/herself and his/her feelings.

14. Use a feelings chart, feelings felt board, or a card game to enhance the client's ability to identify specific feelings.

15. Educate the client in the basics of identifying and labeling feelings, and assist him/her in beginning to identify what he/she is feeling.

7. Increase eye contact with others. (5, 16, 17)

5. Assist the client in becoming aware of how he/she expresses or acts out (e.g., lack of eye contact, social withdrawal, expectation of failure or rejection) negative feelings about himself/herself.

16. Focus attention on the client's lack of eye contact; encourage and reinforce increased eye contact within sessions.

17. Ask the client to increase eye contact with teachers, parents, and other adults; review and process reports of attempts and the feelings associated with them.

8. Identify actions that can be taken to improve self-image. (18, 19, 20)

18. Read with the client *Don't Feed the Monster on Tuesdays!* (Moser). Afterward, assist him/her in identifying things from the book that can be used to keep the monster of self-critical messages away. Then help the client make a chart containing self-esteem-building activities and have him/her record progress on each. Monitor and provide encouragement and affirmation for reported progress.

19. Ask the client to read *My Best Friend Is Me* (available from Childswork/Childsplay) and then make a list of good qualities about himself/herself to share with therapist.

20. Encourage the client to try new activities and to see failure as a learning experience (or assign the exercises "Dixie Overcomes Her Fears" and "Learn from Your Mistakes" from the *Child Psychotherapy Homework Planner,* 2nd ed. by Jongsma, Peterson, and McInnis).

9. Identify and verbalize needs. (21, 22, 23)

21. Assist the client in identifying and verbalizing his/her emotional needs; brainstorm ways to increase the chances of his/her needs being met.

22. Conduct a family session in which the client expresses his/her needs to family and vice versa.

23. Use therapeutic stories (e.g., *Dr. Gardner's Fairy Tales for Today's Children* by Gardner) to help the client identify feelings or needs and to build self-esteem.

10. Increase the frequency of speaking up with confidence in social situations. (24, 25, 26)

24. Use role-playing and behavioral rehearsal to improve the client's assertiveness and social skills.

25. Encourage the client to use the Pretending to Know How (Theiss) method in attempting tasks and facing new situations. Process the client's results, acknowledging his/her competence in following through and reinforcing the self-confidence gained from each experience.

26. Assign the parents to read with the client *Good Friends Are Hard to Find* (Frankel) to help the client build social skills.

11. Identify instances of emotional, physical, or sexual abuse that have damaged self-esteem. (27)

27. Explore for incidents of abuse (emotional, physical, and sexual) and how they have impacted feelings about self (see Sexual Abuse Victim and/or Physical/Emotional Abuse Victim chapters in this *Planner*).

12. Identify negative automatic thoughts and replace them with positive self-talk messages to build self-esteem. (28, 29, 30)

28. Help the client identify his/her distorted negative beliefs about himself/herself and the world.

29. Help the client to identify, and reinforce the use of, more realistic, positive messages about himself/herself and life events.

30. Use the Positive Thinking game (available from Childswork/Childsplay) to promote healthy self-talk and thought patterns. Allow the client to take the game home to play with his/her parent(s).

13. Take responsibility for daily self-care and household tasks that are developmentally age-appropriate. (31, 32)

31. Help the client find and implement daily self-care and household or academic responsibilities that are age-appropriate. Monitor follow-through and give positive feed back when warranted.

32. Have conversation(s) on phone with the client about some recent accomplishment, allowing him/her to initiate the call if he/she chooses and tell about the accomplishment. Give positive feedback, praise, compliments.

14. Identify and discuss the feelings that are associated with successful task accomplishment. (32, 33)

32. Have conversation(s) on phone with the client about some recent accomplishment, allowing him/her to initiate the call if he/she chooses and tell about the accomplishment. Give positive feedback, praise, compliments.

33. Ask the client to participate in The Yarn Drawing Game (see *Directive Group Play Therapy* by Leben), in which a ball of yarn/string is shaped into words, numbers, objects, or a complete picture. The therapist will offer the directive that there is no wrong design to empower the client and will also give encouragement and perspective on the various designs created.

15. Positively acknowledge and verbally accept praise or compliments from others. (34, 35)

34. Use a projective exercise, such as "Magic Act" (Walker), whereby the client selects a colored piece of paper and uses at least three colors of paint to make dots, lines, or a picture. The paper is then folded lengthwise and flattened, with the therapist saying, "Magic picture, what will the client draw today?" The client unfolds the paper and tells what he/she sees in the design. The therapist will emphasize that there is no possible way to make a bad picture.

35. Use neurolinguistic programming or reframing techniques in which messages about self are changed to assist the client in accepting compliments from others.

16. Parents attend a didactic series on positive parenting. (36)

36. Ask the parents to attend a didactic series on positive parenting, afterward processing how they can begin to implement some of these techniques.

17. Parents verbalize realistic expectations and discipline methods for the client. (37, 38)

37. Explore the parents' expectations of the client. Assist, if necessary, in making them more realistic.

38. Train the parents in the three R's (related, respectful, and reasonable) discipline techniques (see

18. Parents identify specific activities for the client that will facilitate development of positive self-esteem. (39)

19. Parents increase positive messages to the client. (36, 40)

Raising Self-Reliant Children in a Self-Indulgent World by Glenn and Nelson) in order to eliminate discipline that results in rebellion, revenge, or reduced self-esteem. Assist in implementation, and coach the parents as they develop and improve their skills using this method.

39. Ask the parents to involve the client in esteem-building activities (e.g., scouting, experiential camps, music, sports, youth groups, enrichment programs).

36. Ask the parents to attend a didactic series on positive parenting, afterward processing how they can begin to implement some of these techniques.

40. Encourage the parents to seek out opportunities to praise, reinforce, and recognize the client's minor or major accomplishments.

__. _____   __. _____
   _____   _____

__. _____   __. _____
   _____   _____

__. _____   __. _____
   _____   _____

DIAGNOSTIC SUGGESTIONS

Axis I:	300.4	Dysthymic Disorder
	314.01	Attention-Deficit/Hyperactivity Disorder, Predominantly Hyperactive-Impulsive Type
	300.23	Social Anxiety Disorder (Social Phobia)
	296.xx	Major Depressive Disorder
	307.1	Anorexia Nervosa
	309.21	Separation Anxiety Disorder

300.02	Generalized Anxiety
995.54	Physical Abuse of Child (Victim)
V61.21	Sexual Abuse of Child
V61.21	Neglect of Child
995.52	Neglect of Child (Victim)
995.53	Sexual Abuse of Child (Victim)

_____   _____

_____   _____

Axis II:

317	Mild Mental Retardation
V62.89	Borderline Intellectual Functioning
V71.09	No Diagnosis

_____   _____

_____   _____

LYING/MANIPULATIVE

BEHAVIORAL DEFINITIONS

1. Repeated pattern of lying to satisfy personal needs or obtain material goods/desired objects.
2. Chronic problem with lying to escape consequences or punishment for misbehavior.
3. Frequent lying to avoid facing responsibilities or performing work/chores.
4. Increase in lying after experiencing a threat to or loss of self-esteem.
5. Numerous lies or exaggerations about deeds or performance in order to boost self-esteem or elevate status in the eyes of peers.
6. Willingness to manipulate or exploit others in order to satisfy personal needs or avoid consequences for misbehavior.
7. Repeated attempts to pit parents and/or peers against each other in order to gratify personal needs or escape punishment.
8. Threatening and intimidating behavior that seeks to meet personal needs at the expense of others.
9. Desire to seek thrills, excitement, or pleasure through acts of manipulation or deception.
10. Persistent refusal to accept responsibility for deceitful or manipulative behavior.
11. Underlying feelings of insecurity or low self-esteem that contribute to the need to lie, falsify information, or manipulate others.
12. Distinction between fantasy and reality is blurred by repeated lies or exaggerations.

—. _____

_____

—. _____

_____

__. _____
   _____

LONG-TERM GOALS

1. Significantly reduce the frequency of lying.
2. Eliminate manipulative and deceptive behavior.
3. Consistently tell the truth, even when facing possible consequences for wrongful actions or irresponsible behavior.
4. Verbalize an acceptance of responsibility for actions or behavior on a regular basis.
5. Verbally identify needs to others, and consistently take steps to meet needs in a healthy, more adaptive manner.
6. Elevate self-esteem, and maintain positive self-image, thus decreasing the need to lie to impress and deceive others.
7. Establish and maintain trusting relationships that provide a sense of security and belonging.

__. _____
   _____

__. _____
   _____

__. _____
   _____

SHORT-TERM OBJECTIVES

1. Identify prior life events that have fostered lying and manipulative behavior. (1, 2, 3)

THERAPEUTIC INTERVENTIONS

1. Gather a detailed developmental and family history of the client to gain insight into the emotional factors, family dynamics, or environmental stressors that contribute to the emergence of his/her lying and manipulative behavior.

2. Assist the client in developing an awareness of prior life events or significant relationships that encouraged or reinforced lying and

manipulative behavior (e.g., parents or family members who lie regularly, overly rigid or punitive parenting, affiliation with peers or siblings who reinforced lying).

3. Explore periods of time when the client demonstrated an increase in lying or acts of manipulation to identify factors that contributed to the emergence of such behavior.

2. Verbally identify current situations and/or people that trigger lying and manipulative behavior. (4)

4. Help the client and his/her parents to identify current life situations or people that trigger lying and manipulative behavior (e.g., threat of being punished, failure experiences, facing criticism).

3. Record incidents of lying, deception, or manipulation. (5, 6, 7)

5. Help the client identify examples of his/her deceitful and manipulative behavior.

6. Assist the client in increasing his/her awareness of deceitful and manipulative behavior by instructing him/her to keep a log of interactions with individuals whom he/she has attempted to deceive or manipulate.

7. Instruct the parents or caregivers to keep a log of times when the client has been caught lying or engaging in manipulative behavior; process entries to explore the factors that contribute to his/her willingness to lie or manipulate.

4. Recognize and list irrational or distorted thoughts that maintain lying and manipulative behavior. (8, 9, 10)

8. Probe the client's thoughts that precede and follow lying or manipulative behavior; assist him/her to correct faulty thinking or irrational thoughts.

9. Identify irrational or distorted thoughts that contribute to the

emergence of lying or manipulative behavior (e.g., "I deserve this
toy, so it doesn't matter if I take
advantage of anyone"; "Nobody
will ever catch me lying"; "This
person is weak and deserves to be
taken advantage of").

10. Counsel the client about replacing
irrational or distorted thoughts
with reality-based or more adaptive ways of thinking (e.g., "I
could get caught lying, and it
would only create more problems
for me"; "It is best to be honest";
"My friends won't want to play
with me if I lie or take advantage
of them").

5. Identify negative consequences
that deceitful/manipulative behavior has for self and others.
(11, 12, 13)

11. Confront the client firmly about
the impact of his/her lying or manipulative behavior, pointing out
consequences for himself/herself
and others.

12. Direct the client to list the
negative effects that lying and
manipulative behavior has on
himself/herself and others (e.g.,
creates mistrust, provokes anger
and hurt in others, leads to social
isolation).

13. Use guided imagery techniques
to help the client visualize the
long-term effects that continued
lying and acts of manipulation
will have on his/her interpersonal
relationships (e.g., termination
of friendships, loss of respect,
frequent arguments with parents
and authority figures).

6. Verbally identify the benefits of
honesty. (14)

14. Teach the client the value of honesty as a basis for building trust
and mutual respect in all relationships.

7. Verbalize an increased sensitivity and/or empathy toward individuals being deceived or manipulated. (15, 16, 17)

15. Inquire into how the client would likely feel if he/she were deceived or manipulated by others; process his/her responses and help him/her empathize with others whom he/she has deceived in the past.

16. Use role reversal or role-playing techniques to help the client become aware of how deceitful or manipulative behavior negatively impacts others.

17. Assign the client the task of observing instances between therapy sessions where others have lied to or manipulated others; instruct him/her to notice the feelings of individuals who have been taken advantage of or manipulated.

8. Increase the frequency of honest and truthful verbalizations. (18, 19)

18. Teach the client mediational and self-control strategies (e.g., "stop, look, listen, and think"; thought-stoppage; assertive communication techniques) to help him/her resist the urge to lie or manipulate others in order to meet needs or avoid consequences.

19. Encourage the parents to praise and reinforce the client for accepting no or unfavorable responses to his/her requests without attempting to lie or manipulate.

9. Parents develop clear rules and follow through with consequences for lying and manipulative behavior. (20, 21, 22, 23)

20. Assist the parents in establishing clearly defined rules and consequences for lying and manipulative behavior; inform the client and have him/her repeat the consequences to demonstrate an understanding of the rules and expectations.

21. Establish a contingency contract with the client and his/her parents that clearly outlines the consequences if he/she is caught lying or manipulating others; have him/her sign the contract, and ask the parents to post it in a visible place in the home.

22. Challenge the parents to remain firm and not give into the client's lies or attempts to manipulate; instruct the parents to assign additional consequences (e.g., time out, removal of privileges or desired objects) if he/she is caught attempting to lie or manipulate to get out of trouble for other misbehaviors.

23. Counsel the parents on how their failure to follow through consistently with limits or consequences reinforces the client's deceptive and manipulative behavior because it communicates a message to him/her that he/she can possibly control the situation or get away with his/her misbehavior.

10. Verbalize an acceptance of responsibility for lying and manipulation by publicly acknowledging and apologizing for deceitful actions. (24, 25)

24. Instruct the parents to require the client to undo lies and manipulation by publicly acknowledging his/her wrongdoings to the individual(s) to whom he/she has lied or manipulated.

25. Direct the client to apologize, either verbally or in writing, to individuals to whom he/she has lied or manipulated.

11. Parents refrain from responding in ways that reinforce the client's lying and manipulative behavior. (23, 26, 27)

23. Counsel the parents on how their failure to follow through consistently with limits or consequences reinforces the client's deceptive and manipulative behavior because it communicates a message

to him/her that he/she can possibly control the situation or get away with his/her misbehavior.

26. Counsel the parents and family members to withdraw attention from the client when he/she attempts to manipulate a situation in the home.

27. Urge the parents to present a united front and prevent splitting by making each other aware of the client's attempts to deceive or manipulate (e.g., self-pity, somatic complaints, inappropriate jokes, lying); encourage the parents to reach a mutually agreed-upon consequence for the deceitful or manipulative behavior.

12. Parents and family members identify factors or stressors that promote or reinforce the client's deceptive and manipulative behavior. (28, 29)

28. Conduct family therapy sessions to explore the dynamics and stressors that promote or reinforce the client's deceptive or manipulative behavior (e.g., modeling of deception, severe criticism, harsh punishment, rejection of the client, substance abuse by the parent).

29. Challenge and confront the parents to cease modeling inappropriate behavior to the client through their own acts of deception or manipulation.

13. Verbalize an understanding of the connection between unmet needs or rejection experiences and a history of lying or manipulation. (30, 31, 32)

30. Explore the connection between the client's unmet needs or past rejection experiences and his/her history of lying and manipulation; assist him/her in identifying more adaptive ways to meet his/her needs for love, affection, or closeness other than through lying or manipulating others.

31. Encourage the client to express his/her feelings of rejection or deprivation; provide support to him/her in directly verbalizing his/her needs for love and affection to his/her parents and significant others.

32. Assist the client in identifying a list of resource people to whom he/she can turn for support and help in meeting unmet needs; encourage him/her to reach out to these individuals for support or help, rather than using deception or manipulation to meet these needs.

14. Identify negative or painful emotions that trigger lying and manipulative behavior. (33, 34)

33. Assist the client in making a connection between his/her underlying painful emotions (e.g., depression, anxiety, insecurity, anger) and lying or manipulative behavior.

34. Teach the client effective communication and assertiveness skills to express his/her painful emotions to others in a more direct and constructive fashion.

15. Increase the frequency of positive social behaviors that help rebuild trust in relationships. (35, 36, 37, 38)

35. Give the client the homework assignment of identifying 5 to 10 positive social behaviors that can help him/her rebuild trust; review the list and encourage him/her to engage in these behaviors.

36. Instruct the parents to observe and record from three to five prosocial or responsible behaviors by the client that help to rebuild trust; encourage the parents to praise and reinforce him/her.

37. Use puppets, dolls, or stuffed animals to create a story that teaches the value of honesty and/or models appropriate ways to rebuild

trust; then ask the client to create a story with similar characters or themes.

38. Brainstorm with the client socially appropriate ways to be sneaky or manipulative (e.g., learn a magic trick; ask peers to solve riddles; design a trick play for basketball team); assign him/her the task of exercising the socially appropriate skill at least once before the next therapy session.

16. Verbally recognize the connection between feelings of low self-esteem and the need to lie or exaggerate about performance or deeds. (39, 40, 41)

39. Assist the client in realizing the connection between underlying feelings of low self-esteem and his/her desire to lie or exaggerate about performance or deeds; help him/her identify more effective ways to improve self-esteem, other than through lying and exaggerated claims.

40. Point out to the client how lies and exaggerated claims are self-defeating as they interfere with his/her ability to establish and maintain close, trusting relationships.

41. Instruct the client to draw pictures of symbols or objects that reflect his/her interests or strengths; encourage him/her to use talents and strengths to improve self-esteem and meet deeper needs for closeness and intimacy.

17. Identify socially appropriate ways to use intelligence to meet needs. (42)

42. Challenge the client to cease channeling intellectual abilities into self-defeating acts of deception and manipulation; encourage him/her to use intelligence in socially appropriate ways (e.g., learn to play chess; play the villain in a school play; make up a story for language arts class).

—. _____   —. _____
    _____   _____
—. _____   —. _____
    _____   _____
—. _____   —. _____
    _____   _____

DIAGNOSTIC SUGGESTIONS

Axis I:	313.81	Oppositional-Defiant Disorder
	312.81	Conduct Disorder, Childhood-Onset Type
	312.82	Conduct Disorder, Adolescent-Onset Type
	312.9	Disruptive Behavior Disorder NOS
	314.01	Attention-Deficit/Hyperactivity Disorder, Combined Type
	309.3	Adjustment Disorder With Disturbance of Conduct
	V71.02	Child or Adolescent Antisocial Behavior
	V61.20	Parent-Child Relational Problem
	300.4	Dysthymic Disorder

_____   _____
_____   _____

| Axis II: | V71.09 | No Diagnosis |

_____   _____
_____   _____

MEDICAL CONDITION

BEHAVIORAL DEFINITIONS

1. A diagnosis of a chronic illness that is not life threatening but necessitates changes in living.
2. A diagnosis of an acute, serious illness that is life threatening.
3. A diagnosis of a chronic illness that eventually will lead to an early death.
4. Sad affect, social withdrawal, anxiety, loss of interest in activities, and low energy.
5. Suicidal ideation.
6. Denial of the seriousness of the medical condition.
7. Refusal to cooperate with recommended medical treatments.

__. _____

_____

__. _____

_____

__. _____

_____

LONG-TERM GOALS

1. Accept the illness and adapt life to necessary changes.
2. Resolve emotional crisis and face terminal illness's implications.
3. Work through the grieving process and face the reality of own death with peace.
4. Accept emotional support from those who care without pushing them away in anger.
5. Resolve depression, fear, and anxiety, finding peace of mind despite the illness.

6. Live life to the fullest extent possible even though time may be limited.
7. Cooperate with the medical treatment regimen without passive-aggressive or active resistance.

__. _____

_____

__. _____

_____

__. _____

_____

SHORT-TERM OBJECTIVES

THERAPEUTIC INTERVENTIONS

▼ 1. Describe history, symptoms, and treatment of the medical condition. (1, 2)

1. Gather a history of the facts regarding the client's medical condition, including symptoms, treatment, and prognosis. ▼

2. With the client's informed consent, contact the treating physician and family members for additional medical information regarding the client's diagnosis, treatment, and prognosis. ▼

▼ 2. Verbalize an understanding of the medical condition, and its consequences. (3)

3. Encourage and facilitate the client in learning about the medical condition from which he or she suffers and its realistic course, including pain management options and chance for recovery. ▼

▼ 3. Comply with the medication regimen and necessary medical procedures, reporting any side effects or problems to physicians or therapists. (2, 4, 5, 6)

2. With the client's informed consent, contact the treating physician and family members for additional medical information regarding the client's diagnosis, treatment, and prognosis. ▼

▼ indicates that the Objective/Intervention is consistent with those found in evidence-based treatments.

4. Monitor and reinforce the client's compliance with the medical treatment regimen. ▼

5. Explore and address the client's misconceptions, fears, and situational factors that interfere with medical treatment compliance. ▼

6. Confront any manipulation, passive-aggressive, and denial mechanisms that block the client's compliance with the medical treatment regimen. ▼

▼ 4. Share feelings triggered by the knowledge of the medical condition and its consequences. (7)

7. Assist the client in identifying, sorting through, and verbalizing the various feelings generated by his/her medical condition (or assign "Gaining Acceptance of Physical Handicap or Illness" or "Dealing with Childhood Asthma" in the *Child Psychotherapy Homework Planner,* 2nd ed. by Jongsma, Peterson, and McInnis). ▼

▼ 5. Family members share with each other the feelings that are triggered by the client's medical condition. (8)

8. Meet with family members to facilitate their clarifying and sharing possible feelings of guilt, anger, helplessness, and/or sibling attention jealousy associated with the client's medical condition (or assign "Coping with a Sibling's Health Problems" in the *Adolescent Psychotherapy Homework Planner,* 2nd ed. by Jongsma, Peterson, and McInnis). ▼

▼ 6. Spend time with family and friends. (9)

9. Assess the effects of the medical condition on the client's social network (or assign "Effects of Physical Handicap or Illness on Self-Esteem and Peer Relations" in the *Adolescent Psychotherapy Homework Planner,* 2nd ed. by Jongsma, Peterson, and McInnis); facilitate the social support available through the client's family and friends. ▼

▼ 7. Identify and grieve the losses or limitations that have been experienced due to the medical condition. (10, 11, 12, 13)

10. Ask the client to list his/her perception of changes, losses, or limitations that have resulted from the medical condition. ▼

11. Educate the client on the stages of the grieving process and answer any questions (or suggest that the child read *Don't Despair on Thursdays!* by Moser). ▼

12. Suggest that the client's parents read a book on grief and loss (e.g., *Good Grief* by Westberg; *How Can It Be All Right When Everything Is All Wrong?* by Smedes; *When Bad Things Happen to Good People* by Kushner) to help them understand and support their child in the grieving process. ▼

13. Assign the client to keep a daily grief journal to be shared in therapy sessions. ▼

▼ 8. Decrease time spent focused on the negative aspects of the medical condition. (14, 15)

14. Suggest that the client set aside a specific time-limited period each day to focus on mourning the medical condition; after the time period is up, have the client resume regular daily activities with agreement to put off thoughts until next scheduled time. ▼

15. Challenge the client to focus his/her thoughts on the positive aspects of his/her life and time remaining, rather than on the losses associated with his/her medical condition; reinforce instances of such a positive focus. ▼

▼ 9. Verbalize acceptance of the reality of the medical condition and its consequences while decreasing denial. (16, 17)

16. Gently confront the client's denial of the seriousness of his/her condition and of the need for compliance with medical treatment procedures. ▼

17. Reinforce the client's acceptance of his/her medical condition. ▼

▼10. Share fearful or depressed feelings regarding the medical condition and develop a plan for addressing them. (18, 19, 20)

▼11. Attend a support group of others diagnosed with a similar illness, if desired. (21)

▼12. Parents and family members attend a support group, if desired. (22)

▼13. Engage in social, productive, and recreational activities that are possible despite the medical condition. (23, 24)

▼14. Learn and implement stress-management skills. (25, 26, 27)

18. Explore and process the client's fears associated with deterioration of physical health, death, and dying. ▼

19. Normalize the client's feelings of grief, sadness, or anxiety associated with his/her medical condition; encourage verbal expression of these emotions. ▼

20. Assess the client for and treat his/her depression and anxiety using relevant cognitive, physiological, and/or behavioral aspects of treatments for those conditions (see Depression and Anxiety chapters in this *Planner*). ▼

21. Refer the client to a support group of others living with a similar medical condition. ▼

22. Refer family members to a community-based support group associated with the client's medical condition. ▼

23. Sort out with the client activities that can still be enjoyed alone and with others. ▼

24. Solicit a commitment from the client to increase his/her activity level by engaging in enjoyable and challenging activities (or assign "Show Your Strengths" in the *Child Psychotherapy Homework Planner*, 2nd ed. by Jongsma, Peterson and McInnis); reinforce such engagement. ▼

25. Teach the client deep muscle relaxation and deep breathing methods along with positive imagery to induce relaxation. ▼

26. Utilize electromyography (EMG) biofeedback to monitor, increase, and reinforce the client's depth of relaxation. ▼

27. Develop and encourage a routine of physical exercise for the client. ▼

▼15. Identify and replace negative self-talk and catastrophizing that is associated with the medical condition. (28, 29)

28. Assist the client in identifying the cognitive distortions and negative automatic thoughts that contribute to his/her negative attitude and hopeless feelings associated with the medical condition (or assign "Bad Thoughts Lead to Depressed Feelings" in the *Adolescent Psychotherapy Homework Planner,* 2nd ed. by Jongsma, Peterson, and McInnis). ▼

29. Generate with the client a list of positive, realistic self-talk that can replace cognitive distortions and catastrophizing regarding his/her medical condition and its treatment. ▼

▼16. Implement positive imagery as a means of triggering peace of mind and reducing tension. (30)

30. Teach the client the use of positive, relaxing, healing imagery to reduce stress and promote peace of mind. ▼

▼17. Client and family identify the sources of emotional support that have been beneficial and additional sources that could be sought. (31, 32)

31. Probe and evaluate the client's, siblings', and parents' sources of emotional support. ▼

32. Encourage the parents and siblings to reach out for support from each other, church leaders, extended family, hospital social services, community support groups, and personal religious beliefs. ▼

▼18. Family members share any conflicts that have developed between them. (33, 34, 35)

33. Explore how each parent is dealing with the stress related to the client's illness and whether conflicts have developed between the parents because of differing response styles. ▼

34. Assess family conflicts using conflict resolution approach to addressing them. ▼

35. Facilitate a spirit of tolerance for individual difference in each person's internal resources and response styles in the face of threat. ▽

▽19. Family members verbalize an understanding of the one's own personal positive presence with the sick child. (36)

36. Stress the healing power in the family's constant presence with the ill child and emphasize that there is strong healing potential in creating a warm, caring, supportive, positive environment for the child. ▽

20. Implement faith-based activities as a source of comfort and hope. (37, 38, 39)

37. Draw out the parents' unspoken fears about the client's possible death; empathize with their panic, helplessness, frustration, and anxiety; reassure them of their God's presence as the giver and supporter of life.

38. Encourage the client to rely upon his/her spiritual faith promises, activities (e.g., prayer, meditation, worship, music) and fellowship as sources of support.

39. Encourage the client to rely on faith-based promises of their God's love, presence, caring, and support to bring peace of mind.

__. _____   __. _____
   _____   _____
__. _____   __. _____
   _____   _____
__. _____   __. _____
   _____   _____

DIAGNOSTIC SUGGESTIONS

Axis I: 316   Psychological Symptoms Affecting
                              (Axis III Disorder)

309.0	Adjustment Disorder With Depressed Mood
309.24	Adjustment Disorder With Anxiety
309.28	Adjustment Disorder With Mixed Anxiety and Depressed Mood
309.3	Adjustment Disorder With Disturbance of Conduct
309.4	Adjustment Disorder With Mixed Disturbance of Emotions and Conduct
296.xx	Major Depressive Disorder
311	Depressive Disorder NOS
300.02	Generalized Anxiety Disorder
300.00	Anxiety Disorder NOS
_____	_____
_____	_____

Axis II:	V71.09	No Diagnosis
	_____	_____
	_____	_____

MENTAL RETARDATION

BEHAVIORAL DEFINITIONS

1. Significantly subaverage intellectual functioning as demonstrated by an IQ score of approximately 70 or below on an individually administered intelligence test.
2. Significant impairments in academic functioning, communication, self-care, home living, social skills, and leisure activities.
3. Difficulty understanding and following complex directions in home, school, or community settings.
4. Short- and long-term memory impairment.
5. Concrete thinking or impaired abstract reasoning abilities.
6. Impoverished social skills as manifested by frequent use of poor judgment, limited understanding of the antecedents and consequences of social actions, and lack of reciprocity in peer interactions.
7. Lack of insight and repeated failure to learn from experience or past mistakes.
8. Low self-esteem as evidenced by frequent self-derogatory remarks (e.g., "I'm so stupid").
9. Recurrent pattern of acting out or engaging in disruptive behaviors without considering the consequences of the actions.

—. _____

_____

—. _____

_____

—. _____

_____

LONG-TERM GOALS

1. Achieve all academic goals identified on the client's individualized educational plan (IEP).
2. Function at an appropriate level of independence in home, residential, educational, or community settings.
3. Develop an awareness and acceptance of intellectual and cognitive limitations but consistently verbalize feelings of self-worth.
4. Parents and/or caregivers develop an awareness and acceptance of the client's intellectual and cognitive capabilities so that they place appropriate expectations on his/her functioning.
5. Consistently comply and follow through with simple directions in a daily routine at home, in school, or in a residential setting.
6. Significantly reduce the frequency and severity of socially inappropriate or acting out behaviors.

__. _____
   _____
__. _____
   _____
__. _____
   _____

SHORT-TERM OBJECTIVES

THERAPEUTIC INTERVENTIONS

1. Complete a comprehensive intellectual and cognitive assessment. (1)

1. Arrange for a comprehensive intellectual and cognitive assessment to determine the presence of Mental Retardation and gain greater insight into the client's learning strengths and weaknesses; provide feedback to the client, parents, and school officials.

2. Complete psychological testing. (2)

2. Arrange for psychological testing to assess whether emotional factors of Attention-Deficit/Hyperactivity Disorder (ADHD) are interfering with the client's intellectual and academic

functioning; provide feedback to the client and parents.

3. Complete neuropsychological testing. (3)

3. Arrange for a neurological examination or neuropsychological testing to rule out possible organic factors that may be contributing to the client's intellectual or cognitive deficits.

4. Complete an evaluation by physical and occupational therapists. (4)

4. Refer the client to physical and occupational therapists to assess perceptual or sensory-motor deficits and determine the need for ongoing physical and/or occupational therapy.

5. Complete a speech/language evaluation. (5)

5. Refer the client to a speech/language pathologist to assess deficits and determine the need for appropriate therapy.

6. The client and his/her parents comply with recommendations made by a multidisciplinary evaluation team at school regarding educational interventions. (6, 7)

6. Attend an individualized educational planning committee (IEPC) meeting with the client's parents, teachers, and other appropriate professionals to determine his/her eligibility for special-education services, design educational interventions, and establish goals.

7. Consult with the client, his/her parents, teachers, and other appropriate school officials about designing effective learning programs or interventions that build on the client's strengths and compensate for weaknesses.

7. Move to an appropriate residential setting. (8)

8. Consult with the client's parents, school officials, or mental health professionals about the client's need for placement in a foster home, group home, or residential program.

8. Parents maintain regular communication with the client's teachers and other appropriate school officials. (9)

9. Encourage the parents to maintain regular communication with the client's teachers or school officials to monitor his/her academic, behavioral, emotional, and social progress.

9. Parents, teachers, and caregivers implement a token economy in the classroom or placement setting. (10)

10. Design a token economy for the classroom or residential program to reinforce on-task behaviors, completion of school assignments, good impulse control, and positive social skills.

10. Parents increase praise and other positive reinforcement toward the client in regard to his/her academic performance or social behaviors. (11, 12, 13)

11. Conduct filial play therapy sessions (i.e., parents are present) to increase the parents' awareness of the client's thoughts and feelings and to strengthen the parent-child bond.

12. Encourage the parents to provide frequent praise and other reinforcement for the client's positive social behaviors and academic performance.

13. Design a reward system or contingency contract to reinforce the client's adaptive or prosocial behaviors.

11. Parents and family cease verbalizations of denial about the client's intellectual and cognitive deficits. (14, 15)

14. Educate the parents about the symptoms and characteristics of Mental Retardation.

15. Confront and challenge the parents' denial surrounding their child's intellectual deficits so they cooperate with recommendations regarding placement and educational interventions.

12. Parents recognize and verbally acknowledge their unrealistic expectations of or excessive pressure on the client. (16, 17)

16. Conduct family therapy sessions to assess whether the parents are placing excessive pressure on the client to function at a level that he/she is not capable of achieving.

17. Confront and challenge the parents about placing excessive pressure on the client.

13. Parents recognize and verbally acknowledge that their pattern of overprotectiveness interferes with the client's intellectual, emotional, and social development. (18, 19)

18. Observe parent-child interactions to assess whether the parents' overprotectiveness or infantilization of the client interferes with his/her intellectual, emotional, or social development.

19. Assist the parents or caregivers in developing realistic expectations of the client's intellectual capabilities and level of adaptive functioning.

14. Increase participation in family activities or outings. (20, 21, 22, 23)

20. Encourage the parents and family members to regularly include the client in outings or activities (e.g., attend sporting events, go ice skating, visit a child's museum).

21. Instruct family members to observe positive behaviors by the client between therapy sessions. Reinforce positive behaviors and encourage the client to continue to exhibit these behaviors.

22. Place the client in charge of a routine or basic task at home to increase his/her self-esteem and feelings of self-worth in the family.

23. Assign homework designed to promote the client's feelings of acceptance and a sense of belonging in the family system, school setting, or community (or assign the "You Belong Here" exercise from the *Child Psychotherapy Homework Planner,* 2nd ed. by Jongsma, Peterson, and McInnis).

15. Perform chores at home, school, or residential program on a daily or regular basis. (24, 25, 26)

24. Assign the client a task in the family (e.g., pick up toys, make bed, help put away clothes) that is appropriate for his/her level of functioning and provides him/her with a sense of responsibility or belonging.

25. Instruct the client to complete a family kinetic drawing to assess how he/she perceives his/her role or place in the family system.

26. Consult with school officials or the residential staff about the client performing a job (e.g., raising the flag, helping to run video equipment) to build self-esteem and provide him/her with a sense of responsibility.

16. Parents agree to and implement an allowance program that helps the client learn to manage money more effectively. (27)

27. Counsel the parents about setting up an allowance plan that seeks to increase the client's responsibilities and help him/her learn simple money-management skills.

17. Take a bath or shower, dress self independently, comb hair, wash hands before meals, and brush teeth on a daily basis. (28)

28. Design and implement a reward system to reinforce desired self-care behaviors such as combing hair, washing dishes, or cleaning the bedroom (or assign the parents to use the "Activities of Daily Living" program from the *Child Psychotherapy Homework Planner,* 2nd ed. by Jongsma, Peterson, and McInnis).

18. Parents consistently implement behavior management techniques to reduce the frequency and severity of temper outbursts or disruptive and aggressive behaviors. (29, 30)

29. Teach the parents effective behavior management techniques (e.g., time outs, removal of privileges) to decrease the frequency and severity of the client's temper outbursts, acting out, and aggressive behaviors.

19. Decrease frequency of impulsive, disruptive, or aggressive behaviors. (31, 32)

20. Recognize and verbally identify appropriate and inappropriate social behaviors. (33)

21. Increase the frequency of identifying and expressing feelings. (34, 35, 36, 37, 38)

30. Encourage the parents to utilize natural, logical consequences for the client's inappropriate social or maladaptive behaviors.

31. Teach the client basic mediational and self-control strategies (e.g., "stop, look, listen, and think") to delay gratification and inhibit impulses.

32. Train the client in the use of guided imagery or relaxation techniques to calm himself/herself down and develop greater control of anger.

33. Utilize role-playing and modeling in individual sessions to teach the client positive social skills. Reinforce new or emerging prosocial behaviors.

34. Educate the client about how to identify and label different emotions.

35. Tell the client to draw faces of basic emotions, then have him/her share times when he/she experienced the different emotions.

36. Teach the client effective communication skills (i.e., proper listening, good eye contact, "I statements") to improve his/her ability to express thoughts, feelings, and needs more clearly.

37. Use puppets, dolls, or stuffed animals to model socially appropriate ways of expressing emotions or relating to other.

38. Use Feelings Poster (available from Childswork/Childsplay) to help the client identify and express different emotions.

22. Express feelings of sadness, anxiety, and insecurity that are related to cognitive and intellectual limitations. (39, 40)

39. Assist the client in coming to an understanding and acceptance of the limitations surrounding his/her intellectual deficits and adaptive functioning.

40. Explore the client's feelings of depression, anxiety, and insecurity that are related to cognitive or intellectual limitations. Provide encouragement and support for the client.

23. Increase the frequency of positive self-statements. (41, 42)

41. Encourage the client to participate in the Special Olympics to build self-esteem.

42. Explore times when the client achieved success or accomplished a goal; reinforce positive steps that the client took to successfully accomplish goals.

24. Express feelings through artwork. (35, 43)

35. Tell the client to draw faces of basic emotions, then have him/her share times when he/she experienced the different emotions.

43. Use art therapy (e.g., drawing, painting, sculpting) with the client in foster care or residential program to help him/her express basic emotions related to issues of separation, loss, or abandonment by parental figures.

—. _____

_____

—. _____

_____

—. _____

_____

—. _____

_____

—. _____

_____

—. _____

_____

DIAGNOSTIC SUGGESTIONS

Axis I:

299.00	Autistic Disorder
299.80	Rett's Disorder
299.80	Asperger's Disorder
299.10	Childhood Disintegrative Disorder

_____   _____

_____   _____

Axis II:

317	Mild Mental Retardation
318.0	Moderate Mental Retardation
318.1	Severe Mental Retardation
318.2	Profound Mental Retardation
319	Mental Retardation, Severity Unspecified
V62.89	Borderline Intellectual Functioning
V71.09	No Diagnosis

_____   _____

_____   _____

OBSESSIVE-COMPULSIVE DISORDER (OCD)

BEHAVIORAL DEFINITIONS

1. Recurrent and persistent ideas, thoughts, or impulses that are viewed as intrusive, senseless, and time-consuming, or that interfere with the client's daily routine, school performance, or social relationships.
2. Failed attempts to ignore or control these thoughts or impulses or neutralize them with other thoughts and actions.
3. Recognition that obsessive thoughts are a product of his/her own mind.
4. Excessive concerns about dirt or unfounded fears of contracting a dreadful disease or illness.
5. Obsessions related to troubling aggressive or sexual thoughts, urges, or images.
6. Persistent and troubling thoughts about religious issues; excessive concern about morality and right or wrong.
7. Repetitive and intentional behaviors that are done in response to obsessive thoughts or increased feelings of anxiety or fearfulness.
8. Repetitive and excessive behavior that is done to neutralize or prevent discomfort or some dreadful situation; however, that behavior is not connected in any realistic way with what it is designed to neutralize or prevent.
9. Recognition of repetitive behaviors as excessive and unreasonable.
10. Cleaning and washing compulsions (e.g., excessive hand washing, bathing, showering, cleaning of household products).
11. Hoarding or collecting compulsions.
12. Checking compulsions (e.g., repeatedly checking to see if door is locked, rechecking homework to make sure it is done correctly, checking to make sure that no one has been harmed).
13. Compulsions about having to arrange objects or things in proper order (e.g., stacking coins in certain order, laying out clothes each evening at same time, wearing only certain clothes on certain days).

__. _____
   _____
__. _____
   _____
__. _____
   _____

LONG-TERM GOALS

1. Significantly reduce time involved with or interference from obsessions.
2. Significantly reduce frequency of compulsive or ritualistic behaviors.
3. Function daily at a consistent level with minimal interference from obsessions and compulsions.
4. Resolve key life conflicts and the emotional stress that fuels obsessive-compulsive behavior patterns.
5. Let go of key thoughts, beliefs, and past life events in order to maximize time free from obsessions and compulsions.

__. _____
   _____
__. _____
   _____
__. _____
   _____

SHORT-TERM OBJECTIVES

1. Describe the nature, history, and severity of obsessive thoughts and/or compulsive behavior. (1)

THERAPEUTIC INTERVENTIONS

1. Assess the nature, severity, and history of the obsessive-compulsive problems using clinical interview with the client and the parents (or assign the exercise "Concerns, Feelings, and Hopes about OCD" in the *Child Psychotherapy Homework Planner,* 2nd ed. by Jongsma, Peterson, and McInnis).

2. Comply with psychological testing evaluation to assess the nature and severity of the obsessive-compulsive problem. (2)

2. Arrange for psychological testing to further evaluate the nature and severity of the client's obsessive-compulsive problem (e.g., *The Children's Yale-Brown Obsessive Compulsive Scale* by Scahill and colleagues, 1997).

▼ 3. Cooperate with an evaluation by a physician for psychotropic medication. (3, 4)

3. Arrange for an evaluation for a prescription of psychotropic medications (e.g., serotonergic medications). ▼

4. Monitor the client for prescription compliance, side effects, and overall effectiveness of the medication; consult with the prescribing physician at regular intervals. ▼

▼ 4. Participate in individual, small group, or family exposure and ritual prevention therapy for obsessions and compulsions. (5)

5. Enroll the client in intensive (e.g., daily) or nonintensive (e.g., weekly), individual, small (closed enrollment) group, or family exposure and ritual-prevention therapy for OCD (e.g., *Treatment of OCD in Children and Adolescents* by Wagner; *OCD in Children and Adolescents* by March and Mulle). ▼

▼ 5. Verbalize an understanding of the rationale for treatment of OCD. (6, 7)

6. Assign the parents to read psychoeducational chapters of books or treatment manuals on the rationale for exposure and ritual prevention therapy and/or cognitive restructuring for OCD (e.g., *Up and Down the Worry Hill* by Wagner; *Brain Lock: Free Yourself from Obsessive-Compulsive Behavior* by Schwartz; *Obsessive-Compulsive Disorder: Help for Children and Adolescents* by Waltz). ▼

▼ indicates that the Objective/Intervention is consistent with those found in evidence-based treatments.

7. Discuss with the client how treatment serves as an arena to desensitize learned fear, reality test obsessive fears and underlying beliefs, and build confidence in managing fears without compulsions (see *Up and Down the Worry Hill* by Wagner). ▼

▼ 6. Identify and replace biased, fearful self-talk and beliefs. (8)

8. Explore the client's schema and self-talk that mediate his/her obsessive fears and compulsive behavior; assist him/her in generating thoughts that correct for the biases (see *Treatment of OCD in Children and Adolescents* by Wagner; or *OCD in Children and Adolescents* by March and Mulle). ▼

▼ 7. Undergo repeated imaginal exposure to feared external and/or internal cues. (9, 10, 11)

9. Assess the nature of any external cues (e.g., persons, objects, situations) and internal cues (thoughts, images, and impulses) that precipitate the client's obsessions and compulsions. ▼

10. Direct and assist the client in construction of a hierarchy of feared internal and external fear cues. ▼

11. Select initial imaginal exposures to the internal and/or external OCD cues that have a high likelihood of being a successful experience for the client; do cognitive restructuring during and after the exposure (see *Treatment of OCD in Children and Adolescents* by Wagner; or *OCD in Children and Adolescents* by March and Mulle). ▼

▼ 8. Complete homework assignments involving in vivo exposure to feared external and/or internal cues. (12)

12. Assign the client a homework exercise in which he/she repeats the exposure to the internal and/or external OCD cues using restructured cognitions between sessions

and records responses (or assign the parents to help the client through the exercise "Reducing the Strength of Compulsive Behaviors" in the *Adult Psychotherapy Homework Planner,* 2nd ed. by Jongsma); review during next session, reinforcing success and providing corrective feedback toward improvement (see *Up and Down the Worry Hill* by Wagner). ▽

▽ 9. Implement relapse prevention strategies for managing possible future anxiety symptoms. (13, 14, 15, 16)

13. Discuss with the client the distinction between a lapse and relapse, associating a lapse with an initial and reversible return of symptoms, fear, or urges to avoid and relapse with the decision to return to fearful and avoidant patterns. ▽

14. Identify and rehearse with the client the management of future situations or circumstances in which lapses could occur. ▽

15. Instruct the client to routinely use strategies learned in therapy (e.g., continued exposure to previously feared external or internal cues that arise) to prevent relapse into obsessive-compulsive patterns. ▽

16. Schedule periodic "maintenance" sessions to help the client maintain therapeutic gains and adjust to life without OCD (see *A Relapse Prevention Program for Treatment of Obsessive Compulsive Disorder* by Hiss, Foa, and Kozak for a description of relapse prevention strategies for OCD). ▽

▽10. Implement the use of the "thought-stopping" technique to reduce the frequency of obsessive thoughts. (17, 18)

17. Teach the client to interrupt obsessive thoughts using the "thought-stopping" technique of shouting STOP to himself/herself

silently while picturing a red traffic signal and then thinking about a calming scene. ▽

18. Assign the client to implement the "thought-stopping" technique on a daily basis between sessions (or assign the parents to help their child through the exercise "Making Use of the Thought-Stopping Technique" in the *Adult Psychotherapy Homework Planner,* 2nd ed. by Jongsma); review the results. ▽

▽11. Increase motivation to resist urge to engage in compulsive behavior or talk about obsessive thoughts. (19)

19. Design a reward system to reinforce client for successfully resisting the urge to engage in compulsive behavior or talk about and openly share obsessive thoughts with others. ▽

▽12. Identify support persons or resources who can help the client manage obsessions/compulsions. (20, 21)

20. Encourage and instruct client to involve support person(s) or a "coach" who can help him/her resist urge to engage in compulsive behavior or take mind off obsessive thoughts. ▽

21. Refer the client and parents to support group(s) to help maintain and support the gains made in therapy. ▽

▽13. Parents provide appropriate support and establish effective boundaries surrounding the client's OCD symptoms. (22, 23, 24, 25, 26)

22. Hold family therapy sessions to identify specific, positive ways that the parents can help the client manage his/her obsessions or compulsions (see *Cognitive-Behavioral Family Treatment of Childhood Obsessive-Compulsive Disorder* by Waters, Barrett, and March). ▽

23. Encourage and instruct parents to remain calm, patient, and supportive when faced with the

client's obsessions or compulsions; discourage parents from reacting strongly with anger or frustration. ▼

24. Assist the family in overcoming the tendency to reinforce the client's OCD; assign "Refocusing" in the *Child Psychotherapy Homework Planner,* 2nd ed. by Jongsma, Peterson, and McInnis. ▼

25. Teach family members problem-solving and communication skills to assist the client's progress through therapy. ▼

26. Design a reward system that reinforces the client for actions that help maintain his/her therapeutic gains. ▼

▼14. Parents identify how they reinforce the client's OCD symptoms. (27, 28)

27. Conduct family therapy sessions to assess the factors contributing to the emergence, maintenance, or exacerbation of OCD symptoms. ▼

28. Teach the parents how being overly protective or reassuring reinforces the client's OCD symptoms and interferes with his/her ability to manage the troubling or distressing thoughts, urges, or images. ▼

15. Verbalize and clarify feelings connected to key life concepts. (29)

29. Encourage, support, and assist the client in identifying and expressing feelings related to key unresolved life issues.

16. Implement the Ericksonian task designed to interfere with OCD. (30)

30. Develop and design an Ericksonian task (e.g., if obsessed with a loss, give the client the task to visit, send a card, or bring flowers to someone who has lost someone) for the client that is centered

17. Engage in a strategic ordeal to overcome OCD impulses. (31)

18. Identify family dynamics that contribute to the emergence, maintenance, or exacerbation of OCD symptoms. (32, 33)

on the obsession or compulsion and assess the results with the client.

31. Create and sell a strategic ordeal that offers a guaranteed cure to help the client with the obsession or compulsion (e.g., instruct client to perform an aversive chore each time an obsessive thought or compulsive behavior occurs). Note that Haley emphasizes that the "cure" offers an intervention to achieve a goal and is not a promise to cure the client in beginning of therapy (see *Ordeal Therapy* by Haley).

32. Obtain detailed family history to identify other family members who have experienced OCD symptoms.

33. Conduct family therapy sessions to address the dynamics contributing to the emergence, maintenance, or exacerbation of OCD symptoms.

__. _____
_____
__. _____
_____
__. _____
_____

__. _____
_____
__. _____
_____
__. _____

DIAGNOSTIC SUGGESTIONS

Axis I: 300.3   Obsessive-Compulsive Disorder
300.00   Anxiety Disorder NOS
300.02   Generalized Anxiety Disorder

296.xx   Major Depressive Disorder

_____   _____

_____   _____

Axis II: V71.09   No Diagnosis

_____   _____

_____   _____

OPPOSITIONAL DEFIANT

BEHAVIORAL DEFINITIONS

1. Displays a pattern of negativistic, hostile, and defiant behavior toward most adults.
2. Often acts as if parents, teachers, and other authority figures are the "enemy."
3. Erupts in temper tantrums (e.g., screaming, crying, throwing objects, thrashing on ground, refusing to move) in defiance of direction from an adult caregiver.
4. Consistently argues with adults.
5. Often defies or refuses to comply with requests and rules, even when they are reasonable.
6. Deliberately annoys people and is easily annoyed by others.
7. Often blames others for own mistakes or misbehavior.
8. Consistently is angry and resentful.
9. Often is spiteful or vindictive.
10. Has experienced significant impairment in social or academic functioning.

—. _____
_____
—. _____
_____
—. _____
_____

LONG-TERM GOALS

1. Display a marked reduction in the intensity and frequency of hostile and defiant behaviors toward adults.

211

2. Terminate temper tantrums and replace with controlled, respectful compliance with directions from authority figures.
3. Replace hostile, defiant behaviors toward adults with those of respect and cooperation.
4. Resolution of the conflict that underlies the anger, hostility, and defiance.
5. Reach a level of reduced tension, increased satisfaction, and improved communication with family and/or other authority figures.
6. Parents learn and implement good child behavioral management skills.

__. _____
   _____
__. _____
   _____
__. _____
   _____

SHORT-TERM OBJECTIVES	THERAPEUTIC INTERVENTIONS
1. Identify situations, thoughts, and feelings that trigger angry feelings, problem behaviors, and the targets of those actions. (1)	1. Thoroughly assess the various stimuli (e.g., situations, people, thoughts) that have triggered the client's anger and the thoughts, feelings, and actions that have characterized his/her anger responses.
2. Cooperate with a medical evaluation to assess possible organic contributors to poor anger control. (2)	2. Refer the client to a physician for a complete physical exam to rule out organic contributors (e.g., brain damage, tumor, elevated testosterone levels) to poor anger control.
3. Complete psychological testing. (3)	3. Conduct or arrange for psychological testing to help in assessing whether a comorbid condition (e.g., depression, Attention-Deficit/Hyperactivity Disorder [ADHD]) is contributing to anger control problems; follow-up accordingly with client and parents regarding treatment options.

▽ 4. Cooperate with a physician evaluation for possible treatment with psychotropic medications and take medications consistently, if prescribed. (4, 5)

4. Assess the client for the need for psychotropic medication to assist in anger and behavioral control, referring him/her, if indicated, to a physician for an evaluation for prescription medication. ▽

5. Monitor the client's prescription compliance, effectiveness, and side effects; provide feedback to the prescribing physician. ▽

▽ 5. Recognize and verbalize how feelings are connected to misbehavior. (6)

6. Actively build the level of trust with the client through consistent eye contact, active listening, unconditional positive regard, and warm acceptance to help increase his/her ability to identify and express feelings instead of acting them out; assist the client in making a connection between his/her feelings and reactive behaviors (or assign "Risk Factors Leading to Child Behavior Problems" in the *Child Psychotherapy Homework Planner*, 2nd ed. by Jongsma, Peterson, and McInnis). ▽

▽ 6. Increase the number of statements that reflect the acceptance of responsibility for misbehavior. (7, 8, 9)

7. Firmly confront the client's oppositional behavior and attitude, pointing out consequences for himself/herself and others. ▽

8. Confront statements in which the client lies and/or blames others for his/her misbehaviors and fails to accept responsibility for his/her actions. ▽

9. Explore and process the factors that contribute to the client's pattern of blaming others (e.g., harsh punishment experiences, family pattern of blaming others). ▽

▽ indicates that the Objective/Intervention is consistent with those found in evidence-based treatments.

▼ 7. Agree to learn alternative ways to think about and manage anger and misbehavior. (10, 11)

10. Assist the client in reconceptualizing anger and opposition as involving different components (cognitive, physiological, affective, and behavioral) that go through predictable phases (e.g., demanding expectations not being met leading to increased arousal and anger leading to acting out) that can be managed. ▼

11. Assist the client in identifying the positive consequences of managing anger and misbehavior (e.g., respect from others and self, co-operation from others, improved physical health); ask the client to agree to learn new ways to conceptualize and manage anger and misbehavior. ▼

▼ 8. Learn and implement calming strategies as part of a new way to manage reactions to frustration. (12)

12. Teach the client calming techniques (e.g., muscle relaxation, paced breathing, calming imagery) as part of a tailored strategy for responding appropriately to angry feelings when they occur. ▼

▼ 9. Identify, challenge, and replace self-talk that leads to anger and misbehavior with self-talk that facilitates more constructive reactions. (13)

13. Explore the client's self-talk that mediates his/her angry feelings and actions (e.g., demanding expectations reflected in should, must, or have to statements); identify and challenge biases, assisting him/her in generating appraisals and self-talk that corrects for the biases and facilitates a more flexible and temperate response to frustration. ▼

▼10. Learn and implement thought-stopping to manage intrusive unwanted thoughts that trigger anger and acting out. (14)

14. Teach the client the "thought-stopping" technique to manage intrusive unwanted thoughts that trigger anger and acting out and assign implementation on a daily basis between sessions; review implementation, reinforcing success

and providing corrective feedback toward improvement. ▼

▼11. Verbalize feelings of frustration, disagreement, and anger in a controlled, assertive way. (15)

15. Use instruction, videotaped or live modeling, and/or role-playing to help develop the client's anger control skills, such as calming, self-statement, assertion skills; if indicated, refer him/her to an anger control group for further instruction. ▼

▼12. Implement problem-solving and/or conflict resolution skills to manage interpersonal problems constructively. (16)

16. Teach the client conflict resolution skills such as empathy, active listening, "I messages," respectful communication, assertiveness without aggression, and compromise (or assign "Filing a Complaint" or "If I could Run My Family" in the *Child Psychotherapy Homework Planner,* 2nd ed. by Jongsma, Peterson, and McInnis); use modeling, roleplaying, and behavior rehearsal to work through several current conflicts. ▼

▼13. Practice using new calming, communication, conflict resolution, and thinking skills in group or individual therapy. (17, 18)

17. Assist the client in constructing and consolidating a client-tailored strategy for managing anger that combines any of the somatic, cognitive, communication, problem-solving, and/or conflict resolution skills relevant to his/her needs. ▼

18. Use any of several techniques (e.g., relaxation, imagery, behavioral rehearsal, modeling, role-playing, feedback of videotaped practice) in increasingly challenging situations to help the client consolidate the use of his/her new anger management skills. ▼

▼14. Practice using new calming, communication, conflict resolution, and thinking skills in homework exercises. (19)

19. Assign the client homework exercises to help him/her practice newly learned calming, assertion, conflict resolution, or cognitive restructuring skills as needed; review and process toward the goal of consolidation. ▼

▼15. Decrease the number, intensity, and duration of angry outbursts, while increasing the use of new skills for managing anger. (20)

20. Monitor the client's reports of angry outbursts toward the goal of decreasing their frequency, intensity, and duration through the client's use of new anger management skills (or assign "Anger Control" or "Child Anger Checklist" in the *Child Psychotherapy Homework Planner,* 2nd ed. by Jongsma, Peterson, and McInnis); review progress, reinforcing success and providing corrective feedback toward improvement. ▼

▼16. Identify social supports that will help facilitate the implementation of new skills. (21)

21. Encourage the client to discuss and/or use his/her new anger and conduct management skills with trusted peers, family, or otherwise significant others who are likely to support his/her change. ▼

▼17. Parents learn and implement Parent Management Training skills to recognize and manage problem behavior of the client. (22, 23, 24, 25, 26)

22. Use a Parent Management Training approach beginning with teaching the parents how parent and child behavioral interactions can encourage or discourage positive or negative behavior and that changing key elements of those interactions (e.g., prompting and reinforcing positive behaviors) can be used to promote positive change (e.g., see *Parenting the Strong-Willed Child* by Forehand and Long; *Living with Children* by Patterson). ▼

23. Teach the parents how to specifically define and identify problem

behaviors, identify their reactions to the behavior, determine whether the reaction encourages or discourages the behavior, and generate alternatives to the problem behavior. ▽

24. Teach parents how to implement key parenting practices consistently, including establishing realistic age-appropriate rules for acceptable and unacceptable behavior, prompting of positive behavior in the environment, use of positive reinforcement to encourage behavior (e.g., praise), use of clear direct instruction, time out, and other loss-of-privilege practices for problem behavior (or assign "Switching from Defense to Offense" in the *Child Psychotherapy Homework Planner,* 2nd ed. by Jongsma, Peterson, and McInnis). ▽

25. Assign the parents home exercises in which they implement and record results of implementation exercises (or assign "Clear Rules, Positive Reinforcement, Appropriate Consequences" in the *Adolescent Psychotherapy Homework Planner,* 2nd ed. by Jongsma, Peterson, and McInnis); review in session, providing corrective feedback toward improved, appropriate, and consistent use of skills. ▽

26. Use Webster-Stratton videotapes to teach parenting techniques (see Webster-Stratton, 1994, 1996). ▽

▽18. Parents and client participate in play sessions in which they use their new rules for appropriate conduct. (27, 28)

27. Conduct Parent-Child Interaction Therapy in which child-directed and parent-directed sessions focus on teaching appropriate child behavior, and parental behavioral

management skills (e.g., clear commands, consistent consequences, positive reinforcement) are developed (see *Parent-Child Interaction Therapy* by Bell and Eyberg). ▽

28. Teach parents to use the time out technique as a consequence for inappropriate behavior; if possible, use a "signal seat" that has a battery-operated buzzer that serves as both a timer and an alert that the child is not staying in the seat (see Hamilton and MacQuiddy, 1984). ▽

▽19. Increase compliance with rules at home and school. (29)

29. Design a reward system and/or contingency contract for the client and meet with school officials to reinforce identified positive behaviors at home and school and deter impulsive or rebellious behaviors. ▽

▽20. Parents verbalize appropriate boundaries for discipline to prevent further occurrences of abuse and to ensure the safety of the client and his/her siblings. (30, 31)

30. Explore the client's family background for a history of neglect and physical or sexual abuse that may contribute to his/her behavioral problems; confront the client's parents to cease physically abusive or overly punitive methods of discipline. ▽

31. Implement the steps necessary to protect the client and siblings from further abuse (e.g., report abuse to the appropriate agencies; remove the client or perpetrator from the home). ▽

▽21. Increase the frequency of civil, respectful interactions with parents/adults. (32)

32. Teach the client the principle of reciprocity, asking him/her to agree to treat everyone in a respectful manner for a 1-week period to see if others will reciprocate by treating him/her with more respect. ▽

▼22. Demonstrate the ability to play by the rules in a cooperative fashion. (33)

33. Play a game (e.g., checkers), first with the client determining the rules (and the therapist holding the client to those rules) and then with rules determined by the therapist. Process the experience and give positive verbal praise to the client for following established rules. ▼

▼23. Increase the frequency of responsible and positive social behaviors. (34, 35)

34. Direct the client to engage in three altruistic or benevolent acts (e.g., read to a developmentally disabled student, mow grandmother's lawn) before the next session to increase his/her empathy and sensitivity to the needs of others. ▼

35. Place the client in charge of tasks at home (e.g., preparing and cooking a special dish for a family get-together, building shelves in the garage, changing oil in the car) to demonstrate confidence in his/her ability to act responsibly (or assign "Share a Family Meal" in the *Child Psychotherapy Homework Planner*, 2nd ed. by Jongsma, Peterson, and McInnis). ▼

24. Identify and verbally express feelings associated with past neglect, abuse, separation, or abandonment. (36)

36. Encourage and support the client in expressing feelings associated with neglect, abuse, separation, or abandonment and help process (e.g., assign the task of writing a letter to an absent parent, use the empty-chair technique, assign "The Lesson of Salmon Rock . . . Fighting Leads to Loneliness" in the *Child Psychotherapy Homework Planner*, 2nd ed. by Jongsma, Peterson, and McInnis).

25. Parents participate in marital therapy. (37)

37. Assess the marital dyad for possible substance abuse, conflict, or triangulation that shifts the

focus from marriage issues to the client's acting out behaviors; refer for appropriate treatment, if needed.

__. _____   __. _____
    _____   _____
__. _____   __. _____
    _____   _____
__. _____   __. _____
    _____   _____

DIAGNOSTIC SUGGESTIONS

Axis I:	312.81	Conduct Disorder, Childhood-Onset Type
	312.82	Conduct Disorder, Adolescent-Onset Type
	313.81	Oppositional Defiant Disorder
	312.9	Disruptive Behavior Disorder NOS
	314.01	Attention-Deficit/Hyperactivity Disorder, Predominantly Hyperactive-Impulsive Type
	314.9	Attention-Deficit/Hyperactivity Disorder NOS
	312.34	Intermittent Explosive Disorder
	V71.02	Child Antisocial Behavior
	V61.20	Parent-Child Relational Problem

_____   _____

_____   _____

| Axis II: | V71.09 | No Diagnosis |

_____   _____

_____   _____

PARENTING

BEHAVIORAL DEFINITIONS

1. Expression of feelings of inadequacy in setting effective limits with their child.
2. Frequently struggle to control their emotional reactions to their child's misbehavior.
3. Increasing conflict between spouses over how to parent/discipline their child.
4. A pattern of lax supervision and inadequate limit setting.
5. A pattern of overindulgence of the child's wishes and demands.
6. A pattern of harsh, rigid, and demeaning behavior toward the child.
7. A pattern of physically and emotionally abusive parenting.
8. One parent is perceived as overindulgent while the other is seen as too harsh.
9. One parent expresses resentment over feeling like the only one who is responsible for the child's supervision, nurture, and discipline.
10. Lack of knowledge regarding reasonable expectations for a child's behavior at a given developmental level.
11. Have been told by others (e.g., school officials. juvenile court, friends) that they need to do something to control their child's negative behavior pattern.
12. Have exhausted their ideas and resources in attempt to deal with their child's behavior.

—. _____
_____

—. _____
_____

—. _____
_____

LONG-TERM GOALS

1. Achieve a level of competent, effective parenting.
2. Reach a realistic view of and approach to parenting and the child's developmental level.
3. Terminate ineffective and/or abusive parenting and implement positive, effective techniques.
4. Establish and maintain a healthy functioning parental team.
5. Resolve childhood issues that prevent effective parenting.
6. Achieve a level of greater family connectedness.

—. _____

_____

—. _____

_____

—. _____

_____

SHORT-TERM OBJECTIVES	THERAPEUTIC INTERVENTIONS
1. Provide information on the marital relationship, child behavior expectations, and style of parenting. (1)	1. Engage the parents through the use of empathy and normalization of their struggles with parenting and obtain information on their marital relationship, child behavior expectations, and parenting style.
2. Identify specific marital conflicts and work toward their resolution. (2, 3)	2. Analyze the data received from the parents about their relationship and parenting and establish or rule out the presence of marital conflicts.
	3. Conduct or refer the parents to marital/relationship therapy to resolve the conflicts that are preventing them from being effective parents.
3. Complete recommended evaluation instruments and receive the results. (4, 5, 6)	4. Administer or arrange for the parents to complete assessment instruments to evaluate their

4. Express feelings of frustration, helplessness, and inadequacy that each experiences in the parenting role. (7, 8, 9)

5. Identify unresolved childhood issues that affect parenting and work toward their resolution. (10, 11)

6. Identify the child's personality/temperament type that causes challenges and develop specific strategies to more effectively deal with that personality/temperament type. (12, 13, 14)

parenting strengths and weaknesses (e.g., the Parenting Stress Index [PSI], the Parent-Child Relationship Inventory [PCRI]).

5. Share results of assessment instruments with the parents and identify issues to begin working on to strengthen the parenting team.

6. Use testing results to identify parental strengths and begin to build the confidence and effectiveness level of the parental team.

7. Create a compassionate, empathetic environment where the parents become comfortable enough to let their guard down and express the frustrations of parenting.

8. Educate the parents on the full scope of parenting by using humor and normalization.

9. Help the parents reduce their unrealistic expectations of themselves.

10. Explore each parent's story of his/her childhood to identify any unresolved issues that are present and to identify how these issues are now affecting the ability to effectively parent.

11. Assist the parents in working through issues from childhood that are unresolved.

12. Have the parents read *The Challenging Child* (Greenspan) and then identify which type of difficult behavior pattern their child exhibits; encourage implementation of several of the parenting methods suggested for that type of child.

13. Expand the parents' repertoire of intervention options by having them read material on parenting difficult children (e.g., *The Difficult Child* by Turecki and Tonner; *The Explosive Child* by Greene; *How to Handle a Hard-to-Handle Kid* by Edwards).

14. Support, empower, monitor, and encourage the parents in implementing new strategies for parenting their child, giving feedback and redirection as needed.

▼ 7. Decrease reactivity to the child's behaviors. (15, 16, 17)

15. Evaluate the level of the parental team's reactivity to the child's behavior and then help them to learn to respond in a more modulated, thoughtful, planned manner (or assign "Picking Your Battles" in the *Child Psychotherapy Homework Planner,* 2nd ed. by Jongsma, Peterson, and McInnis). ▼

16. Help the parents become aware of the "hot buttons" they have that the child can push to get a quick negative response and how this overreactive response reduces their effectiveness as parents. ▼

17. Role-play reactive situations with the parents to help them learn to thoughtfully respond instead of automatically reacting to their child's demands or negative behaviors. ▼

▼ 8. Parents learn and implement Parent Management Training skills to recognize and manage problem behavior of the client. (18, 19, 20, 21, 22)

18. Use a Parent Management Training approach beginning with teaching the parents how parent and child behavioral interactions can encourage or discourage positive or negative behavior and

---

▼ indicates that the Objective/Intervention is consistent with those found in evidence-based treatments.

that changing key elements of those interactions (e.g., prompting and reinforcing positive behaviors) can be used to promote positive change (e.g., *Parenting the Strong-Willed Child* by Forehand and Long; *Living with Children* by Patterson). ▽

19. Teach the parents how to specifically define and identify problem behaviors, identify their reactions to the behavior, determine whether the reaction encourages or discourages the behavior, and generate alternatives to the problem behavior. ▽

20. Teach parents how to implement key parenting practices consistently. including establishing realistic age-appropriate rules for acceptable and unacceptable behavior, prompting of positive behavior in the environment, use of positive reinforcement to encourage behavior (e.g., praise), use of clear direct instruction, time out, and other loss-of-privilege practices for problem behavior. ▽

21. Assign the parents home exercises in which they implement and record results of implementation exercises (or assign "Clear Rules, Positive Reinforcement, Appropriate Consequences" in the *Adolescent Psychotherapy Homework Planner,* 2nd ed. by Jongsma, Peterson, and McInnis); review in session, providing corrective feedback toward improved, appropriate, and consistent use of skills. ▽

22. Use Webster-Stratton videotapes to teach parenting techniques (see Webster-Stratton, 1994, 1996). ▽

▽ 9. Parents and client participate in play sessions in which they use their new rules for appropriate conduct. (23, 24)

23. Conduct Parent-Child Interaction Therapy in which child-directed and parent-directed sessions focus on teaching appropriate child behavior, and parental behavioral management skills (e.g., clear commands, consistent consequences, positive reinforcement) are developed (see *Parent-Child Interaction Therapy* by Bell and Eyberg). ▽

24. Teach parents to use the time out technique as a consequence for inappropriate behavior; if possible, use a "signal seat" that has a battery-operated buzzer that serves as both a timer and an alert that the child is not staying in the seat (see *Self-Administered Behavioral Parent Training* by Hamilton and MacQuiddy). ▽

▽ 10. Parents implement a reward system designed to increase the client's compliance with rules at home and school. (25)

25. Design a reward system and/or contingency contract for the client and assign parents to meet with school officials to reinforce identified positive behaviors at home and school and deter impulsive or disruptive behaviors. ▽

▽ 11. Parents enact appropriate boundaries for discipline, terminating all abusive behaviors. (26, 27)

26. Explore the client's family background for a history of neglect and physical or sexual abuse that may contribute to his/her behavioral problems; confront the client's parents to cease physically abusive or overly punitive methods of discipline and to ensure the safety of the client and his/her siblings. ▽

27. Implement the steps necessary to protect the client or siblings from further abuse (e.g., report abuse to the appropriate agencies; remove the client or perpetrator from the home). ▽

▼12. Parents verbalize a sense of increased skill, effectiveness, and confidence in their parenting. (28, 29, 30)

28. Educate the parents on the numerous key differences between boys and girls, such as rate of development, perspectives, impulse control, and anger, and how to handle these differences in the parenting process. ▼

29. Have the children complete the "Parent Report Card" (Berg-Gross) and then give feedback to the parents; support areas of parenting strength and identify weaknesses that need to be bolstered. ▼

30. Assist the parental team in identifying areas of parenting weaknesses; help the parents improve their skills and boost their confidence and follow-through (or assign "Being a Consistent Parent" in the *Child Psychotherapy Homework Planner*, 2nd ed. by Jongsma, Peterson, and McInnis). ▼

▼13. Partners express verbal support of each other in the parenting process. (31)

31. Help the parents identify and implement specific ways they can support each other as parents and in realizing the ways children work to keep the parents from cooperating in order to get their way. ▼

▼14. Decrease outside pressures, demands, and distractions that drain energy and time from the family. (32, 33)

32. Give the parents permission to not involve their child and themselves in too numerous activities, organizations, or sports. ▼

33. Ask the parents to provide a weekly schedule of their entire family's activities and then evaluate the schedule with them, looking for which activities are valuable and which can possibly be eliminated to create a more focused and relaxed time to parent. ▼

▼15. Develop skills to talk openly and effectively with the children. (34, 35)

34. Use modeling and role-play to teach the parents to listen more than talk to their children and to use open-ended questions that encourage openness, sharing, and ongoing dialogue. ▼

35. Ask the parents to read material on parent-child communication (e.g., *How to Talk So Kids Will Listen and Listen So Kids Will Talk* by Faber and Mazlish; *Parent Effectiveness Training* by Gordon); help them to implement the new communication style in daily dialogue with their children and to see the positive responses each child had to it.

16. Parents verbalize a termination of their perfectionist expectations of the child. (36, 37)

36. Point out to the parents any unreasonable and perfectionist expectations of their child they hold and help them to modify these expectations.

37. Help the parents identify the negative consequences/outcomes that perfectionist expectations have on a child and on the relationship between the parents and the child.

17. Parents and child report an increased feeling of connectedness between them. (38)

38. Assist the parents in removing and resolving any barriers that prevent or limit connectedness between family members and in identifying activities that will promote connectedness such as games or one-on-one time (or assign "Share a Family Meal" in the *Child Psychotherapy Homework Planner,* 2nd ed. by Jongsma, Peterson, and McInnis).

—. _____

_____

—. _____

_____

—. _____

_____

—. _____

_____

—. ————————————————   —. ————————————————
————————————————   ————————————————

DIAGNOSTIC SUGGESTIONS

Axis I:	309.3	Adjustment Disorder With Disturbance of Conduct
	309.4	Adjustment Disorder With Mixed Disturbance of Emotions and Conduct
	V61.21	Neglect of Child
	V61.20	Parent-Child Relational Problem
	V61.1	Partner Relational Problem
	V61.21	Physical Abuse of Child
	V61.21	Sexual Abuse of Child
	313.81	Oppositional Defiant Disorder
	312.9	Disruptive Behavior Disorder NOS
	312.82	Conduct Disorder, Adolescent-Onset Type
	314.01	Attention-Deficit/Hyperactivity Disorder, Combined Type

———————   ————————————————
———————   ————————————————

Axis II:	301.7	Antisocial Personality Disorder
	301.6	Dependent Personality Disorder
	301.81	Narcissistic Personality Disorder
	301.83	Borderline Personality Disorder
	799.9	Diagnosis Deferred
	V71.09	No Diagnosis

———————   ————————————————
———————   ————————————————

PEER/SIBLING CONFLICT

BEHAVIORAL DEFINITIONS

1. Frequent, overt, intense fighting (verbal and/or physical) with peers and/or siblings.
2. Projects responsibility for conflicts onto others.
3. Believes that he/she is treated unfairly and/or that parents favor sibling(s) over himself/herself.
4. Peer and/or sibling relationships are characterized by bullying, defiance, revenge, taunting, and incessant teasing.
5. Has virtually no friends, or a few who exhibit similar socially disapproved behavior.
6. Exhibits a general pattern of behavior that is impulsive, intimidating, and unmalleable.
7. Behaviors toward peers are aggressive and lack a discernible empathy for others.
8. Parents are hostile toward the client, demonstrating a familial pattern of rejection, quarreling, and lack of respect or affection.

___. _____
    _____
___. _____
    _____
___. _____
    _____

LONG-TERM GOALS

1. Compete, cooperate, and resolve conflict appropriately with peers and siblings.
2. Develop healthy mechanisms for handling anxiety, tension, frustration, and anger.
3. Obtain the skills required to build positive peer relationships.
4. Terminate aggressive behavior and replace with assertiveness and empathy.
5. Form respectful, trusting peer and sibling relationships.
6. Parents acquire the necessary parenting skills to model respect, empathy, nurturance, and lack of aggression.
7. Demonstrate consistent prosocial behaviors with all peers and siblings.

—. _____

_____

—. _____

_____

—. _____

_____

SHORT-TERM OBJECTIVES

1. Describe relationship with siblings and friends. (1, 2)

2. Attend and freely participate in play therapy session. (3, 4, 5, 6)

THERAPEUTIC INTERVENTIONS

1. Actively build level of trust with client through consistent eye contact, active listening, unconditional positive regard, and warm acceptance to help increase the client's ability to identify and express feelings.

2. Explore the client's perception of the nature of his/her relationships with siblings and peers; assess the degree of denial regarding conflict and projection of the responsibility for conflict onto others.

3. Employ psychoanalytic play therapy approaches (e.g., explore and gain understanding of the

etiology of unconscious conflicts, fixations, or arrests; interpret resistance, transference, or core anxieties) to help the client work through and resolve issues with the sibling and/or peers.

4. Employ ACT model (Landreth) in play therapy sessions to *acknowledge* the client's feelings, to *communicate* limits, and to *target* more appropriate alternatives to ongoing conflicts and aggression with peers and/or siblings.

5. Interpret the feelings expressed in play therapy and relate them to anger and aggressive behaviors toward siblings and/or peers.

6. Create scenarios with puppets, dolls, or stuffed animals that model and/or suggest constructive ways to handle/manage conflicts with siblings or peers.

3. Decrease the frequency and intensity of aggressive actions toward peers or siblings. (7, 8, 9, 10)

7. Guide the parents in utilizing the Playing Baby game (see Schaefer in *101 Favorite Play Therapy Techniques* by Kaduson and Schaefer) in which the child is given an allotted time each day (30 minutes) to be a baby and have mother/parents cater to his/her every need. After the allotted time, client is again treated in an age-appropriate manner as a regular member of the family.

8. Utilize the "Tearing Paper" exercise (see Daves in *101 Favorite Play Therapy Techniques*), in which the therapist places several phone books and Sunday papers in the center of the room and instructs the family to tear

the paper into small pieces and throw them in the air. The only two conditions are that they must clean up and not throw paper at one another. During cleanup, the therapist reinforces verbally their follow-through in cleaning up and processes how it felt for family/siblings to release energy in this way and how could they do it in other situations at home.

9. Teach the client the Stamping Feet and Bubble Popping method (see Wunderlich in *101 Favorite Play Therapy Techniques*) of releasing angry and frustrating feelings that are part of everyday life and emphasize that what is important is how we choose to handle them. Then talk about how the "anger goes through his/her fingers into the air."

10. Instruct the parents and teachers in social learning techniques of ignoring the client's aggressive acts, except when there is danger of physical injury, while making a concerted effort to attend to and praise all nonaggressive, cooperative, and peaceful behavior.

4. Identify verbally and in writing how he/she would like to be treated by others. (11, 12, 13)

11. Educate the client about feelings, focusing on how others feel when they are the focus of aggressive actions and then asking how the client would like to be treated by others.

12. Ask the client to list the problems that he/she has with siblings and to suggest concrete solutions (or assign the client and parents the exercise "Negotiating a Peace

5. Recognize and verbalize the feelings of others as well as her/his own. (14, 15, 16)

6. Increase socially appropriate behavior with peers and siblings. (17, 18, 19)

Treaty" from the *Child Psychotherapy Homework Planner,* 2nd ed. by Jongsma, Peterson, and McInnis).

13. Play The Helping, Sharing, and Caring Game (Gardner) with the client and/or family to develop and expand feelings of respect for self and others.

14. Use therapeutic stories (e.g., *Dr. Gardner's Fairy Tales for Today's Children* by Gardner) to increase awareness of feelings and ways to cooperate with others.

15. Refer the client to a peer therapy group whose objectives are to increase social sensitivity and behavioral flexibility through the use of group exercises (strength bombardment, trusting, walking, expressing negative feelings, etc.).

16. Use The Talking, Feeling, and Doing game (available from Creative Therapeutics) to increase the client's awareness of self and others.

17. Use The Anger Control Game (Berg) or a similar game to expose the client to new, constructive ways to manage aggressive feelings.

18. Play with the client The Social Conflict Game (Berg) to assist him/her in developing behavior skills to decrease interpersonal antisocialism with others.

19. Conduct or refer the client to a behavioral contracting group therapy in which contracts for positive

7. Participate in peer group activities in a cooperative manner. (20, 21)

8. Parents facilitate the client's social network building. (22)

9. Identify feelings associated with the perception that parent(s) have special feelings of favoritism toward a sibling. (23)

10. Respond positively to praise and encouragement as evidenced by smiling and expressing gratitude. (24)

11. Parents increase verbal and physical demonstrations of affection and praise to the client. (25)

12. Verbalize an understanding of the pain that underlies the anger. (26)

peer interaction are developed each week and reviewed. Positive reinforcers are verbal feedback and small concrete rewards.

20. Direct the parents to involve the client in cooperative activities (sports, scouts, etc.).

21. Refer the client to an alternative summer camp that focuses on self-esteem and cooperation with peers.

22. Have the parents read *Helping Your Child Make Friends* (Nevick). Then assist them in implementing several of the suggestions with the client to build his/her skills in connecting with others.

23. Help the client work through his/her perception that his/her parents have a favorite child (or assign the "Joseph, His Amazing Technicolor Coat, and More" exercise from the *Child Psychotherapy Homework Planner,* 2nd ed. by Jongsma, Peterson, and McInnis).

24. Use role-playing, modeling, and behavior rehearsal to teach the client to become open and responsive to praise and encouragement.

25. Assist the parents in developing their ability to verbalize affection and appropriate praise to client in family sessions.

26. Probe causes for the client's anger in enduring rejection experiences with family and friends.

13. Family members decrease the frequency of quarreling and messages of rejection. (27, 28, 29, 30)

27. Ask the parents to read *How to End the Sibling Wars* (Bieniek), and then coach them into implementing several of the suggestions. The therapist will follow up by monitoring, encouraging, and redirecting as needed.

28. Work with the parents in family sessions to reduce parental aggression, messages of rejection, and quarreling within the family.

29. Assign the parents to read *Siblings without Rivalry* (Faber and Mazlish) and process key concepts with the therapist. Then have the parents choose two suggestions from the reading and implement them with their children.

30. Assign the parents to read *Between Parent and Child* (Ginott), especially the chapters "Jealousy" and "Children in Need of Professional Help." Process the reading with the therapist, identifying key changes in family structure or personal interactions that will need to occur to decrease the level of rivalry.

14. Parents attend a didactic series on positive parenting. (31)

31. Refer the parents to a positive parenting class.

15. Parents implement a behavior modification plan designed to increase the frequency of cooperative social behaviors. (32, 33)

32. Assist the parents in developing and implementing a behavior modification plan in which the client's positive interaction with peers and siblings is reinforced immediately with tokens that can be exchanged for preestablished rewards. Monitor and give feedback as indicated.

33. Conduct weekly contract sessions with the client and the parents in which the past week's behavior modification contract is reviewed and revised for the following week. Give feedback and model positive encouragement when appropriate.

16. Parents terminate alliances with children that foster sibling conflict. (34)

34. Hold family therapy sessions to assess dynamics and alliances that may underlie peer or sibling conflict.

17. Family members engage in conflict resolution in a respectful manner. (35)

35. Confront disrespectful expression of feelings in family session and use modeling, role-playing, and behavior rehearsal to teach cooperation, respect, and peaceful resolution of conflict.

18. Complete the recommended psychiatric or psychological testing/evaluation. (36)

36. Assess and refer the client for a psychiatric or psychological evaluation.

19. Comply with the recommendations of the mental health evaluations. (37)

37. Assist and monitor the client and the parents in implementing the recommendations of the mental health assessment.

__. _____
   _____
__. _____
   _____
__. _____

__. _____
   _____
__. _____
   _____
__. _____

DIAGNOSTIC SUGGESTIONS

Axis I:	313.81	Oppositional Defiant Disorder
	312.xx	Conduct Disorder
	312.9	Disruptive Behavior Disorder NOS
	314.01	Attention-Deficit/Hyperactivity Disorder, Predominantly Hyperactive-Impulsive Type

	314.9	Attention-Deficit/Hyperactivity Disorder NOS
	V62.81	Relational Problem NOS
	V71.02	Child or Adolescent Antisocial Behavior
	315.00	Reading Disorder
	315.9	Learning Disorder NOS

_____ _____

_____ _____

Axis II: V71.09   No Diagnosis

_____ _____

_____ _____

PHYSICAL/EMOTIONAL ABUSE VICTIM

BEHAVIORAL DEFINITIONS

1. Confirmed self-report or account by others of having been assaulted (e.g., hitting, burning, kicking, slapping, torture) by an older person.
2. Bruises or wounds as evidence of victimization.
3. Self-reports of being injured by a supposed caregiver coupled with feelings of fear and social withdrawal.
4. Significant increase in the frequency and severity of aggressive behaviors toward peers or adults.
5. Recurrent and intrusive distressing recollections of the abuse.
6. Feelings of anger, rage, or fear when in contact with the perpetrator.
7. Frequent and prolonged periods of depression, irritability, anxiety, and/or apathetic withdrawal.
8. Appearance of regressive behaviors (e.g., thumb-sucking, baby talk, bed-wetting).
9. Sleep disturbances (e.g., difficulty falling asleep, refusal to sleep alone, night terrors, recurrent distressing nightmares).
10. Running away from home to avoid further physical assaults.

__. _____
   _____
   _____
__. _____
   _____
   _____
__. _____

LONG-TERM GOALS

1. Terminate the physical abuse.
2. Escape from the environment where the abuse is occurring and move to a safe haven.

3. Rebuild sense of self-worth and overcome the overwhelming sense of fear, shame, and sadness.
4. Resolve feelings of fear and depression while improving communication and the boundaries of respect within the family.
5. Caregivers establish limits on the punishment of the client such that no physical harm can occur and respect for his/her rights is maintained.
6. Client and his/her family eliminate denial, putting the responsibility for the abuse on the perpetrator and allowing the victim to feel supported.
7. Reduce displays of aggression that reflect abuse and keep others at an emotional distance.
8. Build self-esteem and a sense of empowerment as manifested by an increased number of positive self-descriptive statements and greater participation in extracurricular activities.

—. _____

_____

—. _____

_____

—. _____

_____

SHORT-TERM OBJECTIVES	THERAPEUTIC INTERVENTIONS
1. Tell the entire account of the most recent abuse. (1, 2, 3)	1. Actively build the level of trust with the client through consistent eye contact, active listening, unconditional positive regard, and warm acceptance to help him/her increase the ability to identify and express facts and feelings about the abuse.
	2. Explore, encourage, and support the client in verbally expressing and clarifying the facts associated with the abuse.
	3. Use individual play therapy sessions to provide the client with the opportunity to reveal facts and feelings regarding the abuse.

2. Identify the nature, frequency, and duration of the abuse. (2, 4, 5)

2. Explore, encourage, and support the client in verbally expressing and clarifying the facts associated with the abuse.

4. Report physical abuse to the appropriate child protection agency, criminal justice officials, or medical professionals.

5. Consult with the family, a physician, criminal justice officials, or child protection case managers to assess the veracity of the physical abuse charges.

3. Agree to actions taken to protect self and provide boundaries against any future abuse or retaliation. (6, 7, 8)

6. Assess whether the perpetrator or the client should be removed from the client's home.

7. Implement the necessary steps (e.g., removal of the client from the home, removal of the perpetrator from the home) to protect the client and other children in the home from further physical abuse.

8. Reassure the client repeatedly of concern and caring on the part of the therapist and others who will protect him/her from any further abuse.

4. Identify and express the feelings connected to the abuse. (9)

9. Explore, encourage, and support the client in expressing and clarifying his/her feelings toward the perpetrator and self (or assign the homework exercise "My Thoughts and Feelings" in the *Child Psychotherapy Homework Planner*, 2nd ed. by Jongsma, Peterson, and McInnis).

5. Terminate verbalizations of denial or making excuses for the perpetrator. (10, 11, 12, 13)

10. Actively confront and challenge denial within the perpetrator and the entire family system.

11. Confront the client about making excuses for the perpetrator's abuse and accepting blame for it.

12. Reassure the client that he/she did not deserve the abuse but that he/she deserves respect and a controlled response even in punishment situations.

13. Reinforce any and all client statements that put responsibility clearly on the perpetrator for the abuse, regardless of any misbehavior by the client.

6. Perpetrator takes responsibility for the abuse. (14)

14. Hold a family therapy session in which the client and/or therapist confronts the perpetrator with the abuse.

7. Perpetrator asks for forgiveness and pledges respect for disciplinary boundaries. (15)

15. Conduct a family therapy session in which the perpetrator apologizes to the client and/or other family member(s) for the abuse.

8. Perpetrator agrees to seek treatment. (16, 17, 18)

16. Require the perpetrator to participate in a child abusers' psychotherapy group.

17. Refer the perpetrator for a psychological evaluation and treatment.

18. Evaluate the possibility of substance abuse with the perpetrator or within the family; refer the perpetrator and/or family member(s) for substance abuse treatment, if indicated.

9. Parents and caregivers verbalize the establishment of appropriate disciplinary boundaries to ensure protection of the client. (19, 20)

19. Counsel the client's family about appropriate disciplinary boundaries.

20. Ask the parents/caregivers to list appropriate means of discipline or correction; reinforce reasonable actions and appropriate boundaries that reflect respect for the rights and feelings of the child.

10. Family members identify the stressors or other factors that may trigger violence. (21, 22)

21. Construct a multigenerational family genogram that identifies physical abuse within the extended family to help the perpetrator recognize the cycle of violence.

11. Nonabusive parent and other key family members verbalize support and acceptance of the client. (23)

12. Reduce the expressions of rage and aggressiveness that stem from feelings of helplessness related to physical abuse. (24, 25)

13. Decrease the statements of being a victim while increasing the statements that reflect personal empowerment. (26, 27)

14. Increase the frequency of positive self-descriptive statements. (28, 29)

15. Express forgiveness of the perpetrator and others connected with the abuse while insisting on respect for his/her own right to safety in the future. (15, 30, 31)

22. Assess the client's family dynamics and explore for the stress factors or precipitating events that contributed to the emergence of the abuse.

23. Elicit and reinforce support and nurturance of the client from the nonabusive parent and other key family members.

24. Assign the client to write a letter expressing feelings of hurt, fear, and anger to the perpetrator; process the letter.

25. Interpret the client's generalized expressions of anger and aggression as triggered by feelings toward the perpetrator.

26. Empower the client by identifying sources of help against abuse (e.g., phone numbers to call, a safe place to run to, asking for temporary alternate protective placement).

27. Assist the client in writing his/her thoughts and feelings regarding the abuse (or assign the exercise "Letter of Empowerment" in the *Child Psychotherapy Homework Planner,* 2nd ed. by Jongsma, Peterson, and McInnis).

28. Assist the client in identifying a basis for self-worth by reviewing his/her talents, importance to others, and intrinsic spiritual value.

29. Reinforce positive statements that the client has made about himself/herself and the future.

15. Conduct a family therapy session in which the perpetrator apologizes to the client and/or other family member(s) for the abuse.

30. Assign the client to write a forgiveness letter and/or complete

a forgiveness exercise in which he/she verbalizes forgiveness to the perpetrator and/or significant family member(s) while asserting the right to safety. Process this letter.

31. Assign the client a letting-go exercise in which a symbol of the abuse is disposed of or destroyed. Process this experience.

16. Increase socialization with peers and family. (32, 33, 34)

32. Encourage the client to make plans for the future that involve interacting with his/her peers and family.

33. Encourage the client to participate in positive peer groups or extracurricular activities.

34. Refer the client to a victim support group with other children to assist him/her in realizing that he/she is not alone in this experience.

17. Verbalize an understanding of the loss of trust in all relationships that results from abuse by a parent. (35)

35. Facilitate the client expressing loss of trust in adults and relate this loss to the perpetrator's abusive behavior and the lack of protection provided.

18. Increase the level of trust of others as shown by increased socialization and a greater number of friendships. (36, 37)

36. Assist the client in making discriminating judgments that allow for the trust of some people rather than a distrust of all.

37. Teach the client the share-check method of building trust, in which a degree of shared information is related to a proven level of trustworthiness.

19. Verbalize how the abuse has affected feelings toward self. (38, 39)

38. Assign the client to draw pictures that represent how he/she feels about himself/herself.

39. Ask the client to draw pictures of his/her own face that represent

how he/she felt about him-
self/herself before, during, and
after the abuse occurred.

20. Express feelings in play therapy
sessions. (40)

40. Use child-centered play therapy
approaches (e.g., demonstrate
genuine interest, provide unconditional positive regard, reflect
feelings, profess trust in the
client's inner direction) to promote resolution of fear, grief, and
rage.

__. _____   __. _____
_____   _____
__. _____   __. _____
_____   _____
__. _____   __. _____
_____   _____

DIAGNOSTIC SUGGESTIONS

Axis I:	309.81	Posttraumatic Stress Disorder
	308.3	Acute Stress Disorder
	995.54	Physical Abuse of Child (Victim)
	300.4	Dysthymic Disorder
	296.xx	Major Depressive Disorder
	300.02	Generalized Anxiety Disorder
	307.47	Nightmare Disorder
	313.81	Oppositional Defiant Disorder
	312.81	Conduct Disorder, Childhood-Onset Type
	300.6	Depersonalization Disorder
	300.15	Dissociative Disorder NOS

_____
_____

Axis II:	V71.09	No Diagnosis

_____
_____

POSTTRAUMATIC STRESS DISORDER (PTSD)

BEHAVIORAL DEFINITIONS

1. Exposure to threats of death or serious injury, or subjection to actual injury, that resulted in an intense emotional response of fear, helplessness, or horror.
2. Intrusive, distressing thoughts or images that recall the traumatic event.
3. Disturbing dreams associated with the traumatic event.
4. A sense that the event is recurring, as in illusions or flashbacks.
5. Intense distress when exposed to reminders of the traumatic event.
6. Physiological reactivity when exposed to internal or external cues that symbolize the traumatic event.
7. Avoidance of thoughts, feelings, or conversations about the traumatic event.
8. Avoidance of activities, places, or people associated with the traumatic event.
9. Inability to recall some important aspect of the traumatic event.
10. Lack of interest and participation in formerly meaningful activities.
11. A sense of detachment from others.
12. Inability to experience the full range of emotions, including love.
13. A pessimistic, fatalistic attitude regarding the future.
14. Sleep disturbance.
15. Irritability or angry outbursts.
16. Lack of concentration.
17. Hypervigilance.
18. Exaggerated startle response.
19. Symptoms have been present for more than 1 month.
20. Sad or guilty affect and other signs of depression.
21. Verbally and/or physically violent threats or behavior.

—· _____
   _____
—· _____
   _____
—· _____
   _____

LONG-TERM GOALS

1. Recall the traumatic event without becoming overwhelmed with negative emotions.
2. Interact normally with friends and family without irrational fears or intrusive thoughts that control behavior.
3. Return to pretrauma level of functioning without avoiding people, places, thoughts, or feelings associated with the traumatic event.
4. Display a full range of emotions without experiencing loss of control.
5. Develop and implement effective coping skills that allow for carrying out normal responsibilities and participating in relationships and social activities.

—· _____
   _____
—· _____
   _____
—· _____
   _____

SHORT-TERM OBJECTIVES

1. Describe the history and nature of PTSD symptoms. (1, 2)

THERAPEUTIC INTERVENTIONS

1. Establish rapport with the client toward building a therapeutic alliance.

2. Assess the client's frequency, intensity, duration, and history of PTSD symptoms and their impact on functioning (or assign the

"PTSD Incident Report" in the *Child Psychotherapy Homework Planner,* 2nd ed. by Jongsma, Peterson, and McInnis; or "Describe Your PTSD Symptoms" in the *Adolescent Psychotherapy Homework Planner II* by Jongsma, Peterson, and McInnis; or see *The Anxiety Disorders Interview Schedule for Children—Parent Version* or *Child Version* by Silverman and Albano).

2. Complete psychological tests designed to assess and/or track the nature and severity of PTSD symptoms. (3)

3. Administer or refer the client for administration of psychological testing to assess for the presence or strength of PTSD symptoms (e.g., Clinician-Administered PTSD Scale–Child and Adolescent Version [CAPS-C] by Nader, Blake, Kriegler, and Pynoos).

3. Describe the traumatic event in as much detail as possible. (4)

4. Gently and sensitively explore the client's recollection of the facts of the traumatic incident and his/her emotional reactions at the time (or utilize "Describe the Trauma and Your Feelings" in the *Adolescent Psychotherapy Homework Planner II* by Jongsma, Peterson, and McInnis).

4. Verbalize the symptoms of depression, including any suicidal ideation. (5)

5. Assess the client's depth of depression and suicide potential and treat appropriately, taking the necessary safety precautions as indicated (see Depression chapter in this *Planner*).

▼ 5. Cooperate with an evaluation by a physician for psychotropic medication. (6, 7)

6. Assess the client's need for medication (e.g., selective serotonin reuptake inhibitors) and arrange for prescription if appropriate. ▼

▼ indicates that the Objective/Intervention is consistent with those found in evidence-based treatments.

▼ 6. Participate, with or without parents, in individual or group therapy sessions focused on PTSD. (8)

7. Monitor and evaluate the client's psychotropic medication prescription compliance and the effectiveness of the medication on his/her level of functioning. ▼

8. Conduct group or individual therapy sessions consistent with Multimodality Trauma Treatment or Trauma-Focused Cognitive Behavioral Therapy—include parents if helpful (see *Cognitive Behavioral Treatment for Pediatric Posttraumatic Stress Disorder* by Amaya-Jackson and colleagues). ▼

▼ 7. Parents verbalize an accurate understanding of PTSD and how it develops. (9, 10)

9. Discuss with the client's parents a biopsychosocial model of PTSD, including that it results from exposure to trauma and results in intrusive recollection, unwarranted fears, anxiety, and a vulnerability to others negative emotions such as shame, anger, and guilt; normalize the client's experiences (see *Traumatic Stress Disorders* by Davidson and March). ▼

10. Assign the client's parents to read psychoeducational chapters of books or treatment manuals on PTSD that explain its features and development. ▼

▼ 8. Verbalize an understanding of the rationale for treatment of PTSD. (11, 12)

11. Discuss how coping skills, cognitive restructuring, and exposure help build confidence, desensitize and overcome fears, and see one's self, others, and the world in a less fearful and/or depressing way. ▼

12. Assign the client's parents to read about anxiety management, stress

inoculation, cognitive restructuring, and/or exposure-based therapy in chapters of books or treatment manuals on PTSD (e.g., *The PTSD Workbook* by Williams and Poijula). ▼

▼ 9. Learn and implement calming and coping strategies to managing emotional reactions related to trauma. (13)

13. Teach the client strategies from Anxiety Management Training or Stress Inoculation Training such as relaxation, breathing control, covert modeling (i.e., imagining the successful use of the strategies), and/or role-playing (i.e., with therapist or trusted other) for managing fears until a sense of mastery is evident (see *Cognitive Behavioral Psychotherapy* by Francis and Beidel; or *Clinical Handbook for Treating PTSD* by Meichenbaum). ▼

▼ 10. Learn and implement anger management techniques. (14)

14. Teach the client anger management techniques (see *Overcoming Situational and General Anger* by Deffenbacher and McKay; or the Anger Management chapter in this *Planner*). ▼

▼ 11. Identify, challenge, and replace fearful self-talk with reality-based, positive self-talk. (15, 16)

15. Explore the client's schema and self-talk that mediate his/her trauma-related fears; identify and challenge biases; assist him/her in generating appraisals that correct for the biases and build confidence. ▼

16. Assign the client a homework exercise in which he/she identifies fearful self-talk and creates reality-based alternatives; review and reinforce success, providing corrective feedback for failure. ▼

▽12. Participate in imaginal and in vivo exposure to trauma-related memories until talking or thinking about the trauma does not cause marked distress. (17, 18, 19)

17. Direct and assist the client in constructing a detailed narrative description of the trauma(s) for imaginal exposure (or assign "Finding My Triggers" in the *Child Psychotherapy Homework Planner,* 2nd ed. by Jongsma, Peterson, and McInnis); construct a fear and avoidance hierarchy of feared and avoided trauma-related stimuli for in vivo exposure. ▽

18. Have the client undergo imaginal exposure to the trauma by having him/her describe a traumatic experience at an increasing but client-chosen level of detail; repeat until associated anxiety reduces and stabilizes, recording the session and having the client listen to it between sessions (see *Cognitive Behavioral Treatment for Pediatric Posttraumatic Stress Disorder* by Amaya-Jackson and colleagues); review and reinforce progress, problem-solve obstacles. ▽

19. Assign the client a homework exercise in which he/she repeats the narrative exposure or does in vivo exposure to environmental stimuli as rehearsed in therapy; ask him/her to record responses; review and reinforce progress. ▽

▽13. Learn and implement thought-stopping to manage intrusive unwanted thoughts. (20)

20. Teach the client thought-stopping in which he/she internally voices the word STOP and/or imagines something representing the concept of stopping (e.g., a stop sign or light) immediately upon noticing unwanted trauma or otherwise negative unwanted thoughts. ▽

▼14. Implement relapse prevention strategies for managing possible future trauma-related symptoms. (21, 22, 23, 24)

21. Discuss with the client the distinction between a lapse and relapse, associating a lapse with an initial and reversible return of symptoms, fear, or urges to avoid and relapse with the decision to return to fearful and avoidant patterns. ▼

22. Identify and rehearse with the client the management of future situations or circumstances in which lapses could occur. ▼

23. Instruct the client to routinely use strategies learned in therapy (e.g., cognitive restructuring, social skills, exposure) while building social interactions and relationships. ▼

24. Develop a "coping card" or other reminder on which coping strategies and other important information (e.g., "Pace your breathing," "Focus on the task at hand," "You can manage it," "It will go away") are recorded for the client's later use. ▼

▼15. Family members learn skills that strengthen and support the client's positive behavior change. (25, 26, 27)

25. Involve the family in the treatment of the client, teaching them developmentally appropriate treatment goals, how to give support as the client faces his/her fears, and how to prevent reinforcing the client's fear and avoidance; offer encouragement, support, and redirection as required. ▼

26. Assist the family members in recognizing and managing their own difficult emotional reactions to the client's experience of trauma. ▼

27. Encourage the family to model constructive skills they have learned and model and praise the therapeutic skills the client is learning (e.g., calming, cognitive restructuring, nonavoidance of unrealistic fears). ▽

16. Cooperate with eye movement desensitization and reprocessing (EMDR) technique to reduce emotional reaction to the traumatic event. (28)

28. Utilize EMDR technique to reduce the client's emotional reactivity to the traumatic event (see *Through the Eyes of a Child: EMDR with Children* by Tinker and Wilson).

17. Implement a regular exercise regimen as a stress release technique. (29)

29. Develop and encourage a routine of physical exercise for the client.

18. Express facts and feelings surrounding the trauma through play therapy and mutual storytelling. (30, 31, 32)

30. Use child-centered play therapy principles (e.g., provide unconditional positive regard, offer nonjudgmental reflection of feelings, display trust in the child's capacity for growth) to help the client identify and express feelings surrounding the traumatic incident.

31. Employ psychoanalytic play therapy approaches (e.g., allow the child to take the lead; explore etiology of unconscious conflicts, fixations, or developmental arrests; interpret resistance, transference, and core anxieties) to help the client express and work through feelings surrounding the traumatic incident.

32. Utilize a mutual storytelling technique whereby the client and therapist alternate telling stories through the use of puppets, dolls, or stuffed animals. Therapist first models constructive steps to take

19. Express facts and feelings through painting or drawing. (33)

20. Sleep without being disturbed by dreams of the trauma. (34)

21. Verbalize hopeful and positive statements regarding the future. (35)

___. _____
_____
___. _____
_____
___. _____
_____

to protect self and feel empowered; the client follows by creating a story with similar characters or themes.

33. Provide the client with materials and ask him/her to draw/paint pictures depicting the trauma and of himself/herself depicting emotions associated with the trauma.

34. Monitor the client's sleep pattern and encourage use of relaxation, positive imagery, and sleep hygiene as aids to sleep (see Sleep Disturbance chapter in this *Planner*).

35. Reinforce the client's positive, reality-based cognitive messages that enhance self-confidence and increase adaptive action.

___. _____
_____
___. _____
_____
___. _____
_____

DIAGNOSTIC SUGGESTIONS

Axis I:	309.81	Posttraumatic Stress Disorder
	309.xx	Adjustment Disorder
	995.54	Physical Abuse of Child (Victim)
	995.53	Sexual Abuse of Child (Victim)
	308.3	Acute Stress Disorder
	296.xx	Major Depressive Disorder

_____
_____

Axis II:	V71.09	No Diagnosis

_____
_____

SCHOOL REFUSAL

BEHAVIORAL DEFINITIONS

1. Persistent reluctance or refusal to attend school because of a desire to remain at home with the parents.
2. Marked emotional distress and repeated complaints (e.g., crying, temper outbursts, pleading with parents not to go to school) when anticipating separation from home to attend school or after arrival at school.
3. Frequent somatic complaints (e.g., headaches, stomachaches, nausea) associated with attending school or in anticipation of school attendance.
4. Excessive clinging or shadowing of parents when anticipating leaving home for school or after arriving at school.
5. Frequent negative comments about school and/or repeated questioning of the necessity of going to school.
6. Persistent and unrealistic expression of fear that a future calamity will cause a separation from his/her parents if he/she attends school (e.g., he/she or parent(s) will be lost, kidnapped, killed, or the victim of an accident).
7. Verbalizations of low self-esteem and lack of confidence that contribute to the fear of attending school and being separated from the parents.
8. Verbalization of a fear of failure, ridicule, or anxiety regarding academic achievement accompanying the refusal to attend school.
9. Excessive shrinking from or avoidance of contact with unfamiliar people for extended periods of time.

—. _____
   _____
   _____

—. _____
   _____
   _____

—. _____
   _____
   _____

LONG-TERM GOALS

1. Attend school on a consistent, full-time basis.
2. Eliminate anxiety and the expression of fears prior to leaving home and after arriving at school.
3. Cease temper outbursts, regressive behaviors, complaints, and pleading associated with attending school.
4. Eliminate somatic complaints associated with attending school.
5. Resolve the core conflicts or traumas contributing to the emergence of the school refusal.
6. Increase the frequency of independent behaviors.
7. Parents establish and maintain appropriate parent-child boundaries, setting firm, consistent limits when the client exhibits temper tantrums and passive-aggressive behaviors associated with attending school.

—. _____
   _____
   _____

—. _____
   _____
   _____

—. _____
   _____

SHORT-TERM OBJECTIVES	THERAPEUTIC INTERVENTIONS
1. Establish a therapeutic alliance and express feelings associated with attending school. (1)	1. Actively build the level of trust with the client through consistent eye contact, active listening, unconditional positive regard, and warm acceptance to increase his/her ability to identify and express feelings regarding school attendance and any known reasons for them.
2. Complete psychological testing and an assessment interview. (2)	2. Arrange for psychological testing of the client to assess the severity of anxiety, depression, or gross psychopathology and to gain greater insight into the underlying dynamics contributing to school refusal; provide feedback to the client and parents.

3. Complete psychoeducational testing. (3)

3. Arrange for psychoeducational testing of the client to rule out the presence of learning disabilities that may interfere with school attendance; provide feedback to the client, parents, and school officials.

4. Comply with a systematic desensitization program and attend school for increasingly longer periods of time. (4)

4. Design and implement a systematic desensitization program to help the client manage his/her anxiety and gradually attend school for longer periods of time.

5. Parents implement a reward system, contingency contract, or token economy focused on school attendance by the client. (5, 6)

5. Develop a reward system or contingency contract to reinforce the client's attending school for increasingly longer periods of time.

6. Design and implement a token economy to reinforce the client's school attendance.

6. Parents and school officials implement a contingency plan to deal with temper tantrums, crying spells, or excessive clinging after arriving at school. (7, 8, 9)

7. Consult with the parents and school officials to develop a plan to manage the client's emotional distress and negative outbursts after arriving at school (e.g., the parent ceases lengthy good-byes, the client goes to the principal's office to calm down).

8. Consult with the teacher in the initial stages of treatment about planning an immediate assignment that will provide the client with an increased chance of success.

9. Use the teacher's aide or a positive peer role model to provide one-on-one attention for the client and decrease the fear and anxiety about attending school.

7. Verbally acknowledge how the fears related to attending school are irrational or unrealistic. (10, 11)

10. Explore the irrational, negative cognitive messages that produce the client's anxiety or fear; assist him/her in identifying the irrational or unrealistic nature of these fears.

11. Assist the client in developing reality-based positive cognitive messages that increase his/her self-confidence to cope with anxiety or fear.

8. Implement relaxation and guided imagery to reduce anxiety. (12)

12. Teach the client relaxation techniques or guided imagery to reduce his/her anxiety and fears.

9. Increase positive statements about accomplishments and experiences at school. (13)

13. Assist the client in identifying and acknowledging his/her accomplishments and positive experiences in school.

10. Decrease the frequency of verbalized somatic complaints. (14, 15, 16)

14. Consult with the parents and school officials to develop a contingency plan to manage the client's somatic complaints (e.g., ignore them, take the client's temperature matter-of-factly, redirect the client to task, send the client to the nurse's office).

15. Refocus the client's discussion from physical complaints to emotional conflicts and the expression of feelings.

16. Conduct family therapy sessions to assess the dynamics, including secondary gain that may be contributing to the emergence of the somatic complaints associated with school refusal.

11. Increase the time spent between the client and the disengaged parent in play, school, or work activities. (17, 18)

17. Ask the client to draw a picture of a house; then instruct him/her to pretend that he/she lives in the house and describe what it is like to live there; process the

client's responses to assess family dynamics, focusing on role of the disengaged parent.

18. Give a directive to the disengaged parent to transport the client to school in the morning; contact the parent's employer, if necessary, to gain permission for this.

12. Parents reinforce the client's autonomous behaviors and set limits on overly dependent behaviors. (19, 20, 21)

19. Encourage the parents to reinforce the client's autonomous behaviors (e.g., attending school, working alone on school assignments) and set limits on overly dependent behaviors (e.g., client insisting that the parent enter the classroom).

20. Stress to the parents the importance of remaining calm and not communicating anxiety to the client.

21. Praise and reinforce the parents for taking positive steps to help the client overcome his/her fears or anxieties about attending school.

13. Parents cease sending inconsistent messages about school attendance and begin to set firm, consistent limits on excessive clinging, pleading, crying, and temper tantrums. (19, 22, 23)

19. Encourage the parents to reinforce the client's autonomous behaviors (e.g., attending school, working alone on school assignments) and set limits on overly dependent behaviors (e.g., client insisting that the parent enter the classroom).

22. Counsel the parents about setting firm, consistent limits on the client's temper outbursts, manipulative behaviors, or excessive clinging.

23. Instruct the parents to write a letter to the client that sends a clear message about the importance

of attending school and reminds him/her of coping strategies that he/she can use to calm fears or anxieties. Place the letter in a notebook and have the client read the letter at appropriate times during school day when he/she begins to feel afraid or anxious (or assign the parents to complete the "Letter of Encouragement" in the *Child Psychotherapy Homework Planner,* 2nd ed. by Jongsma, Peterson, and McInnis).

14. Enmeshed or overly protective parent identifies overly dependent behaviors. (24, 25)

24. Identify how enmeshed or overly protective parents reinforce the client's dependency and irrational fears.

25. Use a paradoxical intervention (e.g., instruct the enmeshed parent to spoon-feed the client each morning) to work around the family's resistance and disengage the client from an overly protective parent.

15. Identify positive coping strategies to help decrease anxiety, fears, and emotional distress. (26, 27)

26. Explore for days or periods of time in which the client was able to attend school without exhibiting significant distress. Identify and reinforce coping strategies that the client used to attend school without displaying excessive fear or anxiety.

27. Anticipate possible stressors or events (e.g., illness, school holidays, vacations) that might cause fears and anxiety about attending school to reappear. Identify coping strategies and contingency plans (e.g., relaxation techniques, positive self-talk, disengaged parent transporting the client to school) that the client and family can use to overcome fears or anxiety.

16. Identify and express the feelings connected with past unresolved separation, loss, or trauma. (28, 29, 30)

17. Implement assertiveness skills to reduce social anxiety and cope with ridicule. (31, 32, 33)

18. Increase the frequency and duration of time spent in independent play or activities away from the parents or home. (34, 35, 36)

28. Assess whether the client's anxiety and fear about attending school are associated with a previously unresolved separation, loss, trauma, or unrealistic danger.

29. Explore, encourage, and support the client in verbally expressing and clarifying his/her feelings associated with a past separation, loss, trauma, or realistic danger.

30. Assign the older child to write a letter to express his/her feelings about a past separation, loss, trauma, or danger; process it with the therapist.

31. Train the client in assertiveness to reduce social anxiety and/or fear of ridicule.

32. Use Stand Up for Yourself (Shapiro) game in therapy sessions to help teach the client assertiveness skills that can be used at school.

33. Assign readings to teach the client effective ways to deal with aggressive or intimidating peers at school (e.g., *Why Is Everybody Always Picking on Me? A Guide to Understanding Bullies for Young People* by Webster-Doyle; *How to Handle Bullies, Teasers, and Other Meanies* by Cohen-Posey).

34. Encourage the client's assertive participation in extracurricular and positive peer group activities.

35. Give the client a directive to spend a specified period of time with his/her peers after school or on weekends.

36. Give the client a directive to initiate three social contacts per week with unfamiliar people or when placed in new social settings.

19. Express feelings about attending school through play, mutual storytelling, and art. (37, 38, 39, 40)

37. Employ psychoanalytic play therapy approaches (e.g., allow the child to take the lead; explore the etiology of unconscious conflicts, fixation, or developmental arrests; interpret resistance, transference, and core anxieties) to help the client work through and resolve issues contributing to school refusal.

38. Use mutual storytelling technique: The client and therapist alternate telling stories through the use of puppets, dolls, or stuffed animals. The therapist first models appropriate ways to overcome fears or anxieties to face separation or academic challenges; then the client follows by creating a story with similar characters or themes.

39. Direct the client to draw a picture or create a sculpture about what he/she fears will happen when he/she goes to school; discuss whether his/her fears are realistic or unrealistic.

40. Use the Angry Tower technique (see Saxe in *101 Favorite Play Therapy Techniques* by Kaduson and Schaefer) to help the client identify and express underlying feelings of anger that contribute to school refusal: Build a tower out of plastic containers or buckets; place doll on top of tower (doll represents object of anger); instruct the client to throw small fabric ball at the tower while verbalizing feelings of anger.

20. Parent(s) follow through with recommendations regarding medication and therapeutic interventions. (41)

41. Assess overly enmeshed parent for the possibility of having either an anxiety or depressive disorder that may be contributing to the client's

21. Cooperate with a medical evaluation and take medication as prescribed by the physician. (42, 43)

refusal to attend school. Refer the parent for a medication evaluation and/or individual therapy if it is found that the parent has an anxiety or a depressive disorder.

42. Refer the client for a medical examination to rule out genuine health problems that may contribute to his/her school refusal and somatic complaints.

43. Arrange for the client to be evaluated for psychotropic medication; monitor for medication prescription compliance, side effects, and effectiveness.

__. _____   __. _____
    _____   _____
__. _____   __. _____
    _____   _____
__. _____   __. _____
    _____   _____

DIAGNOSTIC SUGGESTIONS

Axis I:	309.21	Separation Anxiety Disorder
	300.02	Generalized Anxiety Disorder
	300.23	Social Anxiety Disorder (Social Phobia)
	296.xx	Major Depressive Disorder
	300.4	Dysthymic Disorder
	300.81	Somatization Disorder
	300.81	Undifferentiated Somatoform Disorder
	309.81	Posttraumatic Stress Disorder

_____   _____
_____   _____

| **Axis II:** | V71.09 | No Diagnosis |

_____   _____
_____   _____

SEPARATION ANXIETY

BEHAVIORAL DEFINITIONS

1. Excessive emotional distress and repeated complaints (e.g., crying, regressive behaviors, pleading with parents to stay, temper tantrums) when anticipating separation from home or close attachment figures.
2. Persistent and unrealistic worry about possible harm occurring to close attachment figures or excessive fear that they will leave and not return.
3. Persistent and unrealistic fears expressed that a future calamity will separate the client from a close attachment figure (e.g., the client or his/her parent will be lost, kidnapped, killed, the victim of an accident).
4. Repeated complaints and heightened distress (e.g., pleading to go home, demanding to see or call a parent) after separation from home or the attachment figure has occurred.
5. Persistent fear of avoidance of being alone as manifested by excessive clinging and shadowing of a close attachment figure.
6. Frequent reluctance or refusal to go to sleep without being near a close attachment figure; refusal to sleep away from home.
7. Recurrent nightmares centering on the theme of separation.
8. Frequent somatic complaints (e.g., headaches, stomachaches, nausea) when separation from home or the attachment figure is anticipated or has occurred.
9. Excessive need for reassurance about safety and protection from possible harm or danger.
10. Low self-esteem and lack of self-confidence that contribute to the fear of being alone or participating in social activities.
11. Excessive shrinking from unfamiliar or new situations.

___. _____
    _____
___. _____
    _____

___. _____

_____

LONG-TERM GOALS

1. Eliminate the anxiety and expression of fears when a separation is antici-pated or occurs.
2. Tolerate separation from attachment figures without exhibiting heightened emotional distress, regressive behaviors, temper outbursts, or pleading.
3. Eliminate the somatic complaints associated with separation.
4. Manage nighttime fears effectively as evidenced by remaining calm, sleeping in own bed, and not attempting to go into the attachment figure's room at night.
5. Resolve the core conflicts or traumas contributing to the emergence of the separation anxiety.
6. Participate in extracurricular or peer group activities and spend time in independent play on a regular, consistent basis.
7. Parents establish and maintain appropriate parent-child boundaries and set firm, consistent limits when the client exhibits temper outbursts or manipulative behaviors around separation points.

___. _____

_____

___. _____

_____

___. _____

_____

SHORT-TERM OBJECTIVES

1. Describe the history and nature of the phobia(s), complete with impact on functioning and at-tempt to overcome it. (1, 2)

THERAPEUTIC INTERVENTIONS

1. Actively build a level of trust with the client that will promote the open showing of thoughts and feelings, especially fearful ones (or assign "Expressions of Fear Through Art" from the *Child Psychotherapy Homework Plan-ner*, 2nd ed. by Jongsma, Peterson, and McInnis).

2. Assess the client's fear and avoidance, including the focus of fear, types of avoidance (e.g., distraction, escape, dependence on others), development, and disability (e.g., *The Anxiety Disorders Interview Schedule for Children—Parent Version* or *Child Version* by Silverman and Albano).

▼ 2. Cooperate with an evaluation by a physician for psychotropic medication. (3, 4)

3. Arrange for an evaluation for a prescription of psychotropic medications if the client requests it or if the client is likely to be noncompliant with gradual exposure. ▼

4. Monitor the client for prescription compliance. side effects, and overall effectiveness of the medication; consult with the prescribing physician at regular intervals. ▼

▼ 3. Verbalize an understanding of information about separation fears and their treatment. (5, 6, 7)

5. Discuss how separation fears are common and natural, but unfounded, are not a sign of weakness, but cause unnecessary distress and disability. ▼

6. Discuss how separation fears are maintained by a "phobic cycle" of unwarranted fear and avoidance that precludes positive, therapeutically corrective experiences being away from attachment figures, and how treatment breaks the cycle by encouraging these experiences (e.g., *Separation Anxiety in Children and Adolescents* by Eisen and Schaefer). ▼

7. Use a storytelling technique to help the client identify his/her fears, their origins, and their

---

▼ indicates that the Objective/Intervention is consistent with those found in evidence-based treatments.

▼ 4. Verbalize an understanding of how thoughts, physical feelings, and behavioral actions contribute to anxiety and its treatment. (8, 9)

resolution (or read and process "Maurice Faces His Fears" from the *Child Psychotherapy Homework Planner,* 2nd ed. by Jongsma, Peterson, and McInnis). ▼

8. Discuss how separation fears involve perceiving unrealistic threats, underestimating coping skills, feeling fear, and avoiding what is threatening, that interact to maintain the problem (e.g., *Helping Your Anxious Child* by Rapee, Spence, Cobham, and Wignall). ▼

9. Discuss how exposure serves as an arena to lessen fear, build confidence, and feel safer by building a new history of success experiences (e.g., *Separation Anxiety in Children and Adolescents* by Eisen and Schaefer). ▼

▼ 5. Learn and implement calming skills to reduce and manage anxiety symptoms. (10, 11, 12)

10. Teach the client anxiety management skills (e.g., staying focused on behavioral goals, muscular relaxation, evenly paced diaphragmatic breathing, positive self-talk) to address anxiety symptoms that may emerge during encounters with phobic objects or situations. ▼

11. Assign the client a homework exercise in which he/she practices daily calming skills; review and reinforce success, providing corrective feedback for failure. ▼

12. Use biofeedback techniques to facilitate the client's success at learning calming skills. ▼

▼ 6. Identify, challenge, and replace fearful self-talk with positive, realistic, and empowering self-talk. (13, 14, 15)

13. Explore the client's schema and self-talk that mediates his/her fear response; challenge the biases; assist him/her in replacing the distorted messages with reality-based, positive self-talk. ▼

14. Use behavioral techniques (e.g., modeling, corrective feedback, imaginal rehearsal, social reinforcement) to train the client in positive self-talk that prepares him/her to endure anxiety symptoms without serious consequences. ▽

15. Assign the client a homework exercise in which he/she identifies fearful self-talk and creates reality-based alternatives (or assign "Tools for Anxiety" in the *Adolescent Psychotherapy Homework Planner II*, by Jongsma, Peterson, and McInnis); review and reinforce success, providing corrective feedback for failure. ▽

▽ 7. Participate in gradual repeated exposure to feared or avoided separation situations. (16, 17, 18, 19, 20)

16. Direct and assist the client in construction of a hierarchy of separation anxiety-producing situations. ▽

17. Select initial exposures that have a high likelihood of being a successful experience for the client; develop a plan for managing the symptoms and rehearse the plan (or assign "Gradually Facing a Phobic Fear" in the *Adolescent Psychotherapy Homework Planner,* 2nd ed. by Jongsma, Peterson, and McInnis). ▽

18. Assign parents to read about situational exposure in books or treatment manuals on separation anxiety (e.g., *Separation Anxiety in Children and Adolescents* by Eisen and Schaefer; *Helping Your Anxious Child* by Rapee, Spence, Cobham, and Wignall). ▽

19. Conduct practice exposures in session with the client or client and attachment figures using

graduated tasks, modeling, and reinforcement of the client's success. ▽

20. Assign the client a homework exercise in which he/she does situational exposures and records responses (see *Separation Anxiety in Children and Adolescents* by Eisen and Schaefer); review and reinforce success or provide corrective feedback toward improvement. ▽

▽ 8. Family members demonstrate support for the client as he/she tolerates more exposure to the separation. (21, 22, 23)

21. Conduct Family Anxiety Management sessions (see *FRIENDS Program for Children* series by Barrett, Lowry-Webster, and Turner) in which the family is taught how to prompt and reward courageous behavior, empathetically ignore excessive complaining and other avoidant behaviors, manage their own anxieties, and model the behavior being taught in session. ▽

22. Assist the family in overcoming the tendency to reinforce the separation anxiety; as the anxiety decreases, teach them constructive ways to reward the client's progress. ▽

23. Teach family members problem-solving and communication skills to assist the client's progress through therapy. ▽

▽ 9. Reduce the frequency and severity of crying, clinging, temper tantrums, and verbalized fears when separated from attachment figures. (24, 25, 26)

24. Counsel the parents about setting firm, consistent limits on the client's temper tantrums and excessive clinging or whining. ▽

25. Design a reward system or establish a contingency contract that reinforces the client for being able to manage separation from his/her parents without displaying excessive emotional distress. ▽

26. Inquire into what the client does differently on days that he/she is able to separate from parents without displaying excessive clinging, pleading, crying, or protesting; process the client's response and reinforce any positive coping mechanisms that are used to manage separations (or assign "Parents' Time Away" in the *Child Psychotherapy Homework Planner,* 2nd ed. by Jongsma, Peterson, and McInnis). ▽

▽10. Increase the client's participation in extracurricular or positive peer group activities away from home. (27, 28)

27. Encourage participation in extracurricular or peer group activities (or assign "Show Your Strengths" in *Child Psychotherapy Homework Planner,* 2nd ed. by Jongsma, Peterson, and McInnis). ▽

28. Utilize behavioral rehearsal and role-play of peer group interaction to teach the client social skills and reduce social anxiety (or assign "Greeting Your Peers" in the *Child Psychotherapy Homework Planner,* 2nd ed. by Jongsma, Peterson, and McInnis). ▽

▽11. Increase the frequency and duration of time spent in independent play away from major attachment figures. (29, 30, 31, 32)

29. Encourage the client to invite a friend for an overnight visit and/or set up an overnight visit at a friend's home; process any fears that arise and reinforce independence. ▽

30. Direct the client to spend gradually longer periods of time in independent play or with friends after school. ▽

31. Encourage the client to safely explore his/her immediate neighborhood in order to foster autonomy (or assign "Explore Your World" exercise in the *Child Psychotherapy Homework Planner,* 2nd ed. by Jongsma, Peterson, and McInnis). ▽

32. Direct the parents to go on a weekly outing without the client. Begin with a 30- to 45-minute outing and gradually increase duration; teach the client effective coping strategies (e.g., relaxation techniques, deep breathing, calling a friend, playing with sibling) to help him/her reduce separation anxiety while parents are away on outing. ▽

▽12. Implement relapse prevention strategies for managing possible future anxiety symptoms. (33, 34, 35, 36)

33. Discuss with the client the distinction between a lapse and relapse, associating a lapse with a temporary and reversible return of symptoms, fear, or urges to avoid and relapse with the decision to return to fearful and avoidant patterns. ▽

34. Identify and rehearse with the client the management of future situations or circumstances in which lapses could occur. ▽

35. Instruct the client to routinely use strategies learned in therapy (e.g., cognitive restructuring, exposure), building them into his/her life as much as possible. ▽

36. Develop a "coping card" on which coping strategies and other important information (e.g., "You're safe," "Pace your breathing," "Focus on the task at hand," "You can manage it," "Stay in the situation," "Let the anxiety pass") are written for the client's later use. ▽

▽13. Parents comply and follow through with recommendations regarding therapy and/or medication evaluations. (37, 38)

37. Assess overly enmeshed parent for the possibility of having either an anxiety or affective disorder; refer parent for medication evaluation and/or individual therapy if he/she is exhibiting symptoms of either an anxiety or affective disorder. ▽

14. Identify and express feelings connected with past separation, loss, abuse, or trauma. (39, 40, 41)

15. Express feelings and fears in play therapy, mutual storytelling, and art. (42, 43, 44)

38. Assess the marital dyad for possible conflict and triangulation of the client into discord. Refer parents for marital counseling if discord is present. ▽

39. Assess whether the client's anxiety and fears are associated with a separation, loss, abuse, trauma, or unrealistic danger.

40. Explore, encourage, and support the client in verbally expressing and clarifying the feelings associated with the separation, loss, trauma, or unrealistic danger.

41. Assign the client to write a letter to express his/her feelings about a past separation, loss, trauma, or danger; process the letter with therapist.

42. Use child-centered play therapy principles (e.g., display genuine interest and unconditional positive regard, reflect feelings in nonjudgmental manner, demonstrate trust in the client's capacity to grow) to promote greater awareness of self and increase motivation to overcome fears about separation.

43. Utilize mutual storytelling technique: The client and therapist alternate telling stories through the use of puppets, dolls, or stuffed animals; the therapist first models appropriate ways to overcome fears or anxieties; then the client follows by creating a story with similar characters or themes.

44. Direct the client to draw a picture or create a sculpture about what he/she fears will happen upon separation from major attachment figures; assess whether the client's fears are irrational or unrealistic.

16. Increase assertive behaviors to deal more effectively and directly with stress, conflict, or responsibilities. (45, 46)

45. Play The Stand Up for Yourself Game (Shapiro) in therapy sessions to teach the client assertiveness skills.

46. Refer the client to group therapy to help him/her develop positive social skills, overcome social anxieties, and become more assertive.

__. _____

_____

__. _____

_____

__. _____

_____

__. _____

_____

__. _____

_____

DIAGNOSTIC SUGGESTIONS

Axis I:	309.21	Separation Anxiety Disorder
	300.02	Generalized Anxiety Disorder
	300.23	Social Anxiety Disorder (Social Phobia)
	296.xx	Major Depressive Disorder
	300.81	Somatization Disorder
	301.47	Nightmare Disorder
	307.46	Sleep Terror Disorder
	309.81	Posttraumatic Stress Disorder
	_____	_____
	_____	_____
Axis II:	V71.09	No Diagnosis
	_____	_____
	_____	_____

SEXUAL ABUSE VICTIM

BEHAVIORAL DEFINITIONS

1. Self-report of being sexually abused.
2. Physical signs of sexual abuse (e.g., red or swollen genitalia, blood in the underwear, constant rashes, a tear in the vagina or rectum, venereal disease, hickeys on the body).
3. Strong interest in or curiosity about advanced knowledge of sexuality.
4. Sexual themes or sexualized behaviors emerge in play or artwork.
5. Recurrent and intrusive distressing recollections or nightmares of the abuse.
6. Acting or feeling as if the sexual abuse were recurring (including delusions, hallucinations, or dissociative flashback experiences).
7. Unexplainable feelings of anger, rage, or fear when coming into contact with the perpetrator or after exposure to sexual topics.
8. Pronounced disturbance of mood and affect (e.g., frequent and prolonged periods of depression, irritability, anxiety, fearfulness).
9. Appearance of regressive behaviors (e.g., thumb-sucking, baby talk, bed-wetting).
10. Marked distrust in others as manifested by social withdrawal and problems with establishing and maintaining close relationships.
11. Feelings of guilt, shame, and low self-esteem.

—. _____

_____

—. _____

_____

—. _____

_____

LONG-TERM GOALS

1. Obtain protection from all further sexual victimization.
2. Work successfully through the issue of sexual abuse with consequent understanding and control of feelings and behavior.
3. Resolve the issues surrounding the sexual abuse, resulting in an ability to establish and maintain close interpersonal relationships.
4. Establish appropriate boundaries and generational lines in the family to greatly minimize the risk of sexual abuse ever occurring in the future.
5. Achieve healing within the family system as evidenced by the verbal expression of forgiveness and a willingness to let go and move on.
6. Eliminate denial in self and the family, placing responsibility for the abuse on the perpetrator and allowing the survivor to feel supported.
7. Eliminate all inappropriate sexual behaviors.
8. Build self-esteem and a sense of empowerment as manifested by an increased number of positive self-descriptive statements and greater participation in extracurricular activities.

—. _____
   _____
—. _____
   _____
—. _____
   _____

SHORT-TERM OBJECTIVES	THERAPEUTIC INTERVENTIONS
1. Tell the entire story of the abuse. (1, 2, 3)	1. Actively build the level of trust with the client through consistent eye contact, active listening, unconditional positive regard, and warm acceptance to help increase his/her ability to identify and express feelings connected to the abuse.
	2. Explore, encourage, and support the client in verbally expressing the facts and clarifying his/her feelings associated with the abuse.

2. Identify the nature, frequency, and duration of the abuse. (4, 5, 6)

3. Using anatomically detailed dolls or puppets, have the client tell and show how he/she was abused. Take great caution not to lead the client's description of the abuse.

4. Report the client's sexual abuse to the appropriate child protection agency, criminal justice officials, or medical professionals.

5. Consult with a physician, criminal justice officials, or child protection case managers to assess the veracity of the sexual abuse charges.

6. Consult with the physician, criminal justice officials, or child protection case managers to develop appropriate treatment interventions for the client.

3. Decrease secrecy in the family by informing key members about the abuse. (7, 8)

7. Facilitate conjoint sessions to reveal the client's sexual abuse to key family members or caregivers.

8. Actively confront and challenge denial of the client's sexual abuse within the family system.

4. Implement steps to protect the client from further sexual abuse. (9, 10, 11, 12)

9. Assess whether the perpetrator should be removed from the home.

10. Implement the necessary steps to protect the client and other children in the home from future sexual abuse.

11. Assess whether the client is safe to remain in the home or should be removed.

12. Empower the client by reinforcing steps necessary to protect himself/herself.

5. Parents establish and adhere to appropriate intimacy boundaries within the family. (13)

6. Identify family dynamics or stressors that contributed to the emergence of sexual abuse. (14, 15, 16, 17)

13. Counsel the client's family members about appropriate intimacy and privacy boundaries.

14. Assess the family dynamics and identify the stress factors or precipitating events that contributed to the emergence of the client's abuse.

15. Assign the client to draw a diagram of the house where the abuse occurred, indicating where everyone slept, and share the diagram with the therapist.

16. Ask the client to draw a picture of a house, then instruct him/her to pretend that he/she lives in that house and describe what it is like to live there; process the client's responses to assess family dynamics and allow for his/her expression of feelings related to abuse.

17. Construct a multigenerational family genogram that identifies sexual abuse within the extended family to help the client realize that he/she is not the only one abused and to help the perpetrator recognize the cycle of boundary violation.

7. Identify and express feelings connected to the abuse. (18, 19, 20, 21)

18. Instruct older child to write a letter to the perpetrator that describes his/her feelings about the abuse; process the letter.

19. Employ art therapy (e.g., drawing, painting, sculpting) to help the client identify and express feelings he/she had toward perpetrator.

20. Use the Angry Tower technique (see Saxe in *101 Favorite Play Therapy Techniques* by Kaduson and Schaefer) to help the client

express feelings of anger about sexual abuse: Build tower out of plastic containers; place small doll on top of tower (doll represents object of anger); instruct the client to throw small fabric ball at tower while verbalizing feelings of anger connected to the abuse.

21. Use guided fantasy and imagery techniques to help the client express suppressed thoughts, feelings, and unmet needs associated with sexual abuse.

8. Decrease expressed feelings of shame and guilt and affirm self as not being responsible for the abuse. (22)

22. Explore and resolve the client's feelings of guilt and shame connected to the sexual abuse (or assign the "You Are Not Alone" exercise in the *Child Psychotherapy Homework Planner,* 2nd ed. by Jongsma, Peterson, and McInnis).

9. Verbalize the way sexual abuse has impacted life and feelings about self. (23, 24)

23. Instruct the client to create a drawing or sculpture that reflects how sexual abuse impacted his/her life and feelings about himself/herself.

24. Assess the client for the presence of symptoms of Posttraumatic Stress Disorder (PTSD) and treat appropriately if positive for this syndrome (see PTSD chapter in this *Planner*).

10. Increase the willingness to talk about sexual abuse in the family. (7, 25)

7. Facilitate conjoint sessions to reveal the client's sexual abuse to key family members or caregivers.

25. Assign the parents and family members reading material to increase their knowledge of sexually addictive behavior and learn ways to help the client recover from sexual abuse (e.g., *Out of the Shadows: Understanding Sexual Addictions* by Carnes; *Allies in Healing* by Davis).

11. Nonabusive parent follows through with recommendations to spend greater quality time with client. (26, 27)

26. Give directive to disengaged, non-abusive parent to spend more time with the client in leisure, school, or household activities.

27. Direct the client and the disengaged, nonabusive parent to create a mutual story through the use of puppets, dolls, or stuffed animals, first in filial play therapy sessions and later at home, to facilitate a closer parent-child relationship.

12. Verbally identify the perpetrator as being responsible for the sexual abuse. (28, 29)

28. Hold a therapy session in which the client and/or the therapist confronts the perpetrator with the abuse.

29. Hold a session in which the perpetrator takes full responsibility for the sexual abuse and apologizes to the client and/or other family members.

13. Perpetrator agrees to seek treatment. (30)

30. Require the perpetrator to participate in a sexual offenders' group.

14. Verbalize a desire to begin the process of forgiveness of the perpetrator and others connected with the abuse. (31)

31. Assign the client to write a forgiveness letter and/or complete a forgiveness exercise in which he/she verbalizes forgiveness to the perpetrator and/or significant family members; process the letter.

15. Identify and express feelings about sexual abuse in play therapy and mutual storytelling. (27, 32, 33)

27. Direct the client and the disengaged, nonabusive parent to create a mutual story through the use of puppets, dolls, or stuffed animals, first in filial play therapy sessions and later at home, to facilitate a closer parent-child relationship.

32. Use child-centered play therapy principles (e.g., provide unconditional positive regard, offer

nonjudgmental reflection of feelings, display trust in the child's capacity for growth) to help the client identify and express feelings surrounding sexual abuse.

33. Use mutual storytelling technique: The client and therapist alternate telling stories through the use of puppets, dolls, or stuffed animals; the therapist first models constructive steps to take to protect self and feel empowered; then the client follows by creating a story with similar characters or themes.

16. Identify and express feelings through artwork and therapeutic games. (34, 35, 36)

34. Ask the client to draw pictures of different emotions and then instruct him/her to identify times when he/she experienced the different emotions surrounding the sexual abuse (or assign the "Feelings and Faces" exercise in the *Child Psychotherapy Homework Planner,* 2nd ed. by Jongsma, Peterson, and McInnis).

35. Employ the Color Your Life technique (O'Connor) to improve the client's ability to identify and verbalize feelings related to sexual abuse: Ask the client to match colors to different emotions (e.g., red-angry, blue-sad, black-very sad, yellow-happy) and then fill up a blank page with colors that reflect his/her feelings about sexual abuse.

36. Play Survivor's Journey (available through Courage to Change), a therapeutic game for working with survivors of sexual abuse to help the client feel empowered.

17. Verbally identify self as a survivor of sexual abuse. (37, 38)

37. Assign readings to the client to help him/her express and work through feelings connected to sexual abuse (e.g., *A Very Touching Book . . . For Little People and Big People* by Hindman; *I Can't Talk About It* by Sanford; *It's Not Your Fault* by Jance).

38. Refer the client to a survivor group with other children to assist him/her in realizing that he/she is not alone in having experienced sexual abuse.

18. Increase outside family contacts and social networks. (38, 39)

38. Refer the client to a survivor group with other children to assist him/her in realizing that he/she is not alone in having experienced sexual abuse.

39. Develop a list of resource people outside of the family to whom the client can turn for support and nurturance.

19. Decrease frequency of sexualized or seductive behaviors in interactions with others. (40, 41)

40. Assist the client in making a connection between underlying painful emotions (e.g., fear, hurt, sadness, anxiety) and sexualized or seductive behaviors.

41. Help the client identify more adaptive ways to meet his/her needs other than through sexualized or seductive behaviors.

20. Decrease anxiety associated with testifying in court. (42)

42. Use role-playing and modeling in session to prepare the client for court and decrease anxiety about testifying.

21. Take medication as prescribed by the physician. (43)

43. Refer the client for a psychotropic medication evaluation; monitor medication compliance, effectiveness, and side effects.

__. _____   __. _____
     _____   _____
__. _____   __. _____
     _____   _____
__. _____   __. _____
     _____   _____

DIAGNOSTIC SUGGESTIONS

Axis I:	309.81	Posttraumatic Stress Disorder
	308.3	Acute Stress Disorder
	296.xx	Major Depressive Disorder
	309.21	Separation Anxiety Disorder
	995.53	Sexual Abuse of Child (Victim)
	307.47	Nightmare Disorder
	300.15	Dissociative Disorder NOS
	_____	_____
	_____	_____
Axis II:	V71.09	No Diagnosis
	_____	_____
	_____	_____

SLEEP DISTURBANCE

BEHAVIORAL DEFINITIONS

1. Emotional distress and demands (e.g., crying, leaving bed to awaken parents, demanding to sleep with parents) that accompanies difficulty falling asleep or remaining asleep.
2. Difficulty falling asleep or remaining asleep without significant demands made on the parents.
3. Distress (e.g., crying, calling for parents, racing heart, fear of returning to sleep) resulting from repeated awakening, with detailed recall of extremely frightening dreams involving threats to self or significant others.
4. Repeated incidents of leaving bed and walking about in an apparent sleep state but with eyes open, face blank, lack of response to communication efforts, and amnesia of the incident upon awakening.
5. Abrupt awakening with a panicky scream followed by intense anxiety and autonomic arousal, no detailed dream recall, and unresponsiveness to the efforts of others to give comfort during the episode.
6. Prolonged sleep and/or excessive daytime napping without feeling adequately rested or refreshed but instead continually tired.

__. _____
_____
__. _____
_____
__. _____
_____

LONG-TERM GOALS

1. Fall asleep calmly and stay asleep without any undue reassuring parental presence required.

2. Feel refreshed and energetic during waking hours.
3. Cease anxiety-producing dreams that cause awakening.
4. End abrupt awakening in terror and return to a peaceful, restful sleep pattern.
5. Restore restful sleep with a reduction of sleepwalking incidents.

—. _____

_____

—. _____

_____

—. _____

_____

SHORT-TERM OBJECTIVES

THERAPEUTIC INTERVENTIONS

1. Describe current sleep pattern. (1, 2, 3)

1. Explore and assess the client's presleep and actual sleep patterns.

2. Ask the client and/or parents to keep a written record of presleep activity, sleep time, awakening occurrences, and parental responses to the child; provide a form to chart data.

3. Review the record of the client's presleep and sleep activity to assess for overstimulation, parental reinforcement, and contributing stressors.

2. Cooperate with a physical exam. (4)

4. Refer the client to a physician to rule out any medical or pharmacological causes for the sleep disturbance.

3. Verbalize feelings of depression or anxiety and share the possible causes. (5, 6)

5. Assess the role of depression as a cause of the client's sleep disturbances and treat if necessary (see Depression chapter in this *Planner*).

6. Explore the client's general level of anxiety and treat if necessary (see Anxiety chapter in this *Planner*).

4. Take psychotropic medication as prescribed to assess its effect on sleep. (7, 8)

7. Arrange for an evaluation regarding the need for antidepressant medication for the client to enhance restful sleep.

8. Monitor the client for psychotropic medication prescription compliance, effectiveness, and side effects.

5. Describe stressful experiences and emotional trauma that continue to disturb sleep. (9, 10, 11)

9. Explore for recent traumatic events that have resulted in interference with the client's sleep.

10. Explore for the possibility of sexual abuse to the client that has not been revealed (see Sexual Abuse Victim chapter in this *Planner*).

11. Probe the nature of the client's disturbing dreams and their relationship to current or past life stress.

6. Parents and family members identify sources of conflict or stress within the home. (12, 13)

12. Hold family therapy sessions to assess the level of tension and conflict and its effect on the client's sleep. Assist family members in identifying effective coping strategies to reduce tension and conflict.

13. Meet with the parents alone to assess the degree of stress in their relationship and its possible impact on the child's sleep behavior; refer the parents for conjoint sessions if necessary.

7. Parents develop a practice of setting firm limits on the client's manipulative behavior at bedtime. (14, 15, 16)

14. Meet with the parents to help them set firm limits on the client's manipulative behavior at bedtime.

15. Devise a reward system and/or contingency contract to reinforce the client for sleeping in his/her own bed and ceasing entering into parents' bedroom at night.

16. Brainstorm with the parents a potential list of negative consequences (e.g., earlier bedtime next evening, removal of privileges such as TV or video games) the client will receive if he/she engages in manipulative behavior to avoid going to bed on time. Encourage the parents to select a specific consequence and follow through consistently if the client engages in misbehavior.

8. Parents consistently adhere to a bedtime routine as developed in a family therapy session. (17, 18)

17. Meet with the client and his/her parents to establish a bedtime routine that is calming and attentive, but firm, consistent, and not lengthy; involve him/her in the development process.

18. Assign the parents to keep a written record of adherence to the client's bedtime routine; review the record at future sessions and reinforce successful implementation while redirecting failures.

9. Follow a sleep-induction schedule of events. (19)

19. Reinforce the client's consistent adherence to a calming sleep-induction routine.

10. Remain alone in the bedroom without expressions of fear. (20, 21, 22)

20. Assess the client's fears associated with being alone in the bedroom in terms of their nature, severity, and origin.

21. Help the client and parents establish a nightly ritual that will help to reduce the client's fears and induce calm before going to sleep (e.g., parents tell a bedtime story; build a fortress of stuffed animals around the client's bed; have mother spray perfume on daughter's wrist to remind her of parent's close proximity).

11. Replace irrational thoughts with positive self-talk. (23)

12. Practice deep-muscle relaxation exercises. (24, 25, 26)

13. Utilize biofeedback training to deepen relaxation skills. (27)

14. Express feelings in play therapy. (28, 29)

22. Encourage the parents to allow the family pet to sleep in room with the client at night to reduce nighttime fears and anxiety.

23. Confront the client's irrational fears and teach cognitive strategies (e.g., positive, realistic self-talk) to reduce them.

24. Train the client in deep-muscle relaxation exercises with and/or without audiotape instruction.

25. Use relaxation tapes to train the client in calming himself/herself as preparation for sleep (e.g., Relaxation Imagery for Children by Weinstock, available from Childswork/Childsplay; Magic Island: Relaxation for Kids by Mehling, Highstein, and Delamarter, available from Courage to Change).

26. Teach the client to reduce anxiety and fear after awakening from nightmares by visualizing how a dream can end on a positive note (e.g., visualize mother or father coming to rescue, client calls the police who arrest the intruder, robber, or perpetrator in the dream).

27. Administer electromyographic (EMG) biofeedback to monitor, train, and reinforce the client's successful relaxation response.

28. Use play therapy techniques to assess and resolve the client's emotional conflicts.

29. Interpret the client's play behavior as reflective of his/her feelings toward family members.

__. _____   __. _____
    _____   _____
__. _____   __. _____
    _____   _____
__. _____   __. _____
    _____   _____

DIAGNOSTIC SUGGESTIONS

Axis I: 309.21   Separation Anxiety Disorder
                 312.9   Disruptive Behavior Disorder NOS
                 307.42   Primary Insomnia
                 307.44   Primary Hypersomnia
                 307.45   Circadian Rhythm Sleep Disorder
                 307.47   Nightmare Disorder
                 307.46   Sleep Terror Disorder
                 307.46   Sleepwalking Disorder
                 309.81   Posttraumatic Stress Disorder
                 296.xx   Major Depressive Disorder
                 300.4   Dysthymic Disorder
                 296.xx   Bipolar I Disorder
                 296.89   Bipolar II Disorder
                 296.80   Bipolar Disorder NOS
                 301.13   Cyclothymic Disorder

                 _____   _____

                 _____   _____

Axis II: V71.09   No Diagnosis

                 _____   _____

                 _____   _____

SOCIAL PHOBIA/SHYNESS

BEHAVIORAL DEFINITIONS

1. Hiding, limited, or no eye contact, and/or a refusal or reticence to respond verbally to social overtures from others.
2. Excessive shrinking from or avoidance of contact with unfamiliar people for an extended period of time (i.e., 6 months or longer).
3. Social isolation and/or excessive involvement in isolated activities (e.g., reading, listening to music in his/her room, playing video games).
4. Extremely limited or no close friendships outside of the immediate family members.
5. Hypersensitivity to criticism, disapproval, or perceived signs of rejection from others.
6. Excessive need for reassurance of being liked by others before demonstrating a willingness to get involved with them.
7. Marked reluctance to engage in new activities or take personal risks because of the potential for embarrassment or humiliation.
8. Negative self-image as evidenced by frequent self-disparaging remarks, unfavorable comparisons to others, and a perception of self as being socially unattractive.
9. Lack of assertiveness because of a fear of being met with criticism, disapproval, or rejection.
10. Heightened physiological distress in social settings manifested by increased heart rate, profuse sweating, dry mouth, muscular tension, and trembling.

___. _____
   _____

___. _____
   _____

___. _____
   _____

LONG-TERM GOALS

1. Eliminate anxiety, shyness, and timidity in social settings.
2. Initiate or respond to social contact with unfamiliar people or when placed in new social settings.
3. Interact socially with peers on a consistent basis without excessive fear or anxiety.
4. Achieve a healthy balance between time spent in solitary activity and social interaction with others.
5. Develop the essential social skills that will enhance the quality of interpersonal relationships.
6. Elevate self-esteem and feelings of security in interpersonal, peer, and adult relationships.

—. _____
   _____
   _____
—. _____
   _____
   _____
—. _____
   _____

SHORT-TERM OBJECTIVES

1. Describe the history and nature of social fears and avoidance. (1, 2, 3)

THERAPEUTIC INTERVENTIONS

1. Establish rapport with the client toward building a therapeutic alliance.

2. Assess the client's fear and avoidance, including the focus of fear, types of avoidance (e.g., distraction, escape, dependence on others), development, and disability (e.g., *The Anxiety Disorders Interview Schedule for Children—Parent Version* or *Child Version* by Silverman and Albano).

3. Assess the nature of any stimulus, thoughts, or situations that precipitate the client's social fear and/or avoidance.

2. Complete psychological tests designed to assess the nature and severity of social anxiety and avoidance. (4)

▽ 3. Cooperate with an evaluation by a physician for psychotropic medication. (5, 6)

▽ 4. Participate in a small group therapy for social anxiety, with or without parents, or individual therapy if the group is unavailable. (7)

▽ 5. Verbalize an accurate understanding of the vicious cycle of social anxiety and avoidance. (8, 9)

▽ 6. Verbalize an understanding of the rationale for treatment of social anxiety. (9, 10)

4. Administer a measure of social anxiety to further assess the depth and breadth of social fears and avoidance (e.g., *Social Phobia and Anxiety Inventory for Children* by Beidel, Turner, and Morris).

5. Arrange for an evaluation for a prescription of psychotropic medications. ▽

6. Monitor the client for prescription compliance, side effects, and overall effectiveness of the medication; consult with the prescribing physician at regular intervals. ▽

7. Enroll clients, with parents if desired, in a small (closed enrollment) group for social anxiety or individual therapy if a group cannot be formed (see *Behavioral Treatment of Childhood Social Phobia* by Beidel, Turner, and Morris; *The Treatment of Childhood Social Phobia* by Spence, Donovan, and Brechman-Toussaint). ▽

8. Discuss how social anxiety derives from cognitive biases that overestimate negative evaluation by others, underestimate one's ability to manage, cause distress, and often lead to unnecessary avoidance. ▽

9. Assign the parents to read psychoeducational material on social anxiety and its treatment (e.g., *Helping Your Anxious Child* by Rapee, Spence, Cobham, and Wignall). ▽

9. Assign the client and/or parents to read psychoeducational material on social anxiety and

---

▽ indicates that the Objective/Intervention is consistent with those found in evidence-based treatments.

its treatment (e.g., *Helping Your Anxious Child* by Rapee, Spence, Cobham, and Wignall). ▽

▽ 7. Learn and implement calming and coping strategies to manage anxiety symptoms and focus attention usefully during moments of social anxiety. (11)

10. Discuss how cognitive restructuring and exposure serve as an arena to desensitize learned fear, build social skills and confidence, and reality test biased thoughts. ▽

11. Teach the client relaxation and attentional focusing skills (e.g., staying focused externally and on behavioral goals, muscular relaxation, evenly paced diaphragmatic breathing, ride the wave of anxiety) to manage social anxiety symptoms. ▽

▽ 8. Identify, challenge, and replace fearful self-talk with reality-based, positive self-talk. (12, 13)

12. Explore the client's schema and self-talk that mediate his/her social fear response; challenge the biases; assist him/her in generating appraisals that correct for the biases and build confidence. ▽

13. Assign the client a homework exercise in which he/she identifies fearful self-talk and creates reality-based alternatives; review and reinforce success, providing corrective feedback for failure (see *The Shyness and Social Anxiety Workbook* by Antony and Swinson; *Helping Your Anxious Child* by Rapee, Spence, Cobham, and Wignall). ▽

▽ 9. Participate in gradual repeated exposure to feared social situations. (14, 15)

14. Direct and assist the client in construction of a hierarchy of anxiety-producing situations associated with the phobic response. ▽

15. Select initial in vivo or role-played exposures that have a high likelihood of being a successful experience for the client; do cognitive restructuring within and

after the exposure and use behavioral strategies (e.g., modeling, rehearsal, social reinforcement) to facilitate the exposure (e.g., *The C.A.T. Project Therapist Manual* by Kendall, Choudhury, Hudson, and Webb). ▽

▽10. Participate in gradual repeated exposure to feared social situations in daily life situations. (16)

16. Assign the client a homework exercise in which he/she does an exposure exercise in a daily life situation and records responses; review and reinforce success, providing corrective feedback toward improvement. ▽

▽11. Learn and implement social skills to reduce anxiety and build confidence in social interactions. (17)

17. Use instruction, modeling, and role-playing to build the client's general social and/or communication skills (e.g., *Social Effectiveness Therapy for Children and Adolescents* by Beidel, Turner, and Morris). ▽

▽12. Learn and implement relapse prevention strategies for managing possible future anxiety symptoms. (18, 19, 20, 21)

18. Discuss with the client the distinction between a lapse and relapse, associating a lapse with an initial and reversible return of symptoms, fear, or urges to avoid and relapse with the decision to return to fearful and avoidant patterns. ▽

19. Identify and rehearse with the client the management of future situations or circumstances in which lapses could occur. ▽

20. Instruct the client to routinely use strategies learned in therapy (e.g., cognitive restructuring, social skills, exposure) while building social interactions and relationships. ▽

21. Develop a "coping card" on which coping strategies and other important information (e.g., "Pace your breathing," "Focus on the task at hand," "You can manage it," "It will go away") are written for the client's later use. ▽

▽13. Family members learn skills that strengthen and support the client's positive behavior change. (22, 23, 24)

22. Conduct Family Anxiety Management sessions (see *FRIENDS Program for Children* series by Barrett, Lowry-Webster, and Turner) in which the family is taught how to prompt and reward courageous behavior, empathetically ignore excessive complaining and other avoidant behaviors, manage their own anxieties, and model the behavior being taught in session. ▽

23. Teach the family problem-solving and conflict resolution skills for managing problems among themselves and between them and the client. ▽

24. Encourage the family to model constructive skills they have learned and model and praise the therapeutic skills the client is learning (e.g., calming, cognitive restructuring, nonavoidance of unrealistic fears). ▽

▽14. Increase participation in interpersonal or peer group activities. (25, 26)

25. Encourage the client to participate in extracurricular or positive peer group activities. ▽

26. Instruct the client to invite a friend for an overnight visit and/or set up an overnight visit at a friend's home; process any fears and anxiety that arise. ▽

▽15. Identify strengths and interests that can be used to initiate social contacts and develop peer friendships. (27, 28)

27. Ask the client to list how he/she is like his/her peers; use this list to encourage contact with peers who share interests and abilities (or assign "Greeting Peers" in the *Child Psychotherapy Homework Planner*, 2nd ed. by Jongsma, Peterson, and McInnis). ▽

28. Assist the client in identifying 5–10 of his/her strengths or interests and then instruct the client to utilize three strengths or interests

in the upcoming week to initiate social contacts or develop peer friendships (or assign the "Show Your Strengths" exercise in the *Child Psychotherapy Homework Planner,* 2nd ed. by Jongsma, Peterson, and McInnis). ▽

16. Increase participation in school-related activities. (29)

29. Consult with school officials about ways to increase the client's socialization (e.g., raising the flag with group of peers, tutoring a more popular peer, pairing the client with popular peer on classroom assignments).

17. Verbalize how current social anxiety and insecurities are associated with past rejection experiences and criticism from significant others. (30, 31)

30. Explore for a history of rejection experiences, harsh criticism, abandonment, or trauma that fostered the client's low self-esteem and social anxiety.

31. Encourage and support the client in verbally expressing and clarifying feelings associated with past rejection experiences, harsh criticism, abandonment, or trauma.

18. Express fears and anxiety in individual play therapy sessions or through mutual storytelling. (32, 33, 34)

32. Use child-centered play therapy principles (e.g., provide unconditional positive regard, display genuine interest, reflect feelings and fears, demonstrate trust in child's capacity for self-growth) to help the client overcome his/her social anxieties and feel more confident in social situations.

33. Employ the Ericksonian play therapy technique whereby the therapist speaks through a "wise doll" (or puppet) to an audience or other dolls (or puppet) to teach the client positive social skills that can be used to overcome shyness.

34. Use puppets, dolls, or stuffed animals to model positive social

	skills (e.g., greeting others, introducing self, verbalizing positive statements about self and others) that help the client feel more confident in social interactions.
19. Identify and express feelings in art. (35, 36)	35. Instruct the client to draw a picture or create a sculpture that reflects how he/she feels around unfamiliar people when placed in new social settings.
	36. Instruct the client to draw objects or symbols on a large piece of paper or poster board that symbolize his/her positive attributes; then discuss how the client can use strengths to establish peer friendships.

—. _____   —. _____
   _____   _____
—. _____   —. _____
   _____   _____
—. _____   —. _____
   _____   _____

DIAGNOSTIC SUGGESTIONS

Axis I: 300.23   Social Anxiety Disorder (Social Phobia)
               300.02   Generalized Anxiety Disorder
               309.21   Separation Anxiety Disorder
               300.4   Dysthymic Disorder
               296.xx   Major Depressive Disorder
               300.7   Body Dysmorphic Disorder

               _____   _____

               _____   _____

Axis II: V71.09   No Diagnosis

               _____   _____

               _____   _____

SPECIFIC PHOBIA

BEHAVIORAL DEFINITIONS

1. Describes a persistent and unreasonable fear of a specific object or situation that promotes avoidance behaviors because an encounter with the phobic stimulus provokes an immediate anxiety response.
2. Avoids the phobic stimulus/feared environment or endures it with distress, resulting in interference of normal routines.
3. Acknowledges a persistence of fear despite recognition that the fear is unreasonable.
4. Sleep disturbed by dreams of the feared stimulus.
5. Dramatic fear reaction out of proportion to the phobic stimulus.
6. Parental reinforcement of the phobia by catering to the client's fear.

__. _____
_____
__. _____
_____
__. _____
_____

LONG-TERM GOALS

1. Reduce fear of the specific stimulus object or situation that previously provoked phobic anxiety.
2. Reduce phobic avoidance of the specific object or situation, leading to comfort and independence in moving around in public environment.
3. Eliminate interference in normal routines and remove distress from feared object or situation.
4. Live phobia-free while responding appropriately to life's fears.
5. Resolve the conflict underlying the phobia.

6. Learn to overcome fears of noise, darkness, people, wild animals, and crowds.

__. _____

_____

__. _____

_____

__. _____

_____

SHORT-TERM OBJECTIVES	THERAPEUTIC INTERVENTIONS
1. Describe the history and nature of the phobia(s), complete with impact on functioning and attempt to overcome it. (1, 2)	1. Actively build a level of trust with the client that will promote the open showing of thoughts and feelings, especially fearful ones (or assign "Expressions of Fear Through Art" from the *Child Psychotherapy Homework Planner,* 2nd ed. by Jongsma, Peterson, and McInnis).
	2. Assess the client's fear and avoidance, including the focus of fear, types of avoidance (e.g., distraction, escape, dependence on others), development, and disability (e.g., *The Anxiety Disorders Interview Schedule for Children—Parent Version* or *Child Version* by Silverman and Albano).
2. Complete psychological tests designed to assess features of the phobia. (3)	3. Administer a client-report measure (e.g., from *Measures for Specific Phobia* by Antony) to further assess the depth and breadth of phobic responses.
▼ 3. Cooperate with an evaluation by a physician for psychotropic medication. (4, 5)	4. Arrange for an evaluation for a prescription of psychotropic medications if the client requests it or if the client is likely to be noncompliant with gradual exposure. ▼

▼ indicates that the Objective/Intervention is consistent with those found in evidence-based treatments.

▽ 4. Verbalize an understanding of information about phobias and their treatment. (6, 7, 8)

▽ 5. Verbalize an understanding of how thoughts, physical feelings, and behavioral actions contribute to anxiety and its treatment. (9, 10)

5. Monitor the client for prescription compliance, side effects, and overall effectiveness of the medication; consult with the prescribing physician at regular intervals. ▽

6. Discuss how phobias are very common, a natural but irrational expression of our fight or flight response, are not a sign of weakness, but cause unnecessary distress and disability. ▽

7. Discuss how phobic fear is maintained by a "phobic cycle" of unwarranted fear and avoidance that precludes positive, corrective experiences with the feared object or situation, and how treatment breaks the cycle by encouraging these experiences (see *Mastery of Your Specific Phobia—Therapist Guide* by Craske, Antony, and Barlow, or *Specific Phobias* by Bruce and Sanderson). ▽

8. Use a storytelling technique to help the client identify his/her fears, their origins, and their resolution (or read and process "Maurice Faces His Fears" from the *Child Psychotherapy Homework Planner,* 2nd ed. by Jongsma, Peterson, and McInnis). ▽

9. Discuss how phobias involve perceiving unrealistic threats, bodily expressions of fear, and avoidance of what is threatening that interact to maintain the problem. ▽

10. Discuss how exposure serves as an arena to desensitize learned fear, build confidence, and feel safer by building a new history of success

experiences (e.g., *Helping Your Anxious Child* by Rapee, Spence, Cobham, and Wignall; *Freeing Your Child from Anxiety* by Chansky). ▽

▽ 6. Learn and implement calming skills to reduce and manage anxiety symptoms. (11, 12, 13)

11. Teach the client anxiety management skills (e.g., staying focused on behavioral goals, muscular relaxation, evenly paced diaphragmatic breathing, positive self-talk) to address anxiety symptoms that may emerge during encounters with phobic objects or situations. ▽

12. Assign the client a homework exercise in which he/she practices daily calming skills; review and reinforce success, providing corrective feedback for failure. ▽

13. Use biofeedback techniques to facilitate the client's success at learning calming skills. ▽

▽ 7. Learn and implement applied tension skills to prevent fainting in response to blood, injection, or injury. (14, 15)

14. Teach the client applied tension in which he/she tenses neck and upper torso muscles to curtail blood flow out of the brain to help prevent fainting during encounters with phobic objects or situations involving blood, injection, or injury (see "Applied tension, exposure in vivo, and tension-only in the treatment of blood phobia" in *Behaviour Research and Therapy* by Ost, Fellenius, and Sterner). ▽

15. Assign the client a homework exercise in which he/she practices daily applied tension skills; review and reinforce success, providing corrective feedback for failure. ▽

▼ 8. Identify, challenge, and replace fearful self-talk with positive, realistic, and empowering self-talk. (16, 17, 18)

16. Explore the client's schema and self-talk that mediate his/her fear response; challenge the biases; assist him/her in replacing the distorted messages with reality-based, positive self-talk. ▼

17. Use behavioral techniques (e.g., modeling, corrective feedback, imaginal rehearsal, social re-inforcement) to train the client in positive self-talk that pre-pares him/her to endure anxiety symptoms without serious conse-quences. ▼

18. Assign the client a homework exercise in which he/she identi-fies fearful self-talk and creates reality-based alternatives; review and reinforce success, providing corrective feedback for failure. ▼

▼ 9. Participate in gradual repeated exposure to feared or avoided phobic objects or situations. (19, 20, 21, 22, 23)

19. Direct and assist the client in construction of a hierarchy of anxiety-producing situations as-sociated with the phobic response. ▼

20. Select initial exposures that have a high likelihood of being a suc-cessful experience for the client; develop a plan for managing the symptoms and rehearse the plan (or assign "Gradually Facing a Phobic Fear" in the *Adolescent Psychotherapy Homework Plan-ner*, 2nd ed. by Jongsma, Peterson, and McInnis). ▼

21. Assign the parents to read about situational exposure in books or treatment manuals on spe-cific phobias (e.g., *Helping Your Anxious Child* by Rapee, Spence, Cobham, and Wignall). ▼

22. Conduct exposures with the client using graduated tasks, modeling, and reinforcement of the client's success until they can do the exposures unassisted. ▽

23. Assign the client a homework exercise in which he/she does situational exposures and records responses (see *Mastery of Your Specific Phobia—Client Manual* by Antony, Craske, and Barlow; or *Living with Fear* by Marks); review and reinforce success or provide corrective feedback toward improvement. ▽

▽10. Family members demonstrate support for the client as he/she tolerates more exposure to the phobic stimulus. (24, 25, 26, 27)

24. Conduct Family Anxiety Management sessions (see *FRIENDS Program for Children* series by Barrett, Lowry-Webster, and Turner) in which the family is taught how to prompt and reward courageous behavior, empathetically ignore excessive complaining and other avoidant behaviors, manage their own anxieties, and model the behavior being taught in session. ▽

25. Assist the family in overcoming the tendency to reinforce the client's phobia; as the phobia decreases, teach them constructive ways to reward the client's progress. ▽

26. Teach family members problem-solving and communication skills to assist the client's progress through therapy. ▽

27. Assign the parents to read and discuss with the client psychoeducational material from books or treatment manuals (e.g., see *Helping Your Anxious Child* by Rapee, Spence, Cobham, and Wignall). ▽

▼11. Implement relapse prevention strategies for managing possible future anxiety symptoms. (28, 29, 30, 31)

28. Discuss with the client the distinction between a lapse and relapse, associating a lapse with a temporary and reversible return of symptoms, fear, or urges to avoid and relapse with the decision to return to fearful and avoidant patterns. ▼

29. Identify and rehearse with the client the management of future situations or circumstances in which lapses could occur. ▼

30. Instruct the client to routinely use strategies learned in therapy (e.g., cognitive restructuring, exposure), building them into his/her life as much as possible. ▼

31. Develop a "coping card" on which coping strategies and other important information (e.g., "You're safe," "Pace your breathing," "Focus on the task at hand," "You can manage it," "Stay in the situation," "Let the anxiety pass") are written for the client's later use. ▼

12. Collect pleasant pictures or stories regarding the phobic stimulus and share them in therapy sessions. (32, 33)

32. Use pleasant pictures, readings, or storytelling about the feared object or situation as a means of desensitizing the client to the fear-producing stimulus.

33. Use humor, jokes, riddles, and stories to enable the client to see his/her situation/fears as not as serious as believed and to help instill hope without disrespecting or minimizing his/her fears.

13. Identify the symbolic significance of the phobic stimulus as a basis for fear. (34)

34. Probe, discuss, and interpret the possible symbolic meaning of the client's phobic stimulus object or situation.

14. Verbalize the separate realities of the irrationally feared object or situation and an emotionally painful experience from the past. (35)

15. Verbalize the feelings associated with a past emotionally painful situation that is connected to the phobia. (36, 37)

35. Clarify and differentiate between the client's current irrational fear and past emotionally painful experiences that are evoked by the phobic stimulus.

36. Encourage the client to share feelings from the past through active listening, unconditional positive regard, and questioning.

37. Reinforce the client's insight into the past emotional pain and its connection to present anxiety.

___. _____

_____

___. _____

_____

___. _____

_____

___. _____

_____

___. _____

_____

___. _____

_____

DIAGNOSTIC SUGGESTIONS

Axis I: 300.00   Anxiety Disorder NOS
              300.29   Specific Phobia

___   _____

___   _____

Axis II: V71.09   No Diagnosis

___   _____

___   _____

SPEECH/LANGUAGE DISORDERS

BEHAVIORAL DEFINITIONS

1. Expressive language abilities, as measured by standardized tests, substantially below the expected level.
2. Expressive language deficits, as demonstrated by markedly limited vocabulary, frequent errors in tense, and difficulty recalling words or producing sentences of developmentally appropriate length or complexity.
3. Receptive and expressive language abilities significantly below the expected level as measured by a standardized test.
4. Receptive language deficits, as manifested by difficulty understanding simple words or sentences; certain types of words, such as spatial terms; or longer, complex statements.
5. Deficits in expressive and/or receptive language development that significantly interfere with academic achievement or social communication.
6. Consistent failure to produce developmentally expected speech sounds that significantly interferes with academic achievement or social communication.
7. Repeated stuttering as demonstrated by impairment in the normal fluency and time patterning of speech.
8. Selective mutism as characterized by a consistent failure to speak in specific social situations (e.g., school) despite speaking in other situations.
9. Social withdrawal and isolation in the peer group, school, or social settings where speaking is required.
10. Recurrent pattern of engaging in acting out, aggressive, or negative attention-seeking behaviors when encountering frustration with speech or language problems.

__. _____

_____

__. _____

_____

___. _____

_____

LONG-TERM GOALS

1. Accept the need for and actively cooperate with speech therapy.
2. Achieve the speech and language goals identified in the individualized educational plan (IEP).
3. Improve the expressive and receptive language abilities to the level of capability.
4. Achieve mastery of the expected speech sounds that are appropriate for the age and dialect.
5. Eliminate stuttering; speak fluently and at a normal rate on a regular, consistent basis.
6. Develop an awareness and acceptance of speech/language problems so that there is consistent participation in discussions in the peer group, school, or social settings.
7. Parents establish realistic expectations of their child's speech/language abilities.
8. Resolve the core conflict that contributes to the emergence of selective mutism so that the client speaks consistently in social situations.

___. _____

_____

___. _____

_____

___. _____

_____

SHORT-TERM OBJECTIVES	THERAPEUTIC INTERVENTIONS
1. Complete a speech/language evaluation to determine eligibility for special-education services. (1)	1. Refer the client for a speech/language evaluation to assess the presence of a disorder and determine his/her eligibility for special-education services.
2. Cooperate with a hearing or medical examination. (2)	2. Refer the client for a hearing and/or medical examination to rule out health problems that

may be interfering with his/her speech/language development.

3. Complete neuropsychological testing. (3)

3. Arrange for a neurological examination or neuropsychological evaluation to rule out the presence of organic factors that may contribute to the client's speech/language problem.

4. Comply with a psychoeducational evaluation. (4)

4. Arrange for a psychoeducational evaluation to assess the client's intellectual abilities and rule out the presence of other possible learning disorders.

5. Complete psychological testing. (5)

5. Arrange for psychological testing to determine whether emotional factors or Attention-Deficit/Hyperactivity Disorder (ADHD) are interfering with the client's speech/language development.

6. Take prescribed medication as directed by the physician. (6)

6. Arrange for a medication evaluation if it is determined that an emotional problem and/or ADHD are interfering with speech/language development.

7. Comply with the recommendations made by a multidisciplinary evaluation team at school regarding speech/language or educational interventions. (7, 8)

7. Attend an IEP committee meeting with the client's parents, teachers, and the speech/language pathologist to determine the client's eligibility for special-education services; design intervention strategies that build on the client's strengths and compensate for weaknesses.

8. Consult with the client, his/her parents, teachers, and the speech/language pathologist about designing effective intervention strategies that build on the client's strengths and compensate for weaknesses.

8. Comply with speech therapy and cooperate with the recommendations or interventions offered by the speech/language pathologist. (9)

9. Parents maintain regular communication with teachers and speech/language pathologist. (10)

10. Parents cease verbalizations of denial in the family system about the client's speech/language problem. (11, 12)

11. Parents comply and follow through with reward system to reinforce the client for improvements in speech/language development. (13, 14)

12. Parents increase the time spent with the client in activities that build and facilitate speech/language development. (15, 16, 17)

9. Refer the client to a private speech/language pathologist for extra assistance in improving speech/language abilities.

10. Encourage the parents to maintain regular communication with the client's teachers and the speech/language pathologist to help facilitate speech/language development.

11. Educate the parents about the signs and symptoms of the client's speech/language disorder.

12. Challenge the parents' denial surrounding the client's speech/language problem so that the parents cooperate with the recommendations regarding placement and interventions for the client.

13. Consult with speech/language pathologist about designing a reward system to reinforce the client for achieving goals in speech therapy and mastering new speech behaviors.

14. Encourage the parents to give frequent positive reinforcement to the client for his/her speech/language development.

15. Ask the parents to have the client read to them for 15 minutes four times weekly and then ask the client to retell the story to build his/her vocabulary, using a reward system to maintain the client's interest and motivation (or assign the "Home-Based Reading and Language Program" in the *Child Psychotherapy Homework Planner,* 2nd ed. by Jongsma, Peterson, and McInnis).

16. Give a directive for the client and his/her family to go on a weekly outing; afterward, require the client to share his/her feelings about the outing to increase his/her expressive and receptive language abilities (or assign the "Tell All About It" exercise in the *Child Psychotherapy Treatment Planner,* 2nd ed. by Jongsma, Peterson, and McInnis).

17. Instruct the parents to sing songs (e.g., nursery rhymes, lullabies, popular songs, songs related to the client's interest) with the client to help him/her feel more comfortable with his/her verbalizations in the home.

13. Parents recognize and verbally acknowledge their unrealistic expectations for or excessive pressure on the client to develop speech/language abilities. (18, 19, 20)

18. Observe parent-child interactions to assess how family communication patterns affect the client's speech/language development.

19. Assist the client and his/her parents to develop an understanding and acceptance of the limitations surrounding the speech/language disorder.

20. Confront and challenge the parents about placing excessive or unrealistic pressure on the client to "talk right."

14. Parents recognize and terminate their tendency to speak for the client in social settings. (21, 22)

21. Explore parent-child interactions to determine whether the parents often speak or fill in pauses for the client to protect him/her from feeling anxious or insecure about speech.

22. Encourage the parents to allow the client to take the lead more often in initiating and sustaining conversations.

15. Improve the lines of communication in the family system. (22, 23)

22. Encourage the parents to allow the client to take the lead more often in initiating and sustaining conversations.

23. Teach effective communication skills (e.g., active listening, reflecting feelings, "I statements") to facilitate the client's speech/language development.

16. Increase the frequency of social interactions in which the client takes the lead in initiating or sustaining conversations. (24, 25, 26, 27)

24. Gently confront the client's pattern of withdrawing in social settings to avoid experiencing anxiety about speech problems.

25. Assign the client the task of contributing one comment to classroom discussion each day to increase his/her confidence in speaking before others.

26. Assign the client the task of sharing toys or objects during show-and-tell to increase his/her expressive language abilities.

27. Consult with speech/language pathologist and teachers about designing a program in which the client orally reads passages of gradually increasing length or difficulty in classroom. Praise and reinforce the client's effort.

17. Decrease level of anxiety associated with speech/language problems. (28, 29, 30)

28. Teach the client positive coping mechanisms (e.g., deep-breathing and muscle relaxation techniques, positive self-talk, cognitive restructuring) that can be used when he/she encounters frustration with speech/language problems.

29. Encourage the client to verbalize his/her insecurities about speech/language problems (or assign the client to read and

complete the exercise "Shauna's Song" in the *Child Psychotherapy Homework Planner*, 2nd ed. by Jongsma, Peterson, and McInnis).

30. Use the mutual storytelling technique whereby the client and therapist alternate telling stories through the use of puppets, dolls, or stuffed animals: The therapist first models constructive ways to handle anxiety or frustrations surrounding speech/language problems, then the client follows by telling a story with similar characters or themes.

18. Decrease the frequency and severity of aggressive acting out and negative attention-seeking behaviors due to speech/language frustration. (31)

31. Teach the client self-control strategies (e.g., cognitive restructuring, positive self-talk, "stop, look, listen, and think") to inhibit the impulse to act out when encountering frustration with speech/language problems.

19. Decrease the frequency and severity of dysfluent speech. (32, 33, 34)

32. Teach the client effective anxiety-reduction techniques (relaxation, positive self-talk, cognitive restructuring) to decrease anticipatory anxiety in social settings and help control stuttering.

33. Assign the client to initiate three social contacts per day with peers to help him/her face and work through anxieties and insecurities related to stuttering in the presence of peers (see the "Greeting Peers" exercise in the *Child Psychotherapy Treatment Planner*, 2nd ed. by Jongsma, Peterson, and McInnis).

34. Use role-playing and positive coping strategies (e.g., positive self-talk, cognitive restructuring) to extinguish the client's anxiety

that triggers stuttering in various social settings (e.g., reading in front of class, talking on the phone, introducing self to unfamiliar peer).

20. Comply with systematic desensitization program to decrease the rate of speech and control stuttering. (35)

35. Consult with a speech/language pathologist about designing an in vivo desensitization program (e.g., using deep-muscle relaxation while exposing the client to gradually more anxiety-producing situations) to help the client overcome anxiety associated with stuttering.

21. Express feelings in individual play therapy sessions and artwork. (36, 37)

36. Employ psychoanalytic play therapy approaches (e.g., allow child to take lead; explore etiology of unconscious conflicts, fixations, or developmental arrests; interpret resistance, transference, and core anxieties) to help the client work through his/her feelings surrounding past loss, trauma, or victimization that contributes to selective mutism.

37. Use art therapy (drawing, painting, sculpting) in early stages of therapy to establish rapport and help the client with selective mutism begin to express his/her feelings through artwork.

22. Verbalize an understanding of how selective mutism is associated with past loss, trauma, or victimization. (38, 39)

38. Assess the family dynamics that contribute to the client's refusal to use speech in some situations.

39. Explore the client's background history of loss, trauma, or victimization that contributed to the emergence of selective mutism.

__. _____

_____

__. _____

_____

___. _____   ___. _____
    _____   _____
___. _____   ___. _____
    _____   _____

DIAGNOSTIC SUGGESTIONS

Axis I: 315.31   Expressive Language Disorder
                315.32   Mixed Receptive-Expressive Language Disorder
                315.39   Phonological Disorder
                307.0   Stuttering
                307.9   Communication Disorder NOS
                313.23   Selective Mutism
                309.21   Separation Anxiety Disorder
                300.23   Social Phobia

                _____
                _____

Axis II: 317   Mild Mental Retardation
                V62.89   Borderline Intellectual Functioning
                V71.09   No Diagnosis

                _____
                _____

Appendix A

BIBLIOTHERAPY SUGGESTIONS

Many references are made throughout the chapters to a therapeutic homework resource that was developed by the authors as a corollary to the *Child Psychotherapy Treatment Planner* (Jongsma, Peterson, and McInnis). This frequently cited homework resource book is:

Jongsma, A., Peterson, L. M., and McInnis, W. (2006). *Child Psychotherapy Homework Planner, 2nd Ed.* New York: Wiley.

GENERAL

Breiner, J. (1989). Training Parents as Change Agents for Their Developmentally Disabled Children. In C. E. Schaefer and J. M. Briesmeister (Eds.), *Handbook of Parent Training: Parents as Co-therapists for Children's Behavior Problems* (pp. 269–304). New York: Wiley.

James, B. (1989). *Treating Traumatized Children.* New York: Lexington Books.

Landreth, G. (1991). *Play Therapy: The Art Of The Relationship.* Muncie, IN: Accelerated Development, Inc.

Leland, H. (1983). Play Therapy for Mentally Retarded and Developmentally Disabled Children. In C. E. Schaefer and K. J. O'Connor (Eds.), *Handbook of Play Therapy* (pp. 436–54). New York: Wiley.

Martin, M., and Greenwood-Waltman, C. (Eds.). (1995). *Solve Your Child's School-Related Problems.* New York: HarperCollins.

Mendell, A. E. (1983). Play Therapy with Children of Divorced Parents. In C. E. Schaeffer and K. J. O'Connor (Eds.), *Handbook of Play Therapy* (pp. 320–54). New York: Wiley.

Millman, H., and Schaeffer, C. (1977). *Therapies for Children: A Handbook of Effective Treatments for Problem Behaviors.* San Francisco: Jossey-Bass.

Millman, H., Schaefer, C., and Cohen, J. (1980). *Therapies for School Behavioral Problems.* San Francisco: Jossey-Bass.

O'Connor, K. J. (1983). The Color Your Life Technique. In C. E. Schaeffer and

K. J. O'Connor (Eds.), *Handbook of Play Therapy* (pp. 251–58). New York: Wiley.

O'Connor, K. J. (1991). *The Play Therapy Primer: An Integration of Theories and Techniques.* New York: Wiley.

Saxe, S. (1997). The Angry Tower. In H. Kaduson and C. Schaeffer (Eds.), *101 Favorite Play Therapy Techniques* (pp. 246–49). Northvale, NJ: Jason Aronson, Inc.

Wadeson, H. (1980). *Art Psychotherapy.* New York: Wiley.

Watson, G. S., and Gross, A. M. (1997). Mental Retardation and Developmental Disorders. In R. T. Ammerman and M. H. Herson (Eds.), *Handbook of Prevention and Treatment with Children and Adolescents* (pp. 495–520). New York: Wiley.

General Self-Help Books Source

http://www.bookinhand.com.au/catandprice.htm

ACADEMIC UNDERACHIEVEMENT

Bloom, J. (1990). *Help Me to Help My Child.* Boston: Little Brown & Co.

Martin, M., and Greenwood-Waltman, C. (Eds.). (1995). *Solve Your Child's School-Related Problems.* New York: HarperCollins.

Pennington, B. (1991). *Diagnosing Learning Disorders.* New York: Guilford.

Romain, T. (1997) . *How to Do Homework without Throwing Up.* Minneapolis, MN: Free Spirit Publishing.

Schumm, J. (2005). *How to Help Your Child with Homework.* Minneapolis, MN: Free Spirit Publishing.

Silverman, S. (1998). *13 Steps to Better Grades.* Plainview, NY: Childswork/Childsplay, LLC.

Smith, S. (1979). *No Easy Answers.* New York: Bantam Books.

ADOPTION

Burlingham-Brown, B. (1994). *Why Didn't She Keep Me?* South Bend, IN: Langford.

Covey, S. (1997). *The 7 Habits of Highly Effective Families: Building a Beautiful Family Culture in a Turbulent World.* New York: Golden Books.

Girard, L. W. (1986). *Adoption Is for Always.* Niles, IL: Albert Whitmore & Co.

Jewett, C. (1982). *Helping Children Cope with Separation and Loss.* Harvard, MA: Harvard Common Press.

Kranz, L. (1995). *All About Me and More About Me.* Norland, AZ: Keepsakes.

Krementz, J. (1996). *How It Feels to Be Adopted.* New York: Alfred Knopf.

Medina, L. (1984). *Making Sense of Adoption.* New York: Harper & Row.

Schooler, J. (1993). *The Whole Life Adoption Book.* Colorado Springs, CO: Pinon Press.

Stinson, K. (1998). *I Feel Different.* Los Angeles: Manson Western Co.

ANGER MANAGEMENT

Canter, L., and Canter, P. (1988). *Assertive Discipline for Parents.* New York: Harper Collins.

Deffenbacher, J. and McKay, M. (2000a). *Overcoming Situational and General Anger: A Protocol for the Treatment of Anger Based on Relaxation, Cognitive Restructuring, and Coping Skills Training.* Oakland, CA: New Harbinger.

Deffenbacher, J. L., and McKay, M. (2000b). *Overcoming Situational and General Anger: Client Manual (Best Practices for Therapy).* Oakland, CA: New Harbinger.

Forehand, R., and Long, N. (1996). *Parenting the Strong-Willed Child.* Chicago: Contemporary Books.

Green, R. (1998). *The Explosive Child.* New York: HarperCollins.

Kaye, D. (1991). *Family Rules: Raising Responsible Children.* New York: St. Martin's Press.

Maag, J.W. (1996). *Parenting without Punishment: Making Problem Behavior Work for You.* Philadelphia: Charles Press.

Moser, A. (1991). *Don't Rant and Rave on Wednesdays!* Kansas City, MO: Landmark Editions.

Patterson, G. R. (1976). *Living with Children: New Methods for Parents and Teachers.* Champaign, IL: Research Press.

Patterson, G. R. (1982). *Coercive Family Process.* Eugene, OR: Castalia.

Patterson, R. J. (2000). *The Assertiveness Workbook: How to Express Your Ideas and Stand up for Yourself at Work and in Relationships.* Oakland, CA: New Harbinger.

Phelan, T. (1995). *1-2-3 Magic: Training Your Preschoolers and Preteens to Do What You Want.* Glen Ellyn, IL: Child Management, Inc.

Shapiro, L. E. (1996). *The Very Angry Day that Amy Didn't Have.* Plainview, NY: Childswork/Childsplay, LLC.

Shapiro, L. E. (1995). *Sometimes I Like to Fight, But I Don't Do It Much Anymore.* Plainview, NY: Childswork/Childsplay, LLC.

Shapiro, L. E. (1995). *How I Learned to Control My Temper.* Plainview, NY: Childswork/Childsplay, LLC.

Shapiro, L. E. (1994). *Anger Control Tool Kit: All the Information You Need to Help the Angry Child in School and at Home* [video and book]. King of Prussia, PA: Center for Applied Psychology.

Shore, H. (1994). *The Angry Monster Workbook.* Plainview, NY: Childswork/Childsplay, LLC.

Whitehouse, E., and Pudney, W. (1996). *A Volcano in My Tummy: Helping Children to Handle Anger: A Resource Book for Parents, Caregivers and Teachers.* Gabriola Island, British Columbia, Canada: New Society Publishing.

ANXIETY

Allen, J., and Klein, R. (1997). *Ready . . . Set . . . R.E.L.A.X.* Watertown, WI: Inner Coaching.

Block, D. (1993). *Positive Self-Talk for Children*. New York: Bantam Books.

Crist, J. J. (2004). *What to Do When You're Scared and Worried: A Guide for Kids*. Minneapolis, MN: Free Spirit Publishing.

Dacey, J. S., and Fiore, L. B. (2001). *Your Anxious Child: How Parents and Teachers Can Relieve Anxiety in Children*. San Francisco: Jossey-Bass.

Deaton, W. (1993). *My Own Thoughts*. Alameda, CA: Hunter House.

Elkind, D. (1981). *The Hurried Child: Growing Up Too Fast Too Soon*. New York: Addison-Wesley.

Huebner, D. (2005). *What to Do When You Worry Too Much*. Washington, DC: Magination Press.

Manassis, K. (1996). *Keys to Parenting Your Anxious Child*. Hauppauge, NY: Barron's.

Marks, I. M. (2001). *Living with Fear, 2nd Ed*. London: McGraw-Hill.

McCauley, C. S., and Schachter, R. (1988). *When Your Child Is Afraid*. New York: Simon & Schuster.

Moser, A. (1988). *Don't Pop Your Cork on Mondays!* Kansas City, MO: Landmark Editions.

Rapee, R., Spense, S., Cobham, V., and Wignal, A. (2000). *Helping Your Anxious Child: A Step-by-Step Guide for Parents*. Oakland. CA: New Harbinger.

Wagner, A. P. (2000). *Up and Down the Worry Hill*. Rochester, NY: Lighthouse Press.

Wagner, A. P. (2002). *Worried No More: Help and Hope for Anxious Children*. Rochester, NY: Lighthouse Press.

Zinbarg, R. E., Craske, M. G., Barlow, D. H., and O'Leary, T. (1993). *Mastery of Your Anxiety and Worry—Client Guide*. San Antonio, TX: Psychological Corporation.

ATTACHMENT DISORDER

Ayres, A. J. (2005). *Sensory Integration and the Child*. Los Angeles: Western Psychological Services.

Gil, E. (1983). *Outgrowing the Pain*. Rockville, MD: Laurel Press.

Greenspan, S. (1995). *The Challenging Child*. Reading. MA: Perseus Books.

Jewett, C. (1982). *Helping Children Cope with Separation and Loss*. Harvard, MA: Harvard Common Press.

Kranowitz, C., and Miller, C. (2005). *The Out-of-Sync Child*. New York: Berkley Publishing.

Moser, A. (1994). *Don't Rant and Rave on Wednesdays!* Kansas City, MO: Landmark Editions.

Moser, A. (1998). *Don't Despair on Thursdays!* Kansas City, MO: Landmark Editions.

Turecki, S. (1985). *The Difficult Child*. New York: Bantam Books.

ATTENTION-DEFICIT/HYPERACTIVITY DISORDER (ADHD)

Barkley, R. A. (2000). *Taking Charge of ADHD: The Complete Authoritative Guide for Parents*. New York: Guilford.

Barkley, R. A. (2006). *Attention-Deficit Hyperactivity Disorder: A Handbook for Diagnosis and Tratment, 3rd Ed.* New York: Guilford.

Barkley, R. A., and Murphy, K. R. (2006). *Attention-Deficit Hyperactivity Disorder: A Clinical Workbook, 3rd Ed.* New York: Guilford

Brown, T. E. (2005). *Attention Deficit Disorder: The Unfocused Mind in Children and Adults.* New Haven, CT: Yale University Press.

DuPaul, G. J., and Stoner, G. (2003). *ADHD in the Schools: Assessment and Intervention Strategies.* New York: Guilford.

Flick, G. L. (1996). *Power Parenting for ADD/ADHD Children: A Practical Parent's Guide for Managing Difficult Behaviors.* Englewood Cliffs, NJ: Prentice Hall.

Flick, G. L. (2002). *ADD/ADHD Behavior.* New York: Wiley.

Ingersoll, B. (1988). *Your Hyperactive Child.* New York: Doubleday.

Parker, H. (1992). *The ADD Hyperactivity Handbook for Schools.* Plantation, FL: Impact Publications.

Phelan, T. (1995). *1-2-3 Magic: Training Your Preschoolers and Preteens to Do What You Want.* Glen Ellyn, IL: Child Management, Inc.

Power, T. G., Karustis, J. L., and Habboushe, D. F. (2001). *Homework Success for Children with ADHD: A Family-School Intervention Program.* New York: Guilford.

Quinn, P., and Stern, J. (1991). *Putting on the Brakes.* New York: Magination Press.

Rief, S. (2002). *The ADHD Book of Lists: A Practical Guide for Helping Children and Teens with ADD.* New York: Wiley.

Rief, S. (2005). *How to Reach and Teach Children with ADD/ADHD: Practical Techniques, Strategies, and Interventions.* San Diego, CA: Educational Resource Specialists.

Saxe, S. (1997). The Angry Tower. In H. Kaduson and C. Schaefer (Eds.), *101 Favorite Play Therapy Techniques* (pp. 246–49). Northvale, NJ: Jason Aronson, Inc.

Shapiro, L. E. (1993). *Sometimes I Drive My Mom Crazy, But I Know She's Crazy About Me.* King of Prussia, PA: Center for Applied Psychology.

Shapiro, L. E. (1996). *The Very Angry Day that Amy Didn't Have.* Plainview, NY: Childswork/Childsplay, LLC.

Silver, L. (1992). *Dr. Larry Silver's Advice to Parents on Attention Deficit Hyperactivity Disorder.* New York: American Psychiatric Press.

Silverman, S. (1998). *13 Steps to Better Grades.* Plainview, NY: Childswork/Childsplay, LLC.

Steven, W. H., and McCluskey, K. W. (1996). *Strategies for Desperate Parents: Managing the Challenges of Attention Deficit and Misbehavior.* Lewiston, NY: Marvin Melnyk Associates.

AUTISM/PERVASIVE DEVELOPMENTAL DISORDER

Brill, M. (1994). *Keys to Parenting the Child with Autism.* Hauppauge, NY: Barron's.

Etlinger, R., and Tomassi, M. (2005). *To Be Me.* Los Angeles: Creative Therapy Store.

Koegel, R. L., and Koegel, L. K. (2006). *Pivotal Response Treatments for Autism Communication, Social, and Academic Development.* Baltimore: Brookes.

Marcus, L. M., and Schopler, E. (1989). Parents as Co-therapists with Autistic Children. In C. E. Schaeffer and J. M. Briesmeister (Eds.), *Handbook of Parent Training: Parents as Co-therapists for Children's Behavior Problems* (pp. 337–60). New York: Wiley.

Rimland, B. (1964). *Infantile Autism.* New York: Appleton Century Crofts.

Siegel, B. (1996). *The World of the Autistic Child.* New York: Oxford.

Simons, J., and Olsihi, S. (1987). *The Hidden Child.* Bethesda, MD: Woodbine House.

Tillon-Jameson, A. (2004). *The Everything Parents' Guide to Children with Autism.* Holbrook, MA: Adams Media Corp.

BLENDED FAMILY

Brown, M. (1947). *Stone Soup.* New York: Simon & Schuster.

Covey, S. (1997). *The 7 Habits of Highly Effective Families.* New York: Golden Books.

Fassler, D., Lash, M., and Ives, S. (1988). *Changing Families.* Burlington, VT: Waterfront Books.

Newman, M. C. (1992). *Stepfamily Realities.* Oakland, CA: New Harbinger.

Schab, L., and Van Patter, B. (1994). *My Dad is Getting Married Again.* King of Prussia, PA: Childswork/Childsplay, LLC.

Seuss, Dr. (1961). *The Sneetches and Other Stories.* New York: Random House.

Visher, E., and Visher, J. (1982). *How To Win As a Stepfamily.* New York: Brunner/Mazel.

BULLYING

Eastman, M. (1994). *Taming the Dragon in Your Child.* New York: Wiley.

Morrison, T. (2002). *The Book of Mean People.* Winnipeg, Canada: Hyperion.

Pagona, S., and Pantel, C. (2004). *Eliminating Bullying.* Chapin, SC: Youth Light, Inc.

Shapiro, L. (1994). *The Very Angry Day that Amy Didn't Have.* Plainview, NY: Childswork/Childsplay, LLC.

Shapiro, L. (1995). *Sometimes I Like to Fight, but I Don't Do It Much Anymore.* Plainview, NY: Childswork/Childsplay, LLC.

Voors, W. (2000). *The Parents' Book About Bullying.* Center City, MN: Hazelden Information Education.

CONDUCT DISORDER/DELINQUENCY

Canter, L., and Canter, P. (1988). *Assertive Discipline for Parents.* New York: HarperCollins.

Carr, T. (2001). *131 Creative Strategies for Reaching Children with Anger Problems.* Minneapolis, MN: Educational Media Corp.

Deffenbacher, J., and McKay, M. (2000a). *Overcoming Situational and General Anger:*

A Protocol for the Treatment of Anger Based on Relaxation, Cognitive Restructuring, and Coping Skills Training. Oakland, CA: New Harbinger.

Deffenbacher, J. L., and McKay, M. (2000b). *Overcoming Situational and General Anger: Client Manual (Best Practices for Therapy).* Oakland, CA: New Harbinger.

Forehand, R., and Long, N. (1996). *Parenting the Strong-Willed Child.* Chicago: Contemporary Books.

Greene, R. (1998). *The Explosive Child.* New York: HarperCollins.

Maag, J. W. (1996). *Parenting without Punishment: Making Problem Behavior Work for You.* Philadelphia: Charles Press.

Metcalf, L. (1997). *Parenting Towards Solutions.* Englewood Cliffs, NJ: Prentice Hall

Patterson, G. R. (1976). *Living with Children: New Methods for Parents and Teachers.* Champaign, IL: Research Press.

Patterson, G. R. (1982). *Coercive Family Process.* Eugene, OR: Castalia.

Patterson, R. J. (2000). *The Assertiveness Workbook: How to Express Your Ideas and Stand up for Yourself at Work and in Relationships.* Oakland, CA: New Harbinger.

Phelan, T. (1995). *1-2-3 Magic: Training Your Preschoolers and Preteens to Do What You Want.* Glen Ellyn, IL: Child Management, Inc.

Saxe, S. (1997). The Angry Tower. In H. Kaduson and C. Schaefer (Eds.), *101 Favorite Play Therapy Techniques* (pp. 246–49). Northvale, NJ: Jason Aronson, Inc.

Shapiro, L. E. (1996). *The Very Angry Day that Amy Didn't Have.* Plainview, NY: Childswork/Childsplay, LLC.

Shapiro, L. E. (1995). *Sometimes I Like to Fight, but I Don't Do It Much Anymore.* Plainview, NY: Childswork/Childsplay, LLC.

Shapiro, L. E. (1994). *Anger Control Tool Kit: All the Information You Need to Help the Angry Child in School and at Home* (video and book). King of Prussia, PA: Center for Applied Psychology.

Shore, H. (1991). *The Angry Monster.* King of Prussia, PA: Center for Applied Psychology.

DEPRESSION

Barbara D. (1996). *Lonely, Sad and Angry: A Parent's Guide to Depression in Children and Adolescents.* New York: Doubleday.

Barnard, M. (2003). *Helping Your Depressed Child.* Oakland, CA: New Harbinger.

Black, C., (1979). *My Dad Loves Me, My Dad Has a Disease.* Denver, CO: MAC.

Burns, D. D. (1999). *Feeling Good: The New Mood Therapy.* New York: HarperCollins.

Cytryn, L., McKnew, D. H., and Weiner, J. M. (1998). *Growing Up Sad: Childhood Depression and Its Treatment.* New York: W. W. Norton.

Fassler, D. G., and Dumas, L. S. (1998). *"Help Me, I'm Sad:" Recognizing, Preventing, and Treating Childhood and Adolescent Depression.* New York: Penguin.

Gottlieb, P. (1994). *A Parent's Guide to Childhood and Adolescent Depression.* New York: Dell.

Graham P., and Hughes, C. (1995). *So Young. So Sad. So Listen.* London: Gaskell.

Ingersoll, B., and Goldstein, S. (1995). *Lonely, Sad and Angry: A Parent's Guide to Depression in Children and Adolescents.* New York: Doubleday.

Kerns, L. (1993). *Helping Your Depressed Child.* Rocklin, CA: Prima.

Merrell, K. W. (2001). *Helping Students Overcome Depression and Anxiety: A Practical Guide.* New York: Guilford.

Miller, J. A. (1999). *The Child Depression Sourcebook.* New York: McGraw-Hill.

Moser, A. (1994). *Don't Rant and Rave on Wednesdays!* Kansas City, MO: Landmark Editions.

Ratcliffe, J. (2002). *Sometimes I Get Sad (but Now I Know What Makes Me Happy).* King of Prussia, PA: Childswork/Childsplay, LLC.

DISRUPTIVE/ATTENTION-SEEKING

Canter, L., and Canter, P. (1988). *Assertive Discipline for Parents.* New York: Harper-Collins.

Kaye, D. (1991). *Family Rules: Raising Responsible Children.* New York: St. Martin's Press.

Phelan, T. (1995). *1-2-3 Magic: Training Your Preschoolers and Preteens to Do What You Want.* Glen Ellyn, IL: Child Management, Inc.

Shapiro, L. E. (1995). *How I Learned to Think Things Through.* Plainview, NY: Childswork/Childsplay, LLC.

DIVORCE REACTION

Gardner, R. (1971). *The Boys and Girls Book About Divorce.* New York: Bantam.

Grollman, E. (1975). *Talking About Divorce.* Boston: Beacon Press.

Ives S., Fassler, D., and Lash, M. (1985). *The Divorce Workbook.* Burlington, VT: Waterfront.

Levins, S. (2005). *Was It the Chocolate Pudding? A Story for Little Kids About Divorce.* Washington, DC: Magination Press.

Lowry, D., and Matthews, B. (2001). *What Can I Do? A Book for Children of Divorce.* Washington, DC: Magination Press.

Phelan, T. (1995). *1-2-3 Magic: Training Your Preschoolers and Preteens to Do What You Want.* Glen Ellyn, IL: Child Management, Inc.

Ransom, J., and Finney, K. (2000). *I Don't Want to Talk About It.* Washington, DC: Magination Press.

Rotes, E. (Ed.). (1981). *The Kids' Book of Divorce.* New York: Vintage.

Tolon, M., and Brown, L. (1986). *Dinosaur's Divorce: A Guide for Changing Families.* Boston: Atlantic Monthly Press.

Wadeson, H. (1995). *The Dynamics of Art Psychotherapy.* New York: Wiley.

ENURESIS/ENCOPRESIS

Azrin, N. H., and Basalel, V. A. (1979). *A Parents' Guide to Bedwetting Control.* New York: Simon & Schuster.

Houts, A. C., and Liebhert, R. M. (1984). *Bedwetting: A Guide for Parents and Children.* Springfield, IL: Charles C. Thomas.

Houts, A. C., and Mellon, M. W. (1989). Home-Based Treatment for Primary Enuresis. In C. E. Schaefer and J. M. Briesmeister (Eds.), *Handbook of Parent Training: Parents as Co-therapists for Children's Behavior Problems* (pp. 60–80). New York: Wiley.

Ilg, F., Ames, L., and Baker, S. (1981). *Child Behavior: Specific Advice on Problems of Child Behavior.* New York: Harper & Row.

Mack, A., and Wilensky, D. (1990). *Dry All Night: The Picture Book Technique that Stops Bedwetting.* Boston: Little Brown & Co.

Whitehouse, E., and Pudney, W. (1996). *A Volcano in My Tummy: Helping Children to Handle Anger: A Resource Book for Parents, Caregiviers and Teachers.* Gabriola Island, British Columbia: New Society Publishing.

To order alarm: Palco Laboratories, 9030 Sequel Avenue, Santa Cruz, CA 95062, Telephone (800) 346-4488.

FIRE SETTING

Green, R. (1998). *The Explosive Child.* New York: HarperCollins.

Millman, H., and Schaefer, C. (1977). *Therapies for Children: A Handbook of Effective Treatments for Problem Behaviors.* San Francisco: Jossey-Bass.

Shore, H. (1994). *The Angry Monster Workbook.* Plainview, NY: Childswork/Childsplay, LLC.

Whitehouse, E., and Pudney, W. (1996). *A Volcano in My Tummy: Helping Children to Handle Anger: A Resource Book for Parents, Caregivers and Teachers.* Gabriola Island, British Columbia, Canada: New Society Publishing.

GENDER IDENTITY DISORDER

Bradley, S., and Zucker, K. (1995). *Gender Identity Disorder and Psychosexual Problems in Children and Adolescents.* New York: Guilford.

GRIEF/LOSS UNRESOLVED

Gof, B. (1969). *Where Is Daddy?* Boston: Beacon Press.

Grollman, E. (1967). *Explaining Death to Children.* Boston: Beacon Press.

Mellonie, B., and Ingpen, R. (1983). *Lifetimes.* New York: Bantam Books.

Moser, A. (1996). *Don't Despair on Thursday.* Kansas City, MO: Landmark Editions.

Nystrom, C. (1990). *Emma Says Goodbye.* Batavia, IL: Lion Publishing Co.

O'Toole, D. (1989). *Aarvy Aardvark Finds Hope.* Burnsville, NC: Compassion Books.

Romzin, T. (1999). *What on Earth Do You Do When Someone Dies?* Minneapolis, MN: Free Spirit Publishing.

Temes, R. (1992). *The Empty Place.* Dallas, TX: New Horizons.

LOW SELF-ESTEEM

Block, D. (1993). *Positive Self-Talk for Children.* New York: Bantam Books.

Briggs, D. (1970). *Your Child's Self-Esteem.* Garden City, NY: Doubleday.

Dobson, J. (1974). *Hide or Seek: How to Build Self-Esteem in Your Child.* Old Tappan, NJ: Revell Co.

Loomans, D., and Loomans, J. (1994). *Full Esteem Ahead.* Fort Collins, CO: Kramer, Inc.

Moser, A. (1991). *Don't Feed the Monster on Tuesday!* Kansas City, MO: Landmark Editions.

Sanford, D. (1986). *Don't Look at Me.* Portland, OR: Multnomah Press.

Shapiro, L. (1993). *The Building Blocks of Self-Esteem.* King of Prussia, PA: Center for Applied Psychology.

LYING/MANIPULATIVE

Moser, A. (1999). *Don't Tell a Whopper on Fridays!* Kansas City, MO: Landmark Editions.

MEDICAL CONDITION

Babcock, E. (1997). *When Life Becomes Precious: A Guide for Loved Ones and Friends of Cancer Patients.* New York: Bantam Books.

Bluebond-Langner, M. (1996). *In the Shadow of Illness.* Princeton, NJ: Princeton University Press.

Fromer, M. (1998). *Surviving Childhood Cancer: A Guide for Families.* Oakland, CA: New Harbinger.

Gosselin, K., and Freedman, M. (1998a). *Taking Asthma to School.* Princeton, NJ: Jayjo Books.

Gosselin, K., and Freedman, M. (1998b). *Taking Diabetes to School.* Princeton, NJ: Jayjo Books.

Gosselin, K., and Freedman, M. (1998c). *Taking Seizure Disorder to School.* Princeton, NJ: Jayjo Books.

Huntley, T. (1991). *Helping Children Grieve.* Minneapolis, MN: Augsburg Fortress.

Keene, N., Hobbie, W., and Ruccione, K. (2000). *Childhood Cancer Survivors: A Practical Guide to Your Future.* Sebastopol, CA: O'Reilly and Associates.

Krisher, T. (1992). *Kathy's Hats: A Story of Hope.* Morton Grove, IL: Albert Whitman & Co.

MacLellan, S. (1998). *Amanda's Gift.* Roswell, GA: Health Awareness Communications, Inc.

Woznick, L. (2002). *Living with Childhood Cancer: A Practical Guide to Help Parents Cope.* Washington, DC: American Psychological Association.

MENTAL RETARDATION

Huff, M., and Gibby, R. (1958). *The Mentally Retarded Child.* Boston: Allyn & Bacon.

Millman, J., and Schaefer, C. (1977). *Therapies for Children: A Handbook of Effective Treatments for Behaviors.* San Francisco: Jossey-Bass.

Sanford, D. (1986). *Don't Look at Me.* Portland, OR: Multnomah Press.

Trainer, M. (1991). *Differences in Common.* Rockville, MD: Woodbine House.

Watson, G. S., and Gross, A. M. (1997). Mental Retardation and Developmental Disorders. In R. T. Ammerman and M. H. Herson (Eds.), *Handbook of Prevention and Treatment with Children and Adolescents* (pp. 495–520). New York: Wiley.

OBSESSIVE-COMPULSIVE DISORDER (OCD)

Chansky, T. E. (2000). *Freeing Your Child from Obsessive Compulsive Disorder: Powerful, Practical Solutions to Overcome Your Child's Fears, Worries, and Phobias.* New York: Random House.

Fitzgibbons, L., and Pedrick, C. (2003). *Helping Your Child with OCD.* Oakland, CA: New Harbinger.

Hyman, B., and Pedrick, C. (2005). *The OCD Workbook.* Oakland, CA: New Harbinger.

Niner, H. (2004). *Mr. Worry: A Story About OCD.* Morton Grove, IL: A. Whitman & Co.

Schwartz, J. (1996). *Brain Lock: Free Yourself from Obsessive-Compulsive Behavior.* New York: Regan Books/HarperCollins.

Wagner, A. P. (2000). *Up and Down the Worry Hill: A Children's Book About Obsessive-Compulsive Disorder and Its Treatment.* Rochester, NY: Lighthouse Press.

Wagner, A. P. (2002). *What to Do When Your Child Has Obsessive-Compulsive Disorder: Strategies and Solutions.* Rochester, NY: Lighthouse Press.

Waltz, M. (2000). *Obsessive Compulsive Disorder: Help for Children and Adolescents.* Sebastopol, CA: O'Reilly and Associates.

OPPOSITIONAL DEFIANT

Abern, A. (1994). *Everything I Do You Blame on Me.* Plainview, NY: Childswork/Childsplay, LLC.

Barkley, R., and Benton, C. (1998). *Your Defiant Child: Eight Steps to Better Behavior.* New York: Guilford.

Dobson, J. (1978). *The Strong-Willed Child.* Wheaton, IL: Tyndale House.

Gardner, R. (1990). *The Girls and Boys Book About Good and Bad Behavior.* Cresskill, NJ: Creative Therapeutics.

Greenspan, S. (1995). *The Challenging Child.* Reading, MA: Perseus Books.

Kaye, K. (1991). *Family Rules: Raising Responsible Children.* New York: St. Martin's Press.

Riley, D. (1997). *The Defiant Child: A Parent's Guide to Oppositional Defiant Disorder.* New York: Taylor.

Wenning, K. (1996). *Winning Cooperation from Your Child.* New York: Jason Aronson.

PARENTING

Ciavola, D. (2003). *50 Great Tips, Tricks, and Techniques to Connect with Your Teen.* Oakland, CA: New Harbinger.

Cline, F., and Fay, J. (1990). *Parenting with Love and Logic.* Colorado Springs, CO: Navpress.

Deffenbacher, J., and McKay, M. (2000a). *Overcoming Situational and General Anger: A Protocol for the Treatment of Anger Based on Relaxation, Cognitive Restructuring, and Coping Skills Training.* Oakland, CA: New Harbinger.

Deffenbacher, J. L., and McKay, M. (2000b). *Overcoming Situational and General Anger: Client Manual (Best Practices for Therapy).* Oakland, CA: New Harbinger.

Edwards, C. D. (1999). *How to Handle a Hard-to-Handle Kid.* Minneapolis, MN: Free Spirit Publishing.

Faber, A., and Mazlish, E. (1982). *How to Talk So Kids Will Listen and Listen So Kids Will Talk.* New York: Avon.

Forehand, R., and Long, N. (1996). *Parenting the Strong-Willed Child.* Chicago: Contemporary Books.

Gordon, T. (2000). *Parent Effectiveness Training.* New York: Three Rivers Press.

Greene, R. (1998). *The Explosive Child.* New York: HarperCollins.

Greenspan, S. (1995). *The Challenging Child.* Reading, MA: Perseus Books.

Ilg, F., Ames, L., and Baker, S. (1992). *Child Behavior: The Classic Childcare Manual from the Gesell Institute of Human Development.* New York: Harper Perennial.

Maag, J. W. (1996). *Parenting without Punishment: Making Problem Behavior Work for You.* Philadelphia: Charles Press.

Metcalf, L. (1997). *Parenting Towards Solutions.* Englewood Cliffs, NJ: Prentice Hall.

Patterson, G. R. (1976). *Living with Children: New Methods for Parents and Teachers.* Champaign, IL: Research Press.

Patterson, G. R. (1982). *Coercive Family Process.* Eugene, OR: Castalia.

Phelan, T. (1995). *1-2-3 Magic: Training Your Preschoolers and Preteens to Do What You Want.* Glen Ellyn, IL: Child Management, Inc.

Pickhardt, C. (2003). *The Everthing Parents' Guide to Positive Discipline.* Holbrook, MA: Adams Media Corp.

Renshaw-Joslin, K. (1994). *Positive Parenting from A to Z.* New York: Fawcett Books.

Turecki, S., and Tonner, L. (1988). *The Difficult Child.* New York: Bantam Books.

Wenning, K. (1996). *Winning Cooperation from Your Child: A Comprehensive Method to Stop Defiant and Aggressive Behavior in Children.* Dunmore, PA: Jason Aronson.

Windell, J. (1996). *Children Who Say No When You Want Them to Say Yes: Failsafe*

Discipline Strategies for Stubborn and Oppositional Children and Teens. New York: Macmillan.

PEER/SIBLING CONFLICT

Baruch, D. (1949). *New Ways in Discipline.* New York: Macmillan.
Bieniek, D. (1996). *How to End the Sibling Wars.* King of Prussia, PA: Childswork/Childsplay, LLC.
Faber, A., and Mazlish, E. (1982). *How to Talk So Kids Will Listen and Listen So Kids Will Talk.* New York: Avon.
Faber, A., and Mazlish, E. (1987). *Siblings without Rivalry.* New York: W. W. Norton.
Ginott, H. (1965). *Between Parent and Child.* New York: Macmillan.
Nevick, R. (1996). *Helping Your Child Make Friends.* King of Prussia, PA: Childswork/Childsplay, LLC.

PHYSICAL/EMOTIONAL ABUSE VICTIM

Miller, A. (1984). *For Your Own Good.* New York: Farrar Straus Group.
Monahon, C. (1983). *Children and Trauma: A Parent's Guide to Helping Children Heal.* New York: Lexington Press.

POSTTRAUMATIC STRESS DISORDER

Allen, J. (1995). *Coping with Trauma: A Guide to Self-Understanding.* Arlington, VA: American Psychiatric Press.
Brooks, B., and Siegel, P. M. (1996). *The Scared Child: Helping Kids Overcome Traumatic Events.* New York: Wiley.
Carmen, R. (2004). *Helping Kids Heal.* Seattle, WA: Bureau of Youth At Risk.
Carter, W. L. (2002). *It Happened to Me.* Oakland, CA: New Harbinger.
Deblinger, E., and Heflin, A. H. (1996). *Treating Sexually Abused Children and Their Non-offending Parents: A Cognitive-Behavioral Approach.* Thousand Oaks, CA: Sage
Deffenbacher, J., and McKay, M. (2000a). *Overcoming Situational and General Anger: A Protocol for the Treatment of Anger Based on Relaxation, Cognitive Restructuring, and Coping Skills Training.* Oakland, CA: New Harbinger.
Deffenbacher, J. L., and McKay, M. (2000b). *Overcoming Situational and General Anger: Client Manual (Best Practices for Therapy).* Oakland, CA: New Harbinger.
Eifert, G. H., Forsyth, J. P., and McKay, M. (2006). *ACT on Life Not on Anger.* Oakland, CA: New Harbinger.
Flannery, R., Jr. (1995). *Post-Traumatic Stress Disorder: The Victim's Guide to Healing and Recovery.* New York: Crossroad Publishing.
Holmes, M. (2000). *A Terrible Thing Happened.* Washington, DC: Magination Press.
Kennerly, H. (2000). *Overcoming Childhood Trauma: A Self-Help Guide Using Cognitive Behavioral Techniques.* New York: New York University Press.

Matsakis, A. (1996). *I Can't Get Over It: A Handbook for Trauma Survivors, 2nd Ed.* Oakland, CA: New Harbinger.

Williams, M. B., and Poijula, S. (2002). *The PTSD Workbook.* Oakland CA: New Harbinger.

SCHOOL REFUSAL

Martin, M., and Greenwood-Waltman, C. (Eds.). (1995). *Solve Your Child's School-Related Problems.* New York: HarperCollins.

Millman, H., and Schaefer, C. (1977). *Therapies for Children: A Handbook of Effective Treatments for Problem Behaviors.* San Francisco: Jossey-Bass.

Millman, M., Schaefer, C., and Cohen, J. (1980). *Therapies for School Behavioral Problems.* San Francisco: Jossey-Bass.

Webster-Doyle, T. (1999). *Why Is Everybody Always Picking on Me? A Guide to Understanding Bullies for Young People.* Boston: Weatherhill.

Yule, W. (1989). Parent Involvement in the Treatment of the School Phobic Child. In C. E. Schaefer and J. M. Briesmeister (Eds.), *Handbook of Parent Training: Parents as Co-therapists for Children's Behavior Problems* (pp. 223–44). New York: Wiley.

SEPARATION ANXIETY

Eisen, A. R., and Schaefer, C. E. (2005). *Separation Anxiety in Children and Adolescents: An Individualized Approach to Assessment and Treatment.* New York: Guilford.

Fraiberg, S., (1959). *The Magic Years.* New York: Scribners.

Ginott, H. (1965). *Between Parent and Child.* New York: Macmillan.

Ingersoll, B., and Goldstein, S. (1995). *Lonely, Sad and Angry: A Parent's Guide to Depression in Children and Adolescents.* New York: Doubleday.

Kerns, L. (1993). *Helping Your Depressed Child.* Rocklin, CA: Prima.

Kliman, G., and Rosenfeld, A. (1980). *Responsible Parenthood.* New York: Holt, Rinehart, and Winston.

Mikulas, W. L., and Coffman, M. F. (1989). Home-Based Treatment of Childrens' Fear of the Dark. In C. E. Schaefer and J. M. Briesmeister (Eds.), *Handbook of Parent Training: Parents as Co-therapists for Children's Behavior Problems* (pp. 179–202). New York: Wiley.

Rapee, R., Spense, S., Cobham, V., and Wignal, A. (2000). *Helping Your Anxious Child: A Step-by-Step Guide for Parents.* San Francisco: New Harbinger.

SEXUAL ABUSE VICTIM

Carnes, P. (1983). *Out of the Shadows: Understanding Sexual Addictions.* Minneapolis, MN: Comp Care Publications.

Colao, F., and Hosansky, T. (1987). *Your Children Should Know.* New York: Harper & Row.

Davis, L. (1991). *Allies in Healing.* New York: HarperCollins.

Hagan, K., and Case, J. (1988). *When Your Child Has Been Molested.* Lexington, MA: Lexington Books.

Hindman, J. (1983). *A Very Touching Book . . . For Little People and for Big People.* Durkee, OR: McClure-Hindman Associates.

Hoke, S. (1995). *My Body Is Mine, My Feelings Are Mine.* King of Prussia, PA: Childswork/Childsplay, LLC.

Jance, J. (1985). *It's Not Your Fault.* Charlotte, NC: Kidsrights.

Sanford, D. (1986). *I Can't Talk About It.* Portland, OR: Multnomah Press.

SLEEP DISTURBANCE

Ferber, R. (1985). *Solve Your Child's Sleep Problems.* New York: Simon & Schuster.

Ilg, F., Ames, L., and Baker, S. (1981). *Child Behavior: Specific Advice on Problems of Child Behavior.* New York: Harper & Row.

SOCIAL PHOBIA/SHYNESS

Antony, M. M., and Swinson, R. P. (2000). *The Shyness and Social Anxiety Workbook: Proven, Step-by-Step Techniques for Overcoming Your Fear.* Oakland, CA: New Harbinger.

Cain, B. (2000). *I Don't Know Why—I Guess I'm Shy.* Washington, DC: Magination Press.

Lamb-Shapiro, J. (2002). *Sometimes I Don't Like to Talk (But Sometimes I Can't Keep Quiet).* King of Prussia, PA: Childswork/Childsplay, LLC.

Martin, M., and Greenwood-Waltman, C. (Eds.). (1995). *Solve Your Child's School-Related Problems.* New York: HarperCollins.

Millman, M., Schaefer, C., and Cohen, J. (1980). *Therapies for School Behavioral Problems.* San Francisco: Jossey-Bass.

Ollhoff, J., and Ollhoff, L. (2004). *Getting Along: Teaching Social Skills to Children and Youth.* Eden Prairie, MN: Sparra Media Group.

Rapee, R. M. (1998). *Overcoming Shyness and Social Phobia: A Step-by-Step Guide.* Northvale, NJ: Jason Aronson.

Rapee, R., Spense, S., Cobham, V., and Wignal, A. (2000). *Helping Your Anxious Child: A Step-by-Step Guide for Parents.* San Francisco: New Harbinger.

Schneier, F., and Welkowitz, L. (1996). *The Hidden Face of Shyness.* New York: Avon.

Soifer, S., Zgourides, G. D., Himle, J., and Pickering, N. L. (2001). *Shy Bladder Syndrome: Your Step-by-Step Guide to Overcoming Paruresis.* Oakland, CA: New Harbinger.

Webster-Doyle, T. (1998). *Why Is Everybody Always Picking on Me? A Guide to Understanding Bullies for Young People.* Boston: Weatherhill.

Zimbardo, P. (1987). *Shyness: What It Is and What to Do About It.* New York: Addison-Wesley.

SPECIFIC PHOBIA

Antony, M. M., Craske, M. C., and Barlow, D. H. (1995). *Mastery of Your Specific Phobia—Client Manual.* San Antonio, TX: Psychological Corporation.

Block, D. (1993). *Positive Self-Talk for Children.* New York: Bantam Books.

Brown, J. (1995). *No More Monsters in the Closet.* New York: Prince Paperbacks.

Chansky, T. E. (2004). *Freeing Your Child from Anxiety: Powerful, Practical Solutions to Overcome Your Child's Fears, Worries, and Phobias.* New York: Random House.

Garber, S., Garber, M., and Spitzman, R. (1993). *Monsters Under the Bed and Other Childhood Fears.* New York: Villard.

Maier, I. (2005). *When Fuzzy was Afraid of Big and Loud Things.* Washington, DC: Magination Press.

Manassis, K. (1996). *Keys to Parenting Your Anxious Child.* Hauppauge, NY: Barron's.

Marks, I. M. (2001). *Living With Fear, 2nd Ed.* London: McGraw-Hill.

Rapee, R., Spense, S., Cobham, V., and Wignal, A. (2000). *Helping Your Anxious Child: A Step-by-Step Guide for Parents.* San Francisco: New Harbinger.

SPEECH/LANGUAGE DISORDERS

Ainsworth, S., and Fraser, J. (1998). *If Your Child Stutters: A Guide for Parents.* Memphis, TN: Stuttering Foundation of America.

Bryant, J. (2004). *Taking Speech Disorder to School.* Princeton, NJ: Jayjo Books.

Heinze, B. A., and Johnson, K. L. (1987). *Easy Does It: Fluency Activities for School-Aged Stutterers.* East Moline, IL: Linguisystems.

Millman, M., Schaefer, C., and Cohen, J. (1980). *Therapies for School Behavioral Problems.* San Francisco: Jossey-Bass.

Appendix B

PROFESSIONAL REFERENCES FOR EVIDENCE-BASED CHAPTERS

Many references are made throughout the chapters to a therapeutic homework resource that was developed by the authors as a corollary to the *Child Psychotherapy Treatment Planner* (Jongsma, Peterson, and McInnis). This frequently cited homework resource book is:

Jongsma, A., Peterson, L. M., and McInnis, W. (2006). *Child Psychotherapy Homework Planner, 2nd Ed.* New York: Wiley.

GENERAL

Albano, A. M., and Silverman, W. K. (1996). *Clinician's Guide to the Anxiety Disorders Interview Schedule for DSM-IV, Child Version.* Boulder, CO: Graywind Publications.

Antony, M. M., Ledley, D. R., and Heimberg, R. G. (2005). *Improving Outcomes and Preventing Relapse in Cognitive Behavioral Therapy.* New York: Guilford.

Bruce, T. J., and Sanderson, W. C. (2005). Evidence-based psychosocial practices: Past, present, and future. In C. Stout and R. Hayes (Eds.), *The Handbook of Evidence-Based Practice in Behavioral Healthcare: Applications and New Directions.* New York: Wiley.

Chambless, D. L., Baker, M. J., Baucom, D., Beutler, L. E., Calhoun, K. S., Crits-Christoph, P., Daiuto, A., DeRubeis, R., Detweiler, J., Haaga, D. A. F., Johnson, S. B., McCurry, S., Mueser, K. T., Pope, K. S., Sanderson, W. C., Shoham, V., Stickle, T., Williams, D. A., Woody, S. R. (1998). Update on empirically validated therapies: II. *The Clinical Psychologist, 51*(1), 3–16.

Chambless, D. L., and Ollendick, T. H. (2001). Empirically supported psychological interventions: Controversies and evidence. *Annual Review of Psychology, 52,* 685–716.

Chambless, D. L., Sanderson, W. C., Shoham, V., Johnson, S. B., Pope, K. S., Crits-Christoph, P., Baker, M., Johnson, B., Woody, S. R., Sue, S., Beutler, L.,

Williams, D. A., and McCurry, S. (1996). An update on empirically validated therapies. *The Clinical Psychologist, 49*(2), 5–18.

Compton, S. N., March, J. S., Brent, D., Albano, A. M., Weersing, R., and Curry, J. (2004). Cognitive-behavioral psychotherapy for anxiety and depressive disorders in children and adolescents: An evidence-based medicine review. *Journal of the American Academy of Child and Adolescent Psychiatry, 43,* 930–59.

Hesley, J. W., and Hesley, J. G. (2001). *Rent Two Films and Let's Talk in the Morning: Using Popular Movies in Psychotherapy, Second Edition.* New York: Wiley.

Hibbs, E. D., and Jensen, P. S. (Eds.). (1996). *Psychological Treatment for Child and Adolescent Disorders: Empirically Based Strategies for Effective Clinical Practice.* Washington, DC: American Psychological Association.

Joshua, J. Maidman, and DiMenna, D. (2000). *Read Two Books and Let's Talk Next Week: Using Bibliotherapy in Clinical Practice.* New York: Wiley.

Kaslow, N. J., and Thompson, M. P. (1998). Applying the criteria for empirically supported treatments to studies of psychosocial interventions for child and adolescent depression. *Journal of Clinical Child Psychology, 27,* 146–55.

Kearney, C. A. (2001). *School Refusal Behavior in Youth: A Functional Approach to Assessment and Treatment.* Washington, DC: American Psychological Association.

Kearney, C. A., and Albano, A. M. (2000). *When Children Refuse School: A Cognitive-Behavioral Therapy Approach/Therapist's Guide.* Boulder, CO: Graywind Publications.

Kendall, P. C. (1994). Treating anxiety disorders in children: Results of a randomized clinical trial. *Journal of Consulting and Clinical Psychology, 62,* 100–10.

Kendall, P. C., Chu, B. C., Pimentel, S. S., and Choudhury, M. (2000). Treating anxiety disorders in youth. In P. C. Kendall (Ed.), *Child and Adolescent Therapy: Cognitive-Behavioral Procedures, 2nd Ed.* (pp. 235–87). New York: Guilford.

Kendall, P. C., Flannery-Schroeder, E., Panichelli-Mindel, S. M., Southam-Gerow, M., Henin, A., and Warman, M. (1997). Therapy for youths with anxiety disorders: A second randomized clinical trial. *Journal of Consulting and Clinical Psychology, 65,* 366–80.

March, J., and Wells, K. (2003). Combining medication and psychotherapy. In A. Martin, L. Scahill, D. S. Charney, and J. F. Leckman (Eds.), *Pediatric Psychopharmacology: Principles and Practice* (pp. 426–46). London: Oxford University Press.

Marlatt, G., and Gordon, J. R. (1985). *Relapse Prevention: Maintenance Strategies in the Treatment of Addictive Behaviors.* New York: Guilford.

McClellan, J., and Werry, J. S. (2003). Evidence-based treatments in child and adolescent psychiatry: An inventory. *Journal of the American Academy of Child and Adolescent Psychiatry, 42,* 1388–400.

Nathan, P. E., and Gorman, J. M. (Eds.). (2002). *A Guide to Treatments That Work* (Vol. II). New York: Oxford University Press.

Nathan, P. E., and Gorman, J. M. (Eds.). (1998). *A Guide to Treatments That Work.* New York: Oxford University Press.

Norcross, J. C., Santrock, J. W., Campbell, L. F., Smith, T. P., Sommer, R., and Zuckerman, E. L. (2003). *The Authoritative Guide to Self-Help Resources in Mental Health. Revised Edition.* New York: Guilford.

Silverman, W. K. (1987). *Anxiety Disorders Interview Schedule for Children.* Boulder, CO: Graywind Publications.

Silverman, W. K., and Albano, A. M. (1996a). *The Anxiety Disorders Interview Schedule for DSM-IV: Child Interview Schedule.* Boulder, CO: Graywind Publications.

Silverman, W. K., and Albano, A. M. (1996b). *The Anxiety Disorders Interview Schedule for DSM-IV: Parent Interview Schedule.* Boulder, CO: Graywind Publications.

ANGER MANAGEMENT

Bell, S., and Eyberg, S. M. (2002). Parent-child interaction therapy. In L. VandeCreek, S. Knapp, and T. L. Jackson (Eds.). *Innovations in Clinical Practice: A Source Book* (Vol. 20, pp. 57–74). Sarasota, FL: Professional Resource Press.

Deffenbacher, J. L., Oetting, E. R., and DiGiuseppe, R. A. (2002). Principles of empirically supported interventions applied to anger management. *The Counseling Psychologist, 30,* 262–80.

Forgatch, M. S., Bullock, B. M., and Patterson, G. R. (2004). From theory to practice: Increasing effective parenting through role-play: The Oregon model of parent management training (PMTO). In H. Steiner (Ed.), *Handbook of Mental Health Interventions in Children and Adolescents: An Integrated Developmental Approach* (pp. 782–812). San Francisco: Jossey-Bass.

Forgatch, M. S., and DeGarmo, D. S. (1999). Parenting through change: An effective prevention program for single mothers. *Journal of Consulting and Clinical Psychology, 67,* 711–24.

Hamilton, S. B., and MacQuiddy, S. L. (1984). Self-administered behavioral parent training: Enhancement of treatment efficacy using a timeout signal seat. *Journal of Clinical Child Psychology, 13,* 61–69.

Lochman, J. E., Lampron, L. B., Gemmer, T. C., Harris, S. R., and Wyckoff, G. M. (1989). Teacher consultation and cognitive-behavioral interventions with aggressive boys. *Psychology in the Schools, 26,*179–88.

Meichenbaum, D. (1985). *Stress Inoculation Training.* New York: Pergamon Press.

Meichenbaum, D. (1993). Stress inoculation training: A twenty-year update. In R. L. Woolfolk and P. M. Lehrer (Eds.), *Principles and Practices of Stress Management* (pp. 373–406). New York: Guilford.

Meichenbaum, D. (2001). *Treatment of Individuals with Anger Control Problems and Aggressive Behaviors: A Clinical Handbook.* Clearwater, FL: Institute Press.

Novaco, R. (1975). *Anger Control: The Development and Evaluation of an Experimental Treatment.* Lexington, MA: Lexington Books.

Vecchio, T. D., and O'Leary, K. D. (2004). Effectiveness of anger treatments for specific anger problems: A meta-analytic review. *Clinical Psychology Review, 24,* 15–34.

ANXIETY

Barrett, P. M. (1998). Evaluation of cognitive-behavioral group treatments for child-hood anxiety disorders. *Journal of Clinical Child Psychology, 27,* 459–68.

Barrett, P. M., Dadds, M. R., and Rapee, R. M. (1996). Family treatment of child-hood anxiety: A controlled trial. *Journal of Consulting Clinical Psychology, 64,* 333–42.

Barrett, P. M., Duffy, A. L., Dadds, M. R., and Rapee, R. M. (2001). Cognitive-behavioral treatment of anxiety disorders in children: Long-term (6-year) follow-up. *Journal of Consulting Clinical Psychology, 69,* 135–41.

Barrett, P. M., Lowry, H., and Turner, C. (2000a). *Friends Program—Group Leader's Workbook for Youth.* Brisbane, Australia: Australian Academy Press.

Barrett, P. M., Lowry, H., and Turner, C. (2000b). *Friends Program—Participant Workbook for Youth.* Brisbane, Australia: Australian Academy Press.

Barrett, P. M., and Shortt, A. (2003). Parental involvement in the treatment of anx-ious children. In A. E. Kazdin and J. R. Weisz (Eds.), *Evidence-Based Psycho-therapies for Children and Adolescents* (pp. 101–19). New York: Guilford.

Bernstein, D. A., Borkovec, T. D., and Hazlett-Stevens, H. (2000). *New Directions in Progressive Relaxation Training: A Guidebook for Helping Professionals.* West-port, CT: Praeger.

Kendall, P. C., Choudhury, M., Hudson, J., and Webb, A. (2002). *The C.A.T. Project Workbook for the Cognitive-Behavioral Treatment of Anxious Adolescents.* Ard-more, PA: Workbook Publishing.

Kendall, P. C., Choudhury, M., Hudson, J., and Webb, A. (2002). *The C.A.T. Project Therapist Manual.* Ardmore, PA: Workbook Publishing.

Kendall, P. C., Krain, A., and Treadwell, K. R. (1999). Generalized Anxiety Disor-der. In R. T. Ammerman, M. Hersen, and C. G. Last (Eds.), *Handbook of Pre-scriptive Treatments for Children and Adolescents. 2nd Ed.* (pp. 155–71). Boston: Allyn & Bacon.

Mendlowitz, S. L., Manassis, K., Bradley, S., Scapillato, D., Miezitis, S., and Shaw, B. F. (1999). Cognitive-behavioral group treatments in childhood anxiety dis-orders: The role of parental involvement. *Journal of the American Academy of Child and Adolescent Psychiatry, 38,* 1223–29.

Ollendick, T. H. (1987). The fear survey schedule for children–revised. In M. Hersen and A. S. Bellack (Eds.), *Dictionary of Behavioral Assessment Techniques* (pp. 218–20). Elmsford, NY: Pergamon.

Ollendick, T. H., and March, J. C. (2004). *Phobic and Anxiety Disorders in Children and Adolescents: A Clinician's Guide to Effective Psychosocial and Pharmacologi-cal Interventions.* New York: Oxford.

Pina, A. A., Silverman, W. K., Fuentes, R. M., Kurtines, W. M., and Weems, C. F. (2003). Exposure-based cognitive-behavioral treatment for phobic and anxiety disorders: Treatment effects and maintenance for Hispanic/Latino relative to European-American youths. *Journal of the American Academy of Child and Ado-lescent Psychiatry, 42,* 1179–87.

Silverman, W. K., and Albano, A. M. (1996a). *The Anxiety Disorders Interview Schedule for DSM-IV: Child Interview Schedule.* Boulder, CO: Graywind Publi-cations.

Silverman, W. K., and Albano, A. M. (1996b). *The Anxiety Disorders Interview Schedule for DSM-IV: Parent Interview Schedule.* Boulder, CO: Graywind Publications.

ATTENTION-DEFICIT/HYPERACTIVITY DISORDER (ADHD)

American Academy of Child and Adolescent Psychiatry. (1997). Practice parameters for the assessment and treatment of children, adolescents, and adults with attention deficit/hyperactivity disorder. *Journal of the American Academy of Child and Adolescent Psychiatry, 36,* 85S–121S.

Barkley, R. A. (1998). *ADHD: A handbook for Diagnosis and Treatment, 2nd Ed.* New York: Guilford.

Castellanos, F. X. (1999). The psychobiology of attention-deficit/hyperactivity disorder. In H. C. Quay and A. E. Hogan (Eds.), *Handbook of Disruptive Behavior Disorders* (pp. 179–98). New York: Kluwer Academic/Plenum Publishers.

Chronis, A. M., Chacko, A., Fabiano, G. A., Wymbs, B. T., and Pelham, W. E. (2004). Enhancements to the standard behavioral parent training paradigm for families of children with ADHD: Review and future directions. *Clinical Child and Family Psychology Review, 7,* 1–27.

DuPaul, G. J., and Stoner, G. (2003). *ADHD in the Schools: Assessment and Intervention Strategies.* New York: Guilford.

Forgatch, M. S., Bullock, B. M., and Patterson, G. R. (2004). From theory to practice: Increasing effective parenting through role-play: The Oregon model of parent management training (PMTO). In H. Steiner (Ed.), *Handbook of Mental Health Interventions in Children and Adolescents: An Integrated Developmental Approach* (pp. 782–812). San Francisco: Jossey-Bass.

Forgatch, M. S., and DeGarmo, D. S. (1999). Parenting through change: An effective prevention program for single mothers. *Journal of Consulting and Clinical Psychology, 67,* 711–24.

Johnston, C., and Mash, E. J. (2001). Families of children with attention deficit hyperactivity disorder: Review and recommendations for future research. *Clinical Child and Family Psychology Review, 4,* 183–207.

Lahey, B. B., Pelham, W. E., Stein, M. A., Loney, J., Trapani, C., Nugent, K., Kipp, H., Schmidt, E., Lee, S., Cale, M., Gold, E., Hartung, C., Willcutt, E., and Baumann, B. (1998). Validity of DSM-IV attention deficit/hyperactivity disorder for younger children. *Journal of the American Academy of Child and Adolescent Psychiatry, 37,* 695–702.

MTA Cooperative Group. (1999). A 14-month randomized clinical trial of treatment strategies for attention-deficit/hyperactivity disorder. *Archives of General Psychiatry, 56,* 1073–86.

Pelham, W. E. (1999). The NIMH multimodal treatment study for ADHD: Just say yes to drugs alone? *Canadian Journal of Psychiatry, 44,* 981–90.

Pelham, W. E., Fabiano, G. A., Gnagy, E. M., Greiner, A. R., and Hoza, B. (2005). Comprehensive psychosocial treatment for ADHD. In E. Hibbs and P. Jensen (Eds.), *Psychosocial Treatments for Child and Adolescent Disorders: Empirically Based Strategies for Clinical Practice* (pp. 377–409). Washington, DC: American Psychological Association.

Pelham, W. E., Jr., Wheeler, T., and Chronis, A. (1998). Empirically supported psychosocial treatments for attention deficit hyperactivity disorder. *Journal of Clinical Child Psychology, 27,* 190–205.

Webster-Stratton, C. (1994). Advancing videotape parent training: A comparison study. *Journal of Consulting and Clinical Psychology, 62,* 583–93.

AUTISM/PERVASIVE DEVELOPMENTAL DISORDER

Dunlap, G., and Koegel, R. L. (1980) Motivating autistic children through stimulus variation. *Journal of Applied Behavior Analysis, 13,* 619–27.

Kern, L., Vorndran, C. M., Hilt, A., Ringdahl, J. E., Adelman, B. E., and Dunlap, G. (1998). Choice as an intervention to improve behavior: A review of the literature. *Journal of Behavioral Education, 8*(2), 151–69.

Koegel, L. K., Camarata, S., Valdez-Menchaca, M., and Koegel, R. L. (1998). Generalization of question asking in children with autism. *American Journal on Mental Retardation, 102,* 346–57.

Koegel, L. K., Koegel, R. L., Hurley, C., and Frea, W. D. (1992). Improving social skills and disruptive behavior in children with autism through self-management. *Journal of Applied Behavior Analysis, 25*(2), 341–53.

Koegel, R. L., Camarata, S., Koegel, L. K., Ben-Tall, A., and Smith, A. (1998). Increasing speech intelligibility in children with autism. *Journal of Autism and Developmental Disorders, 28,* 241–51.

Koegel, R. L., Dyer, K., and Bell, L. K. (1987). The influence of child-preferred activities on autistic children's social behavior. *Journal of Applied Behavior Analysis, 20,* 243–52.

Koegel, R. L., O'Dell, M. C., and Dunlap, G. (1998). Producing speech use in non-verbal autistic children by reinforcing attempts. *Journal of Autism and Developmental Disorders, 18*(4), 525–38.

Koegel, R. L., Schreibman, L., Johnson, J., O'Neill, R. E., and Dunlap, G. (1984). Collateral effects of parent-training on families with autistic children. In R. F. Dangel and R. A. Polster (Eds.), *Behavioral Parent-Training: Issues in Research and Practice* (pp. 358–78). New York: Guilford.

Koegel, R. L., and Williams, J. (1980). Direct vs. indirect response-reinforcer relationships in teaching autistic children. *Journal of Abnormal Child Psychology, 4,* 537–47.

Lerman, D. C., Iwata, B. A., Rainville, B. Adelinis, J. D., Crosland, K., and Kogan, J. (1997). Effects of reinforcement choice on task responding in individuals with developmental disabilities. *Journal of Applied Behavior Analysis, 30*(3), 411–22.

Matson, J., Benavidez, D., Compton, L., Paclawskyj, J., and Baglio, C. (1996). Behavioral treatment of autistic persons: A review of research from 1980 to the present. *Research in Developmental Disabilities, 17,* 433–65.

CONDUCT DISORDER/DELINQUENCY

Alexander, J. F., and Parsons, B. V. (1973). Short-term behavioral intervention with delinquent families: Impact on family process and recidivism. *Journal of Abnormal Psychology, 81,* 219–25.

Bell, S., and Eyberg, S. M. (2002). Parent-child interaction therapy. In L. Vande-Creek, S. Knapp, and T. L. Jackson (Eds.), *Innovations in Clinical Practice: A Source Book* (Vol. 20, pp. 57–74). Sarasota, FL: Professional Resource Press.

Bernstein, D. A., Borkovec, T. D., and Hazlett-Stevens, H. (2000). *New Directions in Progressive Relaxation Training: A Guidebook for Helping Professionals.* Westport, CT: Praeger.

Borduin, C. M., Mann, B. J., Cone, L. T., Henggeler, S. W., Fucci, B. R., Blaske, D. M., and Williams, R. A. (1995). Multisystemic treatment of serious juvenile offenders: Long-term prevention of criminality and violence. *Journal of Consulting and Clinical Psychology, 63,* 569–78.

Brestan, E. V., and Eyberg, S. M. (1998). Effective psychosocial treatments of conduct-disorders children and adolescents: 29 years, 82 studies, and 5,272 kids. *Journal of Clinical Child Psychology, 27,* 180–89.

Curtis, N. M., Ronan, K. R., and Borduin, C. M. (2004). Multisystemic treatment: A meta-analysis of outcome studies. *Journal of Family Psychology, 18,* 411–19.

Forgatch, M. S., Bullock, B. M., and Patterson, G. R. (2004). From theory to practice: Increasing effective parenting through role-play: The Oregon model of parent management training (PMTO). In H. Steiner (Ed.), *Handbook of Mental Health Interventions in Children and Adolescents: An Integrated Developmental Approach* (pp. 782–812). San Francisco: Jossey-Bass.

Forgatch, M. S., and DeGarmo, D. S. (1999). Parenting through change: An effective prevention program for single mothers. *Journal of Consulting and Clinical Psychology, 67,* 711–24.

Hamilton, S. B., and MacQuiddy, S. L. (1984). Self-administered behavioral parent training: Enhancement of treatment efficacy using a timeout signal seat. *Journal of Clinical Child Psychology, 13,* 61–69.

Henggeler, S. W., Schoenwald, S. K., Borduin, C. M., Rowland, M. D., and Cunningham, P. B. (1998). *Multisystemic Treatment of Antisocial Behavior in Children and Adolescents.* New York: Guilford.

Kazdin, A. E., Esveldt-Dawson, K., French, N. H., and Unis, A. S. (1987a). Problem-solving skills training and relationship therapy in the treatment of antisocial child behavior. *Journal of Consulting and Clinical Psychology, 55,* 76–85.

Kazdin, A. E., Esveldt-Dawson, K., French, N. H., and Unis, A. S. (1987b). Effects of parent management training and problem-solving skills training combined in the treatment of antisocial child behavior. *Journal of the American Academy of Child and Adolescent Psychiatry, 26,* 416–24.

Kazdin, A. E., Siegel, T. C., and Bass, D. (1992). Cognitive problem-solving skills training and parent management training in the treatment of antisocial behavior in children. *Journal of Consulting and Clinical Psychology, 60,* 733–47.

Lochman, J. E., Lampron, L. B., Gemmer, T. C., Harris, S. R., and Wyckoff, G. M. (1989). Teacher consultation and cognitive-behavioral interventions with aggressive boys. *Psychology in the Schools, 26,* 179–88.

Meichenbaum, D. (1985). *Stress Inoculation Training.* New York: Pergamon Press.

Meichenbaum, D. (1993). Stress inoculation training: A twenty-year update. In R. L. Woolfolk and P. M. Lehrer (Eds.), *Principles and Practices of Stress Management* (pp. 373–406). New York: Guilford.

Meichenbaum, D. (2001). *Treatment of Individuals with Anger Control Problems and Aggressive Behaviors: A Clinical Handbook.* Clearwater, FL: Institute Press.

Novaco, R. (1975). *Anger Control: The Development and Evaluation of an Experimental Treatment.* Lexington, MA: Lexington Books.

Webster-Stratton, C. (1994). Advancing videotape parent training: A comparison study. *Journal of Consulting and Clinical Psychology, 62,* 583–93.

Webster-Stratton, C. (1996). Early intervention with videotape modeling: Programs for families of children with oppositional defiant disorder or conduct disorder. In E. D. Hibbs and P. S. Jensen (Eds.), *Psychosocial Treatments for Child and Adolescent Disorders: Empirically-Based Strategies for Clinical Practice* (pp. 435–74). Washington, DC: American Psychological Association.

Webster-Stratton, C., and Hooven, C. (1998). Parent training for child conduct problems. In T. H. Ollendick (Ed.), *Comprehensive Clinical Psychology* (pp. 186–219). Oxford, England: Elsevier Science.

DEPRESSION

Beck, A. T., Rush, A. J., Shaw, B. F., and Emery, G. (1979). *Cognitive Therapy of Depression.* New York: Guilford.

Beidel, D. C., Turner, S. M., and Morris, T. L. (2004). *Social Effectiveness Therapy for Children and Adolescents: Manual.* North Tonawanda, NY: Multi-Health Systems, Inc.

Birmaher, B., Ryan, N., Williamson, D., Brent, D., Kaufman, J., Dahl, R., Perel, J., and Nelson, B. (1996). Childhood and adolescent depression: A review of the past 10 years: Part I. *Journal of the American Academy of Child and Adolescent Psychiatry, 35,* 1427–39.

Clarke, G. N., Rohde, P., Lewinsohn, P., Hops, H., and Seeley, J. (1999). Cognitive-behavioral treatment of adolescent depression: Efficacy of acute group treatment and booster sessions. *Journal of the American Academy of Child and Adolescent Psychiatry, 38,* 272–79.

Kovacs, M. (1980). Rating scales to assess depression in school-aged children. *Acta Paediatrica, 46,* 305–15.

Rossello, J., and Bernal, G. (1999). The efficacy of cognitive-behavioral and interpersonal treatments for depression in Puerto Rican adolescents. *Journal of Consulting and Clinical Psychology, 67,* 734–45.

Sommers-Flanagan, J., and Sommers-Flanagan, R. (1996). Efficacy of antidepressant medication with depressed youth: What psychologists should know. *Professional Psychology: Research and Practice, 27,* 145–53.

Stark, K. D., Rouse, L., and Livingston, R. (1991). Treatment of depression during childhood and adolescence: Cognitive behavioral procedures for the individual and family. In P. Kendall (Ed.), *Child and Adolescent Therapy* (pp. 165–206). New York: Guilford.

Treatment for Adolescents with Depression Study. (2003). Treatment for Adolescents with Depression Study (TADS): Rationale, design, and methods. *Journal of the American Academy of Child Adolescent Psychiatry, 42,* 531–42.

Vostanis P., Feehan, C., Grattan, E., and Bickerton, W. (1996). A randomised controlled out-patient trial of cognitive-behavioural treatment for children and adolescents with depression: 9-month follow-up. *Journal of Affective Disorders, 40,* 105–16.

Zimmerman, M., Coryell, W., Corenthal, C., and Wilson, S. (1986). A self-report scale to diagnose major depressive disorder. *Archives of General Psychiatry, 43,* 1076–81.

ENURESIS/ENCOPRESIS

Houts, A. C., Berman, J. S., and Abramson, H. (1994). The effectiveness of psychological and pharmacological treatments for nocturnal enuresis. *Journal of Consulting and Clinical Psychology, 62,* 737–45.

Houts, A. C., Liebert, R. M., and Padawer, W. (1983). A delivery system for the treatment of primary enuresis. *Journal of Abnormal Child Psychology, 11,* 513–19.

Houts, A. C., Peterson, J. K., and Whelan, J. P. (1986). Prevention of relapse in Full Spectrum home training for primary enuresis: A components analysis. *Behavior Therapy, 17,* 462–69.

Houts, A. C., Whelan, J. P., and Peterson, J. K. (1987). Filmed vs. live delivery of full-spectrum home training for primary enuresis: Presenting the information is not enough. *Journal of Consulting and Clinical Psychology, 55,* 902–6.

Whelan, J. P., and Houts, A. C. (1990) Effects of a waking schedule on primary enuretic children treated with Full-Spectrum Home Training. *Health Psychology, 9,* 164–76.

MEDICAL CONDITION

Rodgers, M., Fayter, D., Richardson, G., Ritchie, G., Lewin, R., and Sowden, A. (2005). *The Effects of Psychosocial Interventions in Cancer and Heart Disease: A Review of Systematic Reviews.* York, England: Centre for Reviews and Dissemination, University of York.

OBSESSIVE-COMPULSIVE DISORDER (OCD)

Albano, A. M., Knox, L. S., and Barlow, D. H. (1995). Obsessive-compulsive disorder. In A. Eisen, C. Kearney, and C. Schafer (Eds.), *Clinical Handbook of Anxiety Disorders in Children and Adolescents* (pp. 282–316). Northvale, NJ: Jason Aronson.

Barrett, P. M., Healy-Farrell, L. J., and March, J. S. (2004). Cognitive-behavioural family based treatment for childhood OCD: A randomized controlled trial. *Journal of American Academy of Child and Adolescent Psychiatry, 43*(1), 46–63.

de Haan, E. K., Hoogduin, A. L., Buitelaar, J. K., and Keijsers, G. (1998). Behavior therapy versus clomipramine for the treatment of obsessive-compulsive disorder in children and adolescents. *Journal of the American Academy of Child and Adolescent Psychiatry, 37,* 1022–29.

Franklin, M. E., Rynn, M., March, J. S., and Foa, E. B. (2002). Obsessive-compulsive disorder. In M. Hersen (Ed.), *Clinical Behavior Therapy: Adults and Children* (pp. 276–303). New York: Wiley.

Hiss, H., Foa, E. B., and Kozak, M. J. (1994). A relapse prevention program for treatment of obsessive-compulsive disorder. *Journal of Consulting and Clinical Psychology, 62*, 801–8.

March, J., and Mulle, K. (1998). *OCD in Children and Adolescents: A Cognitive-Behavioral Treatment Manual*. New York: Guilford.

Pediatric OCD Treatment Study (POTS) Team. (2004). Cognitive-behavior therapy, sertraline and their combination for children and adolescents with obsessive-compulsive disorder: The Pediatric OCD Treatment Study (POTS) randomized controlled trial. *JAMA, 292*, 1969–76.

Scahill, L., M., Riddle, A., McSwiggin-Hardin, M., Ort, S. I., King, R. A., Goodman, W. K., Cicchetti, D., and Leckman, J. F. (1997). Children's Yale-Brown Obsessive-Compulsive Scale: Reliability and validity. *Journal of the American Academy of Child and Adolescent Psychiatry, 36*, 844–52.

Wagner, A. P. (2003). *Treatment of OCD in Children and Adolescents: A Cognitive-Behavioral Therapy Manual*. Rochester, NY: Lighthouse Press.

Waters, T., Barrett, P., and March, J. S. (2001). Cognitive-Behavioral family treatment of childhood obsessive-compulsive disorder. *American Journal of Psychotherapy, 55*(3), 372–87.

OPPOSITIONAL DEFIANT

Bell, S., and Eyberg, S. M. (2002). Parent-child interaction therapy. In L. VandeCreek, S. Knapp, and T. L. Jackson (Eds.), *Innovations in Clinical Practice: A Source Book* (Vol. 20, pp. 57–74). Sarasota, FL: Professional Resource Press.

Bernstein, D. A., Borkovec, T. D., and Hazlett-Stevens, H. (2000). *New Directions in Progressive Relaxation Training: A Guidebook for Helping Professionals*. Westport, CT: Praeger.

Block, J. (1978). Effects of a rational-emotive mental health program on poorly achieving disruptive high school students. *Journal of Counseling Psychology, 25*, 61–65.

Feindler, E. L., Marriott, S. A., and Iwata, M. (1984). Group anger control training for junior high school delinquents. *Cognitive Therapy and Research, 8*, 299–311.

Forgatch, M. S., Bullock, B. M., and Patterson, G. R. (2004). From theory to practice: Increasing effective parenting through role-play: The Oregon model of parent management training (PMTO). In H. Steiner, (Ed.), *Handbook of Mental Health Interventions in Children and Adolescents: An Integrated Developmental Approach* (pp. 782–12). San Francisco: Jossey-Bass.

Forgatch, M. S., and DeGarmo, D. S. (1999). Parenting through change: An effective prevention program for single mothers. *Journal of Consulting and Clinical Psychology, 67*, 711–24.

Hamilton, S. B., and MacQuiddy, S. L. (1984). Self-administered behavioral parent training: Enhancement of treatment efficacy using a timeout signal seat. *Journal of Clinical Child Psychology, 13*, 61–69.

Kazdin, A. E., Esveldt-Dawson, K., French, N. H., and Unis, A. S. (1987a).

Problem-solving skills training and relationship therapy in the treatment of anti-social child behavior. *Journal of Consulting and Clinical Psychology, 55,* 76–85.

Kazdin, A. E., Esveldt-Dawson, K., French, N. H., and Unis, A. S. (1987b). Effects of parent management training and problem-solving skills training combined in the treatment of antisocial child behavior. *Journal of the American Academy of Child and Adolescent Psychiatry, 26,* 416–24.

Kazdin, A. E., Siegel, T. C., and Bass, D. (1992). Cognitive problem-solving skills training and parent management training in the treatment of antisocial behavior in children. *Journal of Consulting and Clinical Psychology, 60,* 733–47.

Lochman, J. E., Lampron, L. B., Gemmer, T. C., Harris, S. R., and Wyckoff, G. M. (1989). Teacher consultation and cognitive-behavioral interventions with aggressive boys *Psychology in the Schools, 26,* 179–88.

Meichenbaum, D. (1985). *Stress Inoculation Training.* New York: Pergamon Press.

Meichenbaum, D. (1993). Stress inoculation training: A twenty-year update. In R. L. Woolfolk and P. M. Lehrer (Eds.), *Principles and Practices of Stress Management* (pp. 373–406). New York: Guilford.

Meichenbaum, D. (2001). *Treatment of Individuals with Anger Control Problems and Aggressive Behaviors: A Clinical Handbook.* Clearwater, FL: Institute Press.

Novaco, R. (1975). *Anger Control: The Development and Evaluation of an Experimental Treatment.* Lexington, MA: Lexington Books.

Peed, S., Roberts, M. and Forehand, R. (1977). Evaluation of the effectiveness of a standardized training program in altering the interaction of mothers and their non-compliant children. *Behavior Modification, 1,* 323–50.

Webster-Stratton, C. (1994). Advancing videotape parent training: A comparison study. *Journal of Consulting and Clinical Psychology, 62,* 583–93.

Webster-Stratton, C. (1996). Early intervention with videotape modeling: Programs for families of children with oppositional defiant disorder or conduct disorder. In E. D. Hibbs and P. S. Jensen (Eds.), *Psychosocial Treatments for Child and Adolescent Disorders: Empirically-based Strategies for Clinical Practice* (pp. 435–74). Washington, DC: American Psychological Association.

Webster-Stratton, C., and Hooven, C. (1998). Parent training for child conduct problems. In T. H. Ollendick (Ed.), *Comprehensive Clinical Psychology* (pp. 186–219). Oxford, England: Elsevier Science.

PARENTING

Bell, S., and Eyberg, S. M. (2002). Parent-child interaction therapy. In L. Vande-Creek, S. Knapp, and T. L. Jackson (Eds.), *Innovations in Clinical Practice: A Source Book* (Vol. 20, pp. 57–74). Sarasota, FL: Professional Resource Press.

Bernal, M. E., Klinnert, M. D., and Schultz, L. A.. (1980). Outcome evaluation of behavioral parent training and client-centered parent counseling for children with conduct problems. *Journal of Applied Behavior Analysis, 13,* 677–91.

Brestan, E. V., and Eyberg, S. M. (1998). Effective psychosocial treatments of conduct-disorders children and adolescents: 29 years, 82 studies, and 5,272 kids. *Journal of Clinical Child Psychology, 27,* 180–89.

Forgatch, M. S., Bullock, B. M., and Patterson, G. R. (2004). From theory to practice: Increasing effective parenting through role-play: The Oregon model of parent management training (PMTO). In H. Steiner (Ed.), *Handbook of Mental Health Interventions in Children and Adolescents: An Integrated Developmental Approach* (pp. 782–812). San Francisco: Jossey-Bass.

Forgatch, M. S., and DeGarmo, D. S. (1999). Parenting through change: An effective prevention program for single mothers. *Journal of Consulting and Clinical Psychology, 67,* 711–24.

Hamilton, S. B., and MacQuiddy, S. L. (1984). Self-administered behavioral parent training: Enhancement of treatment efficacy using a timeout signal seat. *Journal of Clinical Child Psychology, 13,* 61–69.

Webster-Stratton, C. (1994). Advancing videotape parent training: A comparison study. *Journal of Consulting and Clinical Psychology, 62,* 583–93.

Webster-Stratton, C. (1996). Early intervention with videotape modeling: Programs for families of children with oppositional defiant disorder or conduct disorder. In E. D. Hibbs and P. S. Jensen (Eds.), *Psychosocial Treatments for Child and Adolescent Disorders: Empirically-Based Strategies for Clinical Practice* (pp. 435–74). Washington, DC: American Psychological Association.

Webster-Stratton, C., and Hooven, C. (1998). Parent training for child conduct problems. In T. H. Ollendick (Ed.), *Comprehensive Clinical Psychology* (pp. 186–219). Oxford, England: Elsevier Science.

POSTTRAUMATIC STRESS DISORDER (PTSD)

American Academy of Child and Adolescent Psychiatry (AACAP). (1998). Summary of the practice parameters for the assessment and treatment of children and adolescents with posttraumatic stress disorder. *Journal of the American Academy of Child and Adolescent Psychiatry, 37,* 997–1001.

Amaya-Jackson, L., Reynolds, V., Murray, M., McCarthy, G., Nelson, A., and Cherney, M., et al. (2003). Cognitive behavioral treatment for pediatric posttraumatic stress disorder: Protocol and application in school and community settings. *Cognitive and Behavioral Practice, 10,* 204–13.

Cohen, J., Berliner, L., and March, J. (2000). Treatment of PTSD in Children and Adolescents: Guidelines. In E. Foa, J. Davidson, and T. Keane (Eds.), *Effective Treatments for PTSD* (pp. 330–32). New York: Guilford.

Cohen, J., March, J., and Berliner, L. (2000). Treatment of PTSD in Children and Adolescents. In E. Foa, J. Davidson, and T. Keane (Eds.), *Effective Treatments for PTSD* (pp. 106–38). New York: Guilford.

Davidson, J., and J. March. (1996). Traumatic stress disorders. In A. Tasman, J. Kay, and J. Lieberman (Eds.), *Psychiatry, Vol. 2* (pp. 1085–98). Philadelphia: Saunders.

Deblinger, E., and Heflin, A. H. (1996). *Treatment for Sexually Abused Children and Their Non-offending Parents: A Cognitive-Behavioral Approach.* Thousand Oaks, CA: Sage.

Donnelly, C., Amaya-Jackson, L., and March, J. (1999) Psychopharmacology of pediatric posttraumatic stress disorder. *Journal of Child Adolescent Psychopharmacology, 9,* 203–20.

Foa, E. B., Keane, T. M., and Friedman, M. J. (2004). *Effective Treatments for PTSD: Practice Guidelines from the International Society for Traumatic Stress Studies.* New York: Guilford.

Foy, D. W. (Ed.). (1992). *Treating PTSD: Cognitive Behavioral Strategies.* New York: Guilford.

Francis, G., and Beidel, D. (1995). Cognitive Behavioral Psychotherapy. In J. March (Ed.), *Anxiety Disorders in Children and Adolescents* (pp. 321–40). New York: Guilford.

March, J., Amaya-Jackson, L., Murray, M., and Schulte, A. (1998). Cognitive-behavioral psychotherapy for children and adolescents with post-traumatic stress disorder following a single incident stressor. *Journal of the American Academy of Child and Adolescent Psychiatry, 37,* 585–93.

Meichenbaum, D. A. *(1995). Clinical Handbook/Practical Therapist Manual for Assessing and Treating Adults with Post-Traumatic Stress Disorder (PTSD).* Clearwater, FL: Institute Press.

Nader, K., Blake, D., Kriegler, J., and Pynoos, R. (1994). *Clinician Administered PTSD Scale for Children (CAPS-C), Current and Lifetime Diagnosis Version, and Instruction Manual.* Los Angeles: UCLA Neuropsychiatric Institute and National Center for PTSD.

Najavits, L. M. (2002). *Seeking Safety: A Treatment Manual for PTSD and Substance Abuse.* New York: Guilford.

Saunders, B. E., and Hanson, R. F. (Eds.). (2002). *Child Physical and Sexual Abuse: Guidelines for Treatment.* Charleston, SC: Authors.

Silverman, W. K., and Albano, A. M. (1996a). *The Anxiety Disorders Interview Schedule for DSM-IV: Child Interview Schedule.* Boulder, CO: Graywind Publications.

Silverman, W. K., and Albano, A. M. (1996b). *The Anxiety Disorders Interview Schedule for DSM-IV: Parent Interview Schedule.* Boulder, CO: Graywind Publications.

SEPARATION ANXIETY

Barrett, P. M., Dadds, M. R., and Rapee, R. M. (1996). Family treatment of childhood anxiety: A controlled trial. *Journal of Consulting Clinical Psychology, 64,* 333–42.

Barrett, P. M., Duffy, A. L., Dadds, M. R., and Rapee, R. M. (2001). Cognitive-behavioral treatment of anxiety disorders in children: Long-term (6-year) follow-up. *Journal of Consulting Clinical Psychology, 69,* 135–41.

Barrett, P. M., Lowry, H., and Turner, C. (2000a). *Friends Program—Group Leader's Workbook for Youth.* Brisbane, Australia: Australian Academy Press.

Barrett, P. M., Lowry, H., and Turner, C. (2000b). *Friends Program—Participant Workbook for Youth.* Brisbane, Australia: Australian Academy Press.

Barrett, P. M., and Shortt, A. (2003). Parental involvement in the treatment of anxious children. In A. E. Kazdin and J. R. Weisz (Eds.), *Evidence-Based Psychotherapies for Children and Adolescents* (pp. 101–19). New York: Guilford.

Silverman, W. K., and Albano, A. M. (1996a). *The Anxiety Disorders Interview*

Schedule for DSM-IV: Child Interview Schedule. Boulder, CO: Graywind Publications.

Silverman, W. K., and Albano, A. M. (1996b). *The Anxiety Disorders Interview Schedule for DSM-IV: Parent Interview Schedule.* Boulder, CO: Graywind Publications.

SOCIAL PHOBIA/SHYNESS

Albano, A. M. (2003). Treatment of social anxiety in adolescents. In M. Reinecke, F. Datillo, and A. Freeman (Eds.), *Casebook of Cognitive Behavioral Therapy with Children and Adolescents, 2nd Ed.* (pp. 128–61). New York: Guilford.

Barrett, P. M., Lowry, H., and Turner, C. (2000a). *Friends Program—Group Leader's Workbook for Youth.* Brisbane, Australia: Australian Academy Press.

Barrett, P. M., Lowry, H., and Turner, C. (2000b). *Friends Program—Participant Workbook for Youth.* Brisbane, Australia: Australian Academy Press.

Beidel, D. C., Turner, S. M., and Morris, T. L. (2000). Behavioral treatment of childhood social phobia. *Journal of Consulting Clinical Psychology, 68,* 1072–80.

Beidel, D. C., Turner, S. M., and Morris, T. L. (1998). *Social Phobia and Anxiety Inventory for Children.* North Tonawanda, NY: Multi-Health Systems, Inc.

Beidel, D. C., Turner, S. M., and Morris, T. L. (2004). *Social Effectiveness Therapy for Children and Adolescents: Manual.* North Tonawanda, NY: Multi-Health Systems, Inc.

Kendall, P. C., Choudhury, M., Hudson, J., and Webb, A. (2002). *The C.A.T. Project Workbook for the Cognitive-Behavioral Treatment of Anxious Adolescents.* Ardmore, PA: Workbook Publishing.

Spence, S. H., Donovan, C., and Brechman-Toussaint, M. (2000). The treatment of childhood social phobia: The effectiveness of a social skills training-based, cognitive-behavioural intervention, with and without parental involvement. *Journal of Child Psychology and Psychiatry, 41,* 713–26.

SPECIFIC PHOBIA

Antony, M. M. (2001). Measures for specific phobia. In M. M. Antony, S. M. Orsillo, and I. Roemer (Eds.), *Practitioner's Guide to Empirically-Based Measures of Anxiety.* New York: Kluwer Academic/Plenum.

Barrett, P. M. (1998). Evaluation of cognitive-behavioral group treatments for childhood anxiety disorders. *Journal of Clinical Child Psychology, 27,* 459–68.

Barrett, P. M., Dadds, M. R., and Rapee, R. M. (1996). Family treatment of childhood anxiety: A controlled trial. *Journal of Consulting Clinical Psychology, 64,* 333–42.

Barrett, P. M., Duffy, A. L., Dadds, M. R., and Rapee, R. M. (2001). Cognitive-behavioral treatment of anxiety disorders in children: Long-term (6-year) follow-up. *Journal of Consulting Clinical Psychology, 69,* 135–41.

Barrett, P. M., Lowry, H., and Turner, C. (2000a). *Friends Program—Group Leader's Workbook for Youth.* Brisbane, Australia: Australian Academy Press.

Barrett, P. M., Lowry, H., and Turner, C. (2000b). *Friends Program—Participant Workbook for Youth*. Brisbane, Australia: Australian Academy Press.

Bernstein, D. A., Borkovec, T. D., and Hazlett-Stevens, H. (2000). *New Directions in Progressive Relaxation Training: A Guidebook for Helping Professionals*. Westport, CT: Praeger.

Kendall, P. C. (1994). Treating anxiety disorders in children: Results of a randomized clinical trial. *Journal of Consulting and Clinical Psychology, 62,* 100–10.

Kendall, P. C., Chu, B. C., Pimentel, S. S., and Choudhury, M. (2000). Treating anxiety disorders in youth. In P. C. Kendall (Ed.), *Child and Adolescent Therapy: Cognitive-Behavioral Procedures, 2nd Ed.* (pp. 235–87). New York: Guilford.

Kendall, P. C., Flannery-Schroeder, E., Panichelli-Mindel, S. M., Southam-Gerow, M., Henin, A., and Warman, M. (1997). Therapy for youths with anxiety disorders: A second randomized clinical trial. *Journal of Consulting and Clinical Psychology, 65,* 366–80.

Ollendick, T. H., and March, J. C. (2003). *Phobic and Anxiety Disorders in Children and Adolescents: A Clinician's Guide to Effective Psychosocial and Pharmacological Interventions*. New York: Oxford University Press.

Pina, A. A., Silverman, W. K., Fuentes, R. M., Kurtines, W. M., and Weems, C. F. (2003). Exposure-based cognitive-behavioral treatment for phobic and anxiety disorders: Treatment effects and maintenance for Hispanic/Latino relative to European-American youths. *Journal of the American Academy of Child and Adolescent Psychiatry, 42,* 1179–87.

Ost, L. G., Fellenius, J., and Sterner, U. (1991). Applied tension, exposure in vivo, and tension-only in the treatment of blood phobia. *Behaviour Research and Therapy, 29*(6), 561–74.

Silverman, W. K., and Albano, A. M. (1996a). *The Anxiety Disorders Interview Schedule for DSM-IV: Child Interview Schedule*. Boulder, CO: Graywind Publications.

Silverman, W. K., and Albano, A. M. (1996b). *The Anxiety Disorders Interview Schedule for DSM-IV: Parent Interview Schedule*. Boulder, CO: Graywind Publications.

Appendix C

INDEX OF THERAPEUTIC GAMES, WORKBOOKS, TOOL KITS, VIDEOTAPES, AND AUDIOTAPES

PRODUCT	AUTHOR
Anger Control Toolkit	Shapiro et al.
Coping With Anger Target Game	Shapiro
Domino Rally	
Don't Be Difficult	Shapiro
Draw Me Out!	Shapiro
Feelings Poster	Bureau for At Risk Youth
Goodbye Game	
Heartbeat Audiotapes	Lamb
How I Learned to Control My Temper	Shapiro
Let's Work It Out—A Conflict Resolution Tool Kit	Shapiro
Magic Island: Relaxation for Kids	Mehling, Highstein, and Delamarter
My Home and Places	Flood
My Two Homes	Shapiro
No More Bullies Game	Courage to Change
Once Upon a Time Potty Book and Doll Set	Weinstock
Parent Report Card	Berg-Gross
Relaxation Imagery For Children	Weinstock
Stand Up For Yourself	Shapiro
Stop, Relax, and Think	Bridges
Techniques for Working with Oppositional Defiant Disorder in Children Audiotapes	Barkley
The Anger Control Game	Berg
The Angry Monster Workbook	Shore
The Angry Monster Machine	Shapiro
The Anti-Bullying Game	Searle and Strong
The Good Mourning Game	Bisenius and M. Norris
The Helping, Sharing, and Caring Game	Gardner

The Self-Control Patrol Game	Trower
The Social Conflict Game	Berg
The Stand Up for Yourself Game	Shapiro
The Squiggle Wiggle Game	Winnicott
The Talking, Feeling, and Doing Game	Gardner
The Ungame	Zakich
You and Me: A Game of Social Skills	Shapiro

Childswork/Childsplay
P.O. Box 1604
Secaucus, NJ 07096-1604
Phone: 1-800-962-1141
www.childswork.com

Courage to Change
P.O. Box 1268
Newburgh, NY 12551
Phone: 1-800-440-4003

Creative Therapeutics
P.O. Box 522
Cresskill, NJ 67626-0522
Phone: 1-800-544-6162
www.rgardner.com

Western Psychological Services
Division of Manson Western Corporation
12031 Wilshire Boulevard
Los Angeles, CA 90025-1251
Phone: 1-800-648-8857
www.wpspublish.com

Appendix D

INDEX OF DSM-IV-TR CODES ASSOCIATED WITH PRESENTING PROBLEMS

Academic Problem   V62.3
  Academic Underachievement

Acute Stress Disorder   308.3
  Physical/Emotional Abuse
    Victim
  Posttraumatic Stress Disorder
    (PTSD)
  Sexual Abuse Victim

Adjustment Disorder   309.xx
  Posttraumatic Stress Disorder
    (PTSD)

Adjustment Disorder With Anxiety   309.24
  Blended Family
  Divorce Reaction
  Medical Condition

Adjustment Disorder With Depressed Mood   309.0
  Adoption
  Blended Family
  Depression
  Divorce Reaction
  Grief/Loss Unresolved
  Medical Condition

Adjustment Disorder With Disturbance of Conduct   309.3
  Blended Family
  Disruptive/Attention-Seeking
  Divorce Reaction
  Fire Setting
  Lying/Manipulative
  Medical Condition
  Parenting

Adjustment Disorder With Mixed Anxiety and Depressed Mood   309.28
  Divorce Reaction
  Medical Condition

Adjustment Disorder With Mixed Disturbance of Emotions and Conduct   309.4
  Adoption
  Attachment Disorder
  Disruptive/Attention-Seeking
  Divorce Reaction
  Fire Setting
  Grief/Loss Unresolved
  Medical Condition
  Parenting

Anorexia Nervosa   307.1
  Low Self-Esteem

**Antisocial Personality
Disorder**   301.7
  Parenting

**Anxiety Disorder Not
Otherwise Specified**   300.00
  Anxiety
  Medical Condition
  Obsessive-Compulsive
    Disorder (OCD)
  Separation Anxiety
  Specific Phobia

Asperger's Disorder   299.80
  Autism/Pervasive
    Developmental Disorder
  Mental Retardation

**Attention-Deficit/Hyperactivity
Disorder, Combined Type**   314.01
  Academic Underachievement
  Adoption
  Anxiety
  Attention-Deficit/Hyperactivity
    Disorder (ADHD)
  Disruptive/Attention-Seeking
  Enuresis/Encopresis
  Lying/Manipulative
  Parenting

**Attention-Deficit/Hyperactivity
Disorder Not Otherwise
Specified**   314.9
  Anger Management
  Attachment Disorder
  Attention-Deficit/Hyperactivity
    Disorder (ADHD)
  Bullying/Intimidation
    Perpetrator
  Conduct Disorder/Delinquency
  Fire Setting
  Oppositional Defiant Disorder
  Peer/Sibling Conflict

**Attention-Deficit/Hyperactivity
Disorder, Predominantly
Hyperactive-Impulsive Type**   314.01
  Anger Management
  Attention-Deficit/Hyperactivity
    Disorder (ADHD)
  Bullying/Intimidation
    Perpetrator
  Conduct Disorder/Delinquency
  Disruptive/Attention-Seeking

  Low Self-Esteem
  Oppositional Defiant
  Peer/Sibling Conflict

**Attention-Deficit/Hyperactivity
Disorder, Predominantly
Inattentive Type**   314.00
  Academic Underachievement
  Attention-Deficit/Hyperactivity
    Disorder (ADHD)

Autistic Disorder   299.00
  Autism/Pervasive
    Developmental Disorder
  Mental Retardation

Bereavement   V62.82
  Depression
  Grief/Loss Unresolved

**Bipolar Disorder Not
Otherwise Specified**   296.80
  Sleep Disturbance

Bipolar I Disorder   296.xx
  Attention-Deficit/Hyperactivity
    Disorder (ADHD)
  Depression
  Sleep Disturbance

Bipolar II Disorder   296.89
  Depression
  Sleep Disturbance

Body Dysmorphic Disorder   300.7
  Social Phobia/Shyness

**Borderline Intellectual
Functioning**   V62.89
  Academic Underachievement
  Low Self-Esteem
  Mental Retardation
  Speech/Language Disorders

**Borderline Personality
Disorder**   301.83
  Parenting

**Childhood Disintegrative
Disorder**   299.10
  Autism/Pervasive
    Developmental Disorder
  Mental Retardation

Profound Mental Retardation 318.2
Mental Retardation

**Psychological Symptoms
Affecting *(Axis III Disorder)*** 316
Medical Condition

**Psychotic Disorder Not
Otherwise Specified** 298.9
Fire Setting

**Reactive Attachment Disorder
of Infancy or Early Childhood** 313.89
Adoption
Attachment Disorder
Autism/Pervasive
   Developmental Disorder

Reading Disorder 315.00
Academic Underachievement
Peer/Sibling Conflict

**Relational Problem Not
Otherwise Specified** V62.81
Blended Family
Bullying/Intimidation
   Perpetrator
Peer/Sibling Conflict

Rett's Disorder 299.80
Autism/Pervasive
   Developmental Disorder
Mental Retardation

Schizophrenia 295.xx
Autism/Pervasive
   Developmental Disorder

Selective Mutism 313.23
Speech/Language Disorders

Separation Anxiety Disorder 309.21
Divorce Reaction
Low Self-Esteem
School Refusal
Separation Anxiety
Sexual Abuse Victim
Sleep Disturbance
Social Phobia/Shyness
Speech/Language Disorders

Severe Mental Retardation 318.1
Mental Retardation

Sexual Abuse of Child V61.21
Low Self-Esteem
Parenting

**Sexual Abuse of Child
*(if focus of clinical attention
is on the victim)*** 995.53
Low Self-Esteem
Posttraumatic Stress Disorder
   (PTSD)
Sexual Abuse Victim

Sleep Terror Disorder 307.46
Separation Anxiety
Sleep Disturbance

Sleepwalking Disorder 307.46
Sleep Disturbance

**Social Anxiety Disorder
(Social Phobia)** 300.23
Low Self-Esteem
School Refusal
Separation Anxiety
Social Phobia/Shyness
Speech/Language Disorders

Somatization Disorder 300.81
School Refusal
Separation Anxiety

Specific Phobia 300.29
Separation Anxiety
Specific Phobia

**Stereotypic Movement
Disorder** 307.3
Autism/Pervasive
   Developmental Disorder

Stuttering 307.0
Speech/Language Disorders

**Undifferentiated Somatoform
Disorder** 300.81
Divorce Reaction
School Refusal